HEADS' TASKS

a handbook of secondary school administration

Geoffrey Lyons

The NFER-Nelson Publishing Company Ltd

Published by The NFER-Nelson Publishing Company Ltd.,
Windsor, Berks. SL4 1DF
Registered Office: The Mere, Upton Park, Slough, Berks. SL1 2DQ
First published by The NFER Publishing Company, 1976
Reprinted by The NFER-Nelson Publishing Company, 1981
© G. Lyons and the University of Bristol
ISBN 0-85633-068-X

Typeset by Moorgate Typesetting Company Ltd.,
Parkhouse Street, London SE5.
Printed in Great Britain by Grosvenor Press Portsmouth

Distributed in the USA by Humanities Press Inc.,
Hillary House-Fernhill House, Atlantic Highlands,
New Jersey 07716 USA.

ACKNOWLEDGEMENTS

Against a background of a lack of information that adequately described administrative practice in the large secondary comprehensive school, two interrelated research projects* were devised that had as their aim the provision of information and materials to this present project. That all of this work has been accomplished is due to the unstinting help of many people.

I am indebted to all of those who helped with the earlier research projects but particularly for the help I received from Christopher Amos, Bernard Chapman, Kathleen Cooper, Nicholas Gill, Norman Harris, Graham Low, Rosalind Lyons, Sadie Nicholson and Walter Shepperd.

Bill Taylor and Alan Brimer were responsible for the original research proposals and helped to shape and develop the work at many stages, a task taken over by Eric Hoyle in the later stages of the research. I am indebted to them for their practical help, their advice and the encouragement that they have given to me throughout.

This present work has been steered through a number of pilot stages and I am particularly grateful to the help that John Davis, Meredydd Hughes, Dr Jack Kitching, HMI, and Len Watson have given to me in the various stages of piloting. Sue Cathie helped the materials see the light of day and the secretarial staff of the Research Unit have given me much help. Dr Harold Knowlson and Peter Taylor provided their resources to mount pilot courses.

The Regional Management Centre of Bristol Polytechnic provided a financial contribution towards the present research as well as making their course facilities available as a vehicle for piloting teaching materials. I would like to take this opportunity of expressing my thanks to three members of their staff, Peter Holmes, John Haxall and Gordon Hayward-Hicks, for all the help they have given to me.

David Parkes, Head of the Resources Section at the Further Education Staff College and Mr Peter Webb, HMI have been an invaluable source of helpful criticism and encouragement to me. Their ideas and thoughts are found throughout the documents and my debt to them both is enormous.

Since the original conditions of participating in the research was that the anonymity of participating schools and staff would be ensured, I am unable to individually thank them. That these materials exist at all is due to the many hundreds of hours work that these schools so freely gave. Their experiences, their hopes, successes, and freely admitted failures, are all recorded throughout the teaching materials with the hope that training in school administration might in the future become that little bit easier. Without their commitment and the effort they so generously gave this research could never have taken place.

The Department of Education and Science provided the substantial proportion of the funds which allowed this research to take place and I am grateful for this opportunity to express my gratitude to them. However, I must accept responsibility for the opinions expressed throughout as these reflect my own points of view. They do not and were never meant to represent the views of the Department of Education and Science.

*LYONS, G. (1974) *The administrative duties of Head and Senior Teachers in Large Secondary schools*. Report to the Department of Education & Science. University of Bristol .

LYONS, G. *Teacher Careers and Career Perceptions*. Report to the Department of Education & Science.

CONTENTS

Tutors' Handbook

SUMMARY

The documents which form this publication are intended to be self-explanatory but it seems useful to direct the reader's attention to the following points:

1. They are presented as a series of discussion documents that focus upon different aspects of the administrative work of the large secondary school.

Although each document is designed to be complete in itself, they can be combined in a whole series of ways: to enable broader based courses to be mounted; to provide a different focus to be brought to bear upon a particular issue or problem and so forth. One of their main strengths therefore is this flexibility.

2. Although they were initially devised for in-service training of senior and middle management staff of the large secondary comprehensive school, subsequent use has considerably extended this original aim.

3. No attempt has been made to provide a representation of ideal practice. The aim throughout has been to stimulate discussion by raising fundamental issues that underly administrative practice in the school.

4. As such they represent current research and thinking in the field of educational administration in this country.

5. They are designed to be used in a group context. The experience and skills of the members of the group thus becomes one of the most important resources available to the course tutor.

6. The course tutor should be able to identify the theme that lies behind each document. He should however be prepared to use the

document as a springboard, creating role plays, simulations, exercises, in-baskets, and so forth, as a way of extending the material more pertinently to fit the needs of the members of his course. 'Pupil Records' and the 'Staff Recruitment Exercise' are provided as examples of how this may be done.

7. Tutors must guard against schools who merely wish to use these documents as a checklist to update their own procedures, or who attempt to incorporate uncritically the examples portrayed into their own practice.

8. Throughout the documents it has been the intention to describe the work of the school. The practices and strategies portrayed are therefore selected to illustrate school administrative procedures—*they do not and were never intended to reflect 'model' ways of doing work.*

The rest of this handbook develops these points in greater detail. Some background information about the documents is provided as well as making suggestions for their use and for the construction of courses.

INTRODUCTION

For a number of years now there has been a developing interest in the provision of formal training for teachers in the tasks of school administration, to provide them with skills which, not very long ago, teachers were expected to pick up for themselves on the job. Many of those who today occupy senior positions in schools pride themselves on having 'gone in at the deep end and survived', but in the light of the myriad and increasing pressures facing schools in these days, there is a growing awareness of the need for teachers to be trained in school administration.

There are many reasons behind this. The insights to be gained from the social and management sciences, the growing complexity of the goals which the large secondary school in particular seeks to serve, the increased size of these schools which has changed the nature of the task of running them, and the devolving of responsibility to the school in the newer, bigger local education authorities, with the consequent accountability by the school to that authority in terms of the 'management' practices adopted—these are some, amongst the many, reasons behind the awakening concern for the training of school staff in administrative practices.

Until a year or two ago educational administration was not well represented at centres of higher education in England and Wales, particularly as compared with the proliferation of courses found in colleges and universities in Canada, the United States and Australia. The principal development in England and Wales has in fact occurred in 'Management Departments' of polytechnics.

One stumbling block to the development of courses has been a lack of coherent information to illustrate the administrative practices adopted by schools, particularly within the larger and newer secondary comprehensive schools. Assuming that the procedures followed in these schools differ from those associated with the more traditional secondary school, one may well ask what do heads and senior staff of large secondary schools do? and what are the problems involved in running the big school?

To try and provide some information on questions such as these the Department of Education and Science funded a research project* which was based in the Research Unit of the School of Education at the University of Bristol. The project was given the task of monitoring and describing administration in large secondary schools, but was principally concerned with generating materials that could be used for in-service training courses in school administration. The materials presented here are almost wholly derived from this research project.

It is not intended that the teaching materials produced should apply to other than the large secondary comprehensive school.

The brief of the project to conduct a study of the administrative duties of head and senior teachers in large secondary comprehensive schools incorporated a number of sub-goals. These were:

1. To determine the nature of the administrative tasks which are undertaken by head and senior teachers.
2. To determine how the nature and the quantity of these tasks varied throughout the school day, the school week, the school year, and for different members of staff and different types of secondary school.
3. To identify and describe patterns of work in school administration.
4. To examine alternative strategies for task re-distribution.

The material is presented as a series of discussion documents, each one complete in itself and focusing on a particular aspect of the administrative work of the large secondary comprehensive school. Although originally designed for use in a group context in in-service courses for senior and middle management staff, pilot trials have shown that they are potentially useful in a number of contexts—even as a basis for individual study. With this in mind, it is important to make clear at the outset that they do *not* reflect 'model' methods—the practices and strategies portrayed are illustrative of what can and does

---

* LYONS, G. (1974) *The Administrative Tasks of Head and Senior Teachers in Large Secondary Schools*. University of Bristol.

happen, not necessarily what *should* happen. The aim is rather to stimulate discussion by raising basic issues that underline administrative practice in the secondary school. As such, they represent current research and thinking in the field of educational administration in Britain.

It will be apparent to an experienced course tutor, on looking through the material, that different documents can be selected and combined in a variety of ways, either for use in more broadly-based courses, or in order to focus on a particular issue—in fact to suit individual needs. Such flexibility is, I feel, an advantage, although naturally it involves considerable thought on the part of the tutor.

The remainder of this brief handbook develops some of the above points in greater detail, provides some background information, and makes some suggestions for the use of the material and for the construction of possible courses.

The role of the tutor

This book is not a syllabus. It is, rather, a collection of resource materials upon which the course tutor can draw. An additional, and most important, resource is the individual skill of the tutor himself, acting as the catalyst in organizing the students' experience and in throwing in new ideas. His role is obviously a crucial one.

There is extensive scope for tutors in the use of these materials, but the maximum benefit is likely to accrue through involving the teacher *directly* in the problem-solving situation, and by so channelling his experience and expertise that explicit practice can be derived, particularly with reference to the needs of the teacher's own school. Essentially, then, this brief handbook is designed to be read, dispensed with, perhaps referred to occasionally, but not to be adhered to rigidly. The documents themselves are designed to be used as springboards —it is for the tutor to fit the materials to the needs of his students.

One note of caution: tutors must guard against schools that merely wish to use the materials as a checklist to update their own procedures, or who attempt to incorporate uncritically the examples portrayed into their own practice. These are descriptive, not prescriptive—*they do not and were never intended to reflect 'model' ways of doing work*. Their inclusion is to help the tutor expose students, in a controlled learning environment, to the content and consequences of certain procedures.

The course tutor should bring variety to his course. The format suggested above should be supplemented by lectures from outside speakers, or by bringing in expert witnesses for the working groups to interview or by visits to schools or other institutions who represent good practice in the task being studied. Students should be provided with materials that they can take away with them in the form of checklists of procedure, and so on.

The documents should be regarded as a springboard to action, not necessarily complete in themselves. They must on the one hand involve the students in a learning situation, setting tasks, exercises, role plays, simulations, and so on, whilst not pre-empting the tutor's need to do this himself. On the other hand, they must present enough open-ended situations to leave scope for full and forthright discussions of 'issues' and allow an exchange of views.

Tasks, exercises, simulations are principally provided as examples of how the material can be used—the documents concerned with pupil records, and staff recruitment are provided as examples of this use—the course tutor must add to these to orientate the documents to his particular needs. They are urged to treat the materials in whichever way they wish, the tutor must take his own stance. The structure, the suggestions for simulated activities, the questions presented in the documents should all be ignored if the tutor wishes to give the material a different treatment.

He must devise role plays, use video or audio tapes and write in-baskets as means of exploring given themes, e.g. the material can act as a starting point for his course and he might ask his students to add to it. He might suggest that they devise their own list of Major Administrative Tasks, produce an outline of how they think a task should be organized and compare it with the schemes outlined in the documents. Exploring the differences will entail resolving weaknesses, building on strengths and looking to the future to consider how schools should organize themselves.

Those documents relating to Major Administrative Tasks lend themselves readily to cumulative planning exercises, particularly if students are constrained by the consequences of decisions made previously. The outlining of procedures, the distribution of tasks across a school year, the allocation of staff to tasks and the simple costing of the operation in time can prove very profitable, particularly if the student's

involvement allows him to test his assumptions against those of his colleagues and those that are in the documents. Such an exercise also provides an opportunity for a profound exchange of opinion without the student appearing disloyal to his own school. The exposure of effective strategies is only part of the learning situation. The how and when of interlocking aspects of administrative programmes in school, particularly as carried out under pressure, must also be brought out.

Theories of educational administration

The materials in this book are particularly concerned with introducing students to the practical skills of administering a school. Although elements of various theories of administration are implicit in the discussion documents, no single theory is explicitly discussed. Whilst recognizing that the majority of students would be reluctant to become too involved in the study of the various theories of administration, it is nevertheless hoped that some will become interested in this aspect and wish to pursue it further. It is the function of the course tutor to provide the resources for this area of study.

The approach briefly outlined below is 'developmental' in that it assumes a programme of reading and discussion which will, over time, equip students to place the training materials within a framework of theory. But this approach has its disadvantages. It can be too abstract at the outset of a course of practical training and there may be a disjuncture between the theory and the practical activities to which it refers. Tutors may prefer to allow the theory to arise from the work on the materials. In many ways this is likely to be much more motivating for students, but it requires considerable ingenuity on the part of the tutor to link practice to a systematic theory rather than to a series of only loosely related concepts. This will require much experimentation and a capacity to be responsive to the needs of particular groups. If this approach is adopted, the brief outline given below can be seen rather as an end product than as a developmental pattern of study.

Administration is the process whereby the differentiated activities of the members of an organization are co-ordinated in the interests of the whole. It involves leadership, decision-making, communicating, allocating resources and so forth. But administration is not the *whole* of an organization which has other components e.g. a culture, a pattern of informal relationships. Thus the first task may be seen as encouraging students to see administration within this broader organizational context.

There is no adequate single theory of organization, but a number of theories which complement each other. It is important that the student should not focus only upon the *school* as an organization since, although a school is a unique form of organization, it shares *some* common features with factories, hospitals, and other forms of organization. Hence a comparative approach can be illuminating. Some basic works on organizational theory are:

KATZ, D. and KAHN, R. (1966) *The Social Psychology of Organizations.* New York: Wiley.

PERROW, C. (1970) *Organizational Analysis: a Sociological View.* London: Tavistock.

SILVERMAN, D. (1971) *The Theory of Organizations.* London: Heinemann.

Much of the literature on schools as organizations originates from the United States and hence raises the problem of 'translation'. Nevertheless, the following provide a useful overall view:

BIDWELL, C. (1965) 'The School as a formal organization'. In: MARCH, J. G. *Handbook of Organizations.* Chicago: Rand McNally.

CARVER, F. D. and SERGIOVANNI, T. J. (1969) *Organizations and Human Behaviour: Focus on Schools.* New York: McGraw Hill.

For the application of organizational theory to British schools see:

DAVIES, W. B. (1970) 'On the contribution of organizational analysis to the study of educational institutions' (Paper presented to the Annual Conference of the British Sociological Assoc. 1970). In: BROWN, R. (ed) *Knowledge, Education and Cultural Change,* Tavistock.

HOYLE, E. (1969a) 'Organizational theory and educational administration.' In: BARON, G. and TAYLOR, W. *Educational Administration and the Social Sciences.* London: Athlone Press.

HOYLE, E. (1973b) 'The Study of schools as organisations.' In: BUTCHER, H. J. and PONT, H. (Eds) *Educational Research in Britain III.* London: ULP.

Once a student has grasped the concept of the school as a social system of interrelated parts, he can then move on to consider the relevance of administrative theory. There are many approaches and the student will need to appreciate several of them. As with organizational theory, each administrative theory tends to seek an understanding of the administrative process through focusing, on one key variable (e.g. role, leadership, decision-making, system etc) and relating other variables to this. Much of the literature is again North American but can be read with advantage by British students. The following are some of the more important American studies which generated the 'new movement' in educational administration in the 1950s and 1960s that attempted to put educational administration in the context of the social and behavioural sciences:

COLADARCI, A. P. and GETZELS, J. W. (1955) *The Use of Theory in Educational Administration.* Stanford: Stanford University Press.,

GETZELS, J. W., LIPHAM, J. M. and CAMPBELL, R. F. (1968) *Educational Administration as a Social Process:* Theory, research, practice. New York: Harper Row.

GRIFFITHS, D. E. (1959) *Administrative Theory.* New York: Appleton-Century-Crofts.

GRIFFITHS, D. E. (ed) (1964) *Behavioural Science and Educational Administration.* 63rd Yearbook of the National Society for the Study of Education, Part II. Chicago: University of Chicago Press.

HALPIN, A. W. (1966) *Theory and Research in Administration.* NY: Macmillan.

HALPIN, A. W. (1967) *Administrative Theory in Education.* NY: Macmillan.

MILSTEIN, M. M. and BELASCO, J. A. (eds) (1973) *Educational Administration and the Behavioural Sciences:* a systems perspective. Boston: Allyn & Bacon.

Students will get an indication of the development of administrative theory in education by reading the collections of papers presented at the International Intervisitation Programme in Educational Administration, three of which have so far been held triennially. These collections are:

BARON, G., COOPER, D. and WALKER, N. G. (eds) (1969) *Educational Administration: International Perspectives.* Chicago: Rand McNally.

DOWNEY, L. W. and ENNS, F. (1963) *The Social Sciences and Educational Administration.* Calgary: University of Alberta Press.

HUGHES, M. (1975) *Administering Education. International Challenge.* London: Athlone Press.

British works which contain chapters on organizational and administrative theory are:

BARON, G. and TAYLOR, W. (1969) *Educational Administration and the Social Sciences.* London: Athlone Press.

HUGHES, M. G. (1970) *Secondary School Administration: a Management Approach.* Oxford: Pergamon.

In educational administration, as in education generally, linking theory and practice is a highly problematic activity. It is impossible to say to what extent a reading of theory actually influences practice. It may well be that students who read extensively in the theory of organization and administration may only thereby extend their own general education in that they will become aware to some degree of the nature of the different social and behavioural sciences and learn something of the philosophy of the natural and social sciences. And, as with any form of general education, the implications for behaviour are unknown. In reading these theories they will acquire, if not a single guiding theory, at least a familiarity with a set of basic concepts (e.g. personality, role, social interaction, social system) which should enable them to order their perceptions of the organizations in which they work. Again, although one does not really know to what extent improved perception leads to improved administrative performance, one expects that it *should* do so.

Some students might want to familiarize themselves with writing within the 'management' field itself. The following, all published as paperbacks, will provide a good initial introduction:

BROWN, WILFRED (1970) *Exploration in Management.* Harmondsworth: Penguin.

DRUCKER, PETER (1968) *The Practice of Management.* London: Pan.

STEWART, ROSEMARY (1967) *The Reality of Management.* London: Pan.

The aim the materials seek to satisfy

The principal, although not the sole, concern in portraying the different aspects of school administrative procedures and their operational consequences has been to focus the documents upon the problems that schools have in organization. This has been attempted without, it is hoped, shaping the material to represent merely one viewpoint. These documents have not sought to provide the students with skills in interpersonal relationships. However, a point of view which is implicit throughout this work, is that active staff participation in the decision-making process is not only desirable but also, in the large complex secondary school, essential.

It is hoped that the materials provide a basis for the development of a critical awareness on the part of the course membership. They provide a template which enables the teacher to critically examine practices in his own school. The course itself, through the structured intervention of the tutor, should lead the students to a realization of more appropriate practice which might be adopted within their own schools.

The wider context of staff training and staff development is thus the central concern rather than the more direct aspect of training Head Teachers in practical administrative skills.

To do this, the documents serve a number of different aims: (1) they permit a 'sensitizing' to the basic and fundamental issues of school administration; (2) they give staff who are comparatively inexperienced in some of the aspects of school administration a more global perception of this work, and (3) by using the documents as an orientation to existing procedures, allow the outlining of more effective practice for their own schools. Particularly important to the fulfilment of this latter aim is the recognition that one of the principal resources available, besides the individual skills of the respective tutors, is the pooling of the skills and experiences of the individual course members in the pursuit of a collaborative task.

The examples featured in the documents are chosen to represent 'typical' administrative practices in the large school. This should (1) enable a rapid familiarization with the administrative practice portrayed and (2) should ensure that problems identified are likely to have more significant impact. Obviously the examples chosen should 'look' and 'feel' real; some have been selected for their provocative nature.

One further aim which the materials seek to achieve is, to publish research evidence and to provide a background orientation in a field where information has been in short supply.

The nature of the materials

The materials reflect many of the activities undertaken and problems faced by teachers in the tasks of running schools, although they in no way represent the complete range of such activities. They are organized in sections as follows:

1. Tutor's handbook
2. Pupil welfare and guidance systems in schools
3. Pupil careers guidance programme
4. Applications for places in further and higher education
5. Pupil records
6. Transfer, induction and allocation of first year children to classes
7. Pupil subject options
8. Curricular activities
9. Procedures for mounting internal and external examinations
10. Production of a timetable
11. Budget, capitation and requisition procedures
12. Staff development: staffing and staff recruitment simulation
13. Arrangements for student teaching practice
14. Aspects of organization in the large secondary school
15. Communications
16. School office: Secretaries and bursars

In addition:

17. *Bishopston High School* A brief description of a large secondary comprehensive school to facilitate discussion of the above chapters.

In terms of content, there are two types of documents. The first relates to specific major administrative tasks in a school, e.g. 'The allocation and induction of first year children' and 'The production of a timetable', and the second to more generalizable topics such as 'Organization', 'Communications'. However, all are principally concerned with the same fundamental problems of school administration.

The documents make a liberal use of quotes from teachers, bar diagrams, flow charts, checklists of procedures, histograms, tables, pie diagrams, as a way of focusing attention upon a particular aspect of a problem. In this they reflect the reality of the school situation, and make the practices adopted by different schools easier to ascertain.

In providing this focus the documents vary in length, in style and in structure. Those relating to the more complex problems of 'organization' stress the consequences of certain organizational structures; the 'welfare' documents allow some comparison to be made of the efficacy of a selection of the systems found operating; whilst those that present 'major administrative tasks' outline the practice followed by a school, presenting some simple time costing and providing sources of additional information to illustrate further the particular task. The document dealing with 'The Pupil Careers Guidance Programme' provides an example.

A general introduction relates to the reader some of the basic problems of any school-based careers guidance programme. One school's strategy is then outlined by means of a flow diagram; a list of some of the decisions that the school has to make in order to mount its programme is also presented. A costing of this programme is provided by a bar chart. Checklists are presented of detailed aspects of the school's programme, as well as a summary of documents and pro-formas which the programme required and a summary of research findings. Since this school made a heavy use of the 'Youth Employment Service', a diametrically opposed viewpoint about their work is provided by the headmaster of another school. One further aspect, that of pupil involvement, is provided from the findings of another research project. The document in its final section asks the students to consider some simple questions. These relate both to the programme examined and to the practice adopted in the students' own school. This is done with the intention of providing a mechanism whereby some of the more fundamental careers guidance programmes questions may be explored, and of raising the question of the interrelationship of this one programme with other aspects of the work of the school.

The use of materials

As already mentioned, a considerable onus is placed upon the course tutor in devising ways of using these materials with each particular group of students. They have, however, been piloted in various contexts and on the basis of this experience some guidance on their use is given below.

A detailed outline of how one of the chapters, 'The Budget Capitation and Requisition Procedures', can be used is given as an example at the end of this section.

Patterns of use (a variety of patterns is possible)

1. *Self study* Here the tutor has only a very limited responsibility. There may be occasions where a student simply takes the entire package and uses the material as a basis for self study. Although this is a theoretical possibility, it is clearly a last resort, where a student cannot attend a course. The great value of these materials is their use in the context of a group of experienced teachers who can bring their experience to bear upon the problems and issues contained in these materials.

2. *Ad hoc use* The documents may be used separately as individual units each complete in itself thereby providing the focus of discussion on the topic selected by the tutor.

3. *Grouped use* The individual documents may be grouped into a whole series of possible combinations, to give a wider perspective than one document would allow, or to assemble a package that would better represent a substantial section of schools administrative processes, for example: Guidance and Welfare Processes, Curricular Processes. The organization into sections of the individual units given on page 7 suggests some of the possibilities. Further permutations of the units are possible, these clearly depend upon the judgement of the course tutor, and the purpose of the course.

4. *Systematic use* This would involve the use of the materials as a whole as the basis of a complete, self-contained course. Most of the comments made below are based on the assumption that a course is built around the materials.

5. *Topic-based use* Most of the documents lend themselves to a study of the broader issues of school administration. Thus the tutor who mounts a course on 'Communications' for example could, if he wished, use others of the documents as a basis for discussion of communication problems. They could provide examples of the consequences of a given pattern of organizational subdivision, resource allocation, the setting up of an academic board, and so on, thereby presenting a variety of viewpoints.

Course membership

Course tutors who use the materials in a systematic manner will need to give some thought to the membership of the group. The membership may be drawn

(i) entirely from the staff of one school; or
(ii) from the staff of several institutions.

Where the group is of the second type it could take one of two forms:

1. *Homogeneous group* This is appropriate where the intention is to run a 'role workshop' in which students all occupy the same role: heads, deputies, heads of departments, etc., and thereby to some degree share a common background. This shared experience has a number of advantages, notably an ease of communication based on mutual understanding.

2. *Heterogeneous group* This is appropriate where a basic objective of the course is to capitalize on the varying perspectives of administrative tasks of

(a) those with different roles within the school, and
(b) individuals drawn from institutions different in kind.

Thus a course on pupil welfare systems could draw upon social workers, LEA personnel, careers officers and so on, together with those responsibile for pupil welfare within the school. Such an approach would seek to remove mutual misconceptions and encourage the different role occupants to appreciate better the problems of others.

Each approach has its uses, and tutors will have to decide which they wish to adopt. However, one point should be taken into consideration. Whatever type of group the tutor wishes to work with, he must make his purpose clear when he advertises his course and recruits students. Otherwise, some dissatisfaction amongst course members could result.

Group size and staffing

It proves most practical if courses can be arranged to provide a ratio of one tutor to each group of ten students. A practical overall size for a course is 20 students. If the resources and expertise are available to manage a bigger group this number can be exceeded. Given, however, an overall course membership of 20, one of the tutors should function as the course director. Tutors should be available for all working sessions; if possible, one tutor should have 'management' expertise, whilst the other should hold, or have held, a senior position in a comprehensive school and thus be able to speak from experience and a background of 'educational' expertise. This would appear to be the best basic combination and to give the greatest satisfaction to course members. In the case of courses with a bigger membership, the additional tutors can clearly represent different specialisms.

Teaching strategies

Obviously, a whole range of teaching strategies is possible and the tutor will no doubt experiment with various approaches until he finds one which appears to meet the needs of his students. However, as a stimulus to tutors to think about their strategies, the following points are offered for consideration:

1. Course members should be given the materials before the course begins. They should be asked to familiarize themselves with the documents and also to use them as a template for examining practice in their own schools. This is particularly important in the case of course members who are class teachers since they may not have the same degree of familiarity with school procedures as those further up the school hierarchy. This preparation should enable teachers to derive greater benefit from the course since they will have gained more knowledge about how their own schools are run and will therefore be in a stronger position to participate in discussions about comparative practice.

2. The course should open with a plenary session at which the tutor outlines the problem which is to be handled and the strategies to be used.

3. Course members then divide into groups or syndicates in order to work on the problems.

4. The syndicates can operate in one of two ways:
   (a) Each syndicate can work on a common problem in order that solutions can later be compared and discussed;
   (b) Each syndicate can work on a separate task as part of an overall strategy determined by the course or working party.

Clearly in the case of (b) it is essential to establish a clear overall strategy at the outset which is understood by all participants if the task is to be profitable. Scheme (a) is probably more practical.

5. It is valuable if each syndicate nominates a secretary and a chairman to act as spokesman. During the course of their work, syndicates should have access to course tutors as consultants.

6. Tutors should circulate among groups throughout all working sessions.

7. After considering the problem and deciding on a tentative solution—or alternative solutions if there is no group consensus—these syndicates should again come together in plenary session. Where the task is sufficiently complex then a series of intermediary plenary sessions is recommended in order to allow syndicates to exchange interim views and to indicate to each other their progress. In the final plenary session, the students should outline and defend the viewpoints to which their work in syndicates has led.

8. This type of structure formalizes the course sufficiently and gives enough flexibility for supplementary material to be included where necessary. It also allows maximum opportunity for an exchange of views between course members and provides a suitable format within which tasks may be undertaken and tuition given in groups small enough for the needs of individuals to be identified. Small numbers also offer the greatest opportunity for all to contribute to the discussion, and through the pursuit of joint tasks provide reinforcement for those who feel they may be threatened by exposure in a more formal teaching situation.

Supplementary material

The documents provide a basis for the creation of a learning situation in which tasks, exercises, simulations, role plays and so forth, form a part. Perhaps two points need to be made in relation to these approaches.

One is that the tutor should not confine students to the activities set in the documents but should devise his own on the basis of the needs of a particular group. The other is that the use of these tasks, as a means for practical training, simulations etc. should not be allowed to pre-empt the possibility of discussing the issues raised in a more fundamental— even philosophical—manner.

Duration of tasks

The length of time which students will take over each document will vary according to the contents themselves and also the way in which they are used by the tutor. A straightforward discussion of the materials will occupy a two-hour session at least, but if practical or problem-solving tasks are to be followed, then considerably longer is necessary. Obviously, a full two-hour session spent 'in discussion' is not a profitable use of time. Greater variety of approach must be adopted if the course is to be successful. The tutor will need to experiment with the length of time required for each document as he sees fit to use it. (For example, if the practical exercises in the chapter 'Staffing and Staffing Recruitment' are used and job descriptions, shortlisting and interviewing exercises are carried out, then these will occupy *at least* a full weekend's work by the students.) It is important that sufficient time be made available for the completion of the tasks if these are to be carried out effectively and if there is to be a full discussion in the plenary session. The tutor should therefore not only ensure that sufficient time is available but also, especially in the period when he is experimenting with the materials, allow enough flexibility in the planning of the course to allow for adaptability according to the time taken by his students to complete the tasks and discuss them fully.

Additional points

1. *The simulated school: Bishopston High School*

At certain times if the discussion of specific documents is not to be too diffuse or where the discussion of general issues raised by the documents needs to be tightly structured if the session is not to become anecdotal, a common focus is required. This has been provided by a brief outline of a simulated school—Bishopston High School.

The discussion can thus be organized around Bishopston High School in order to ensure that the issues are dealt with more systematically. However, this simulation, based entirely upon one of the schools making the research returns, ought not to be used in such a way as to detract from one of the principle features underlying the presentation of these materials—this is that course members are to use the orientation afforded by the framework of the documents to examine critically the practice followed in their own schools.

2. *Do your own research*

If a course were able to provide the time and the resources, it would prove most rewarding for the students to be set the task of gathering for themselves some of the types of information the documents provide, i.e. outlines of strategies by which the school undertakes a task, simple costing of procedures, and so on. They might if they wished use a document as a model to guide their action, or as a basis for comparison. The difficulties they would encounter in collecting, processing and presenting their information would draw rapid attention to the value bases of much administrative practice and the difficulties the organization has in critically reviewing its programmes—not least because the information it needs to do this is not readily available. They might be able to suggest resolutions to some of the dilemmas that the institution faces.

Were the student able to undertake such a task using his own school, and for a programme or a part of the organization with which he is closely identified, then it is likely that the experience would be particularly valuable.

3. *Survey findings*

As a further orientation to tutors in the design of their courses, attached as an appendix at the end of this handbook, are the findings of a survey conducted by the author in five comprehensive schools, into what serving teachers looked for from short in-service training courses.

An example of how the documents may be used

Below is a brief outline of how one of the chapters 'Budget, Capitation and Requisition Procedures' might be used.

This is presented as an example of possible use. Many other

strategies might be employed, and other issues raised, particularly where the document is interrelated to other documents portraying different aspects of school administration. This outline of the use of one document is presented to give some guidance to tutors as to the way they might use a document on their courses.

The budget, capitation and requisition procedures

Although the document should be circulated in advance so that those on the course can have sufficient time to read it, it is necessary to spend the first twenty minutes or so familiarizing the course members with the contents. To this end, the introduction is best read together, though the tutor should paraphrase the paragraphs expanding or contracting them as he wishes. He should anticipate some of the questions likely to be raised and refer to some of the issues to be dealt with later. For example, the degree to which schools might have progressed beyond the 'traditional' phase referred to, why there should exist the degree of variation that is found in LEA financial provision, what 'virement' means, who in their school retains control of finance and of policy development and what is the relation between the two, and so on.

Some attempt should be made at this stage to obtain views on what questions the course members think they ought to be asking in order to gain a sufficient insight into the complexity of the task so that they will be able to devise an effective strategy. This procedure is a device (a) to explore the degree of knowledge they have, and (b) to bring out into the open some of the opposing values that they possibly hold.

The budgetary procedure for School 1 should then be studied in detail and discussion should continue until all have a sufficient understanding. The course members might be asked about the way the LEA appears to perceive the school budget, the degree of freedom the school appears to have in handling its financial affairs, the apparent role of the head, deputy head, heads of departments and individual members of staff in this procedure and what is the degree of delegation that is implied. The course members should be invited to indicate strengths and weaknesses in the programme—are the budget headings to departments justifiable? what is the reaction of the course to how monies other than capitation are handled? and so on.

The budgetary procedure of School 2 should then be discussed on similar lines to those indicated above. However one useful difference in standpoint which might be adopted is to ask the course to determine the degree to which the procedure followed by School 2 resolves the problems they have outlined as existing for School 1.

The tutor might also like to raise some of the questions presented at the end of the document. Questions 2 and 4 have on pilot courses excited considerable comment.

If there is longer than a two hour session available then the tutor might wish to have the course complete some practical exercises.

Whilst clearly the most pertinent task is to devise a more effective budgetary procedure for their own school, the time absorbing nature of such a task means that the course members should not attempt it without considerable time being available. To attempt this effectively, it is desirable to send working parties to other schools to study their procedures; and to receive lecture inputs and examine witnesses from schools that in the tutor's knowledge adopt good practice, from LEA personnel, management personnel who specialize in budgetary control, and so on.

At a more restricted level, the course in syndicate session might be asked to:

Devise a job description, complete with performance indicators, for a bursar who is to be introduced into School 1; how would they introduce him into this school?

Devise a new requisition card, or consult firms specializing in filing systems to see what equipment for 'at a glance' budgetary control is available;

Determine (a) the composition of a budgetary sub-committee for a school, and (b) the body that sub-committee should report to. They might answer questions such as should parents, governors and pupils be represented on the sub-committee.

The syndicates should in plenary session defend the schemes they propose.

How the materials have been used

Outlined below are some examples of courses with widely differing aims and differing memberships which have been organized using these materials. These are presented merely to exemplify the range of courses which could be organized, and it must be clear that there are many other possibilities.

The materials have been found to have a successful use on courses organized for senior staff of newly formed comprehensive schools, or those just about to become comprehensive. As such the material provides: an orientation to practice, the opportunity for full discussion of the types of problems to be resolved, a comparison with the situation in the student's own school, and the occasion for exchange of knowledge and experience with colleagues. It proves profitable to introduce at a suitable time on such courses a senior member of staff from an established comprehensive school which is known to adopt good practice of the particular topic under discussion. It is, needless to say, the tutor's responsibility to make the appropriate choice.

Those occupying middle management levels in a school or those who perhaps have been recently promoted to a senior position, benefit from a more global orientation to the difficulties of school administration. The material is particularly helpful in this respect if simple problem-solving tasks are asked of the course members. For example, the bar charts which are incorporated in some of the documents dealing with major administrative tasks prove a useful device for questioning: the timing of tasks over a school year; the overloading of key members of staff with responsibility; the problems of delegation; the interrelationship of tasks; the demands which outside agencies make upon schools and upon school calendars, and so on. The more fundamental problems of organization are thus rapidly exposed.

A course on the Professional Training and Development of Teaching Staff in the large school was organized in a more didactic way, using a subset of the materials. Only senior members of staff from established comprehensive schools who intended to set up a scheme of staff development and training within their school were recruited. The course tutors and lecturers were those, who represented a management approach, and those who were operating or planning schemes of staff development in their schools.

Courses which are organized specifically to achieve practical outcomes along the above lines must ensure that the course has sufficient time to consider in depth schemes developed by individual schools. *It would also be profitable if the tutors were subsequently prepared to act as consultant(s) to any school intending to implement a scheme developed on that course.*

The local teachers' centre was chosen as the venue for a course that examined systems of pupil welfare and guidance for three schools which had recently become (or were about to become) comprehensive. A selection of the documents provided the orientation and focus to the initial meeting, after which the teachers were given the brief of returning to their schools to set up working parties to examine present practice. At a subsequent meeting, problems which had proved common to all three schools were discussed, and three tutors were attached, one to each of the three schools, to act as consultants to help the schools review and revise their procedure.

For courses aimed at experienced head teachers of large secondary comprehensive schools, the materials are better used as a rapid orientation to discussion, as a resource base exemplifying practice, and as a way of ensuring that the dialogue proceeds meaningfully on common ground using a common terminology.

The materials have been piloted by other tutors in a diversity of settings. They have been used on courses at the diploma and masters degree levels in polytechnics and universities; on induction courses for probationer teachers; at the initial training level in colleges of education; to educationists from abroad as an orientation to school administration in England and Wales; and by wardens of teachers' centres mounting in-service courses for secondary school staff in their areas.

Further use of the materials

It seems particularly important to extend the use of the materials beyond the somewhat narrow confines so far developed and there are many potential areas of fruitful study. One in particular is to focus upon those tasks which cross the boundaries of the school. Where a task involves institutions or individuals who normally work outside the school and whose loyalties are probably to different reference groups there exists a potential source of conflict. It would be helpful to bring such people together for a discussion of their mutual perspectives on the same problem. A tutor might organize discussions with ancillary and auxiliary staff; involve primary and secondary school staffs working together; involve educational welfare officers, school welfare staff, the school health and psychological services, social workers, the school governors, local authority staff, and so on, in courses designed to explore how they might mutually help and reinforce each other's work.

The material in providing a rapid orientation to practice and a framework for analysis proves an ideal resource base to school working parties who wish to review a particular aspect of their school's administration.

Head teachers who wish to undertake staff development will find the documents a rich source of information and a useful way of initiating a dialogue with members of staff e.g. at the head of department level.

By exposure to carefully selected documents or, sections of them, the young and comparatively inexperienced teacher can be acquainted with the ramifications of administrative practice, not only to his own benefit and development, but to that of the school as well.

There is a clear applicability of the materials at the initial training level and also for other graduate and undergraduate students.

Further uses might involve the teaching of concepts derived from the behavioural sciences, using the materials as orientation and illustration in a planning exercise for a hypothetical school . . .

The responsibility is however the tutor's own. He must select the material he wishes to use on his course, and the treatment he gives to it, in order to match the special needs of his students.

APPENDIX

Some comments from teachers about short duration in-service training courses

One hundred and twenty-two teachers who reflected all grades of staff in five large secondary comprehensive schools had initially, during an interview about career perceptions, been asked whether they had attended any short duration in-service training courses and what effect they thought such courses had upon career prospects.* In answering, comments ranged over a much wider field than that of promotion and offered quite fundamental views on the structure and the organization of in-service training courses. In view of the increasing interest in in-service training for practising teachers it was thought that these comments are worthy of a wider audience.

Answers were unstructured, any teacher being allowed to make as many responses as he or she wished. Comments were coded to indicate those features of courses found particularly satisfactory (positive); those features which were criticized (negative); and those items to which it was impossible to allocate a positive or negative response (general). These are tabulated below. Problems unfortunately exist in interpreting responses made to unstructured questions, and in this context, about the validity to attach to a quantitative weighting, for such responses unfortunately tell us nothing about other responses which the respondent might have made. An interpretation of the views expressed therefore can be no more than impressionistic and with this in mind the first three items in the table are considered together, for although logically distinct they are interrelated.

One point of interest is that, apart from facts relating to promotions,

* *Teacher Careers and Career Perceptions.* Report to the Department of Education and Science.

comments referring to a particular feature are almost wholly positive or almost wholly negative. That a course gives orientation, skills or ideas, or that participation on courses allows teachers to share experience are only referred to as virtues. If a course is to be criticized then it is the presentation, the content, the terms of reference or the times at which courses occur that are singled out for negative comment and criticism.

It is clear that a primary expectation of practising teachers is that a course should be realistically and practically based and offer the teacher something that he can take directly back into the classroom. It should typically: 'Provide thought,' 'give ideas', 'encourage experimentation', 'extend knowledge', 'give information about textbooks, methods, exam. requirements, etc.'. It would also be distinctly encouraging if such a course 'would enthuse you'.

As can be seen in the table, the preponderance of comments fall into this area. Where the expectation is unfulfilled then it seems as if criticism is likely to be directed either at the presentation of the 'course content', or, at the course's 'terms of reference'. 'The way of issuing information is important, not enough printed material and too much note taking', 'courses can be top heavy with too many lectures and not enough discussion time', 'I get home and ask myself what have I gained today—nothing—just new names for old tricks'.

The performance of lecturers, a very delicate area with regard to the professional competence of the audience, came in for specific criticism, 'the teacher was very young and not knowledgeable'. 'Too theoretical, not practical enough'. 'Some of the organizers don't know what they are talking about', 'out of touch'. That the course fails to fulfill its own publicity can be a similar source of frustration: 'the speaker didn't speak on the subject', 'impractical misleading prospectus suggested would give ideas for what could do in school'.

In providing a focus where people of similar interests are drawn together the course becomes a vehicle whereby informal contacts between teachers are fostered, and this contact out of the confines of a lecture room was frequently mentioned as one of the strongest positive features emerging from attendance at short duration in-service courses. 'A valuable part of any course is the discussion that goes on between members of the course, you share problems with other teachers—removes isolation', 'a sense of security meeting other people like your-

Teachers' comments: Short duration in-service training courses

Number of times response mentioned	Postively	Negatively	General	Total
Orientation skills, ideas	58	—	5	63
Presentation	4	32	7	43
Terms of reference	—	12	1	13
Help each other by sharing problems and ideas	38	1	—	39
Promotion	19	12	7	38
Duration and timing external factors	3	13	7	23
Duration and timing internal factors	1	9	2	12
Availability Accessibility	—	7	4	11
Other	12	6	2	20
Totals	135	92	35	262

Number of teachers interviewed = 122
Number of teachers making one or more comments = 116
Number of teachers failing to comment = 6

self, interchange ideas', 'provides the opportunity of standing back from your own school and seeing that other colleagues have same problems'. The fact that a sense of isolation is ameliorated, that security comes from the recognition of sharing similar problems, and that teachers may learn as much from picking each others' brains seems to be of some considerable interest.

Timing presents certain problems, and courses run in school hours can generate particular difficulties. 'Tough on one's colleagues, feels guilty about others covering (her) lessons'. A course 'on the same day each week always hits the same school class', 'one night a week ones are an imposition'. 'Takes a lot of arranging at home to get away for a weekend course'. For a married woman it becomes even more difficult 'with a family and doing schoolwork haven't got time to cope, can't sit down until 8 o'clock at night', and the expected pace of work is important to staff who have already completed a full day's teaching, 'the determination to work people through to 10.30 at night causes difficulty'. A teacher's accessibility to a course appears to be dependent upon geographical accident, those living in large conurbations being more favoured. 'Aren't enough within easy access', 'difficult to find a course (he) is interested in'.

This group of teachers quite clearly appreciated courses which immediately give information or techniques to carry back into the classroom. The course, they suggest, should be kept to the point and, if information needs to be dispensed, then it is advantageous if it can be disseminated in a printed form thus providing the additional bonus of more time to explore the ramifications of what is being offered, for science teachers to practice the use of new apparatus etc. There are many problems associated with 'off the job' training particularly those problems relating to transferring knowledge or techniques gained back into the 'in school' situation. At first hand, 'on the job' training appears to resolve some of these difficulties. A course, however, which fails to provide a context, outside the formally organized lecture or workshop session, in which teachers from different schools are brought together in such a way as to allow them to forge mutual bonds and to exchange experience and ideas, omits by the same token one of the factors which teachers regard as most important in contributing to the success of courses. An understanding of such a consequence and the provision of physical facilities to allow the successful achievement of such an aim seem to be equally necessary.

Pupil Welfare and Guidance Systems in the School

CONTENTS

INTRODUCTION

Pupil welfare and guidance in the school context are concerned certainly with at least three main areas of need, that is, the personal, the academic and the career needs of a pupil. It is self-evident that these are not discrete categories—they come together to form one of the major planks of the work of the school. The interrelationship of the welfare and guidance programmes to the other major plank of the school's work, that is, its curricular processes, immediately raises fundamental questions since the school must make clear where it has determined its priorities are to lie.

In formulating a system to handle the welfare and guidance needs of pupils, it often seems as though schools have reacted to pressures placed upon them rather than designing a system which will cope with all the foreseeable problems. As more schools see the operation of some sort of structured welfare system as part of their function, one of the main problems with which they are faced is whether their system is designed and able to cope with crises or whether it is only able to cope with the routine and mundane.

It also ought to have been decided at what point in the hierarchy responsibility is to be carried, whether and to what degree outside experts are to be used, whether staff are to be trained and, if so, how they are to be trained, how much time is to be made available within the timetable for the welfare operation and, crucial to the effective operation of any decisions made, how much of the budget is to be allocated to this sector of the school's activities. It is suggested that certain schools would operate more effectively if they allocated the major part of their budget to welfare/guidance functions and if teaching activities were regarded as a subservient function to this major aim.

There is in the allocation of resources a tension between the help any individual child may need and the developmental needs of all the children. In order to discharge the latter effectively, it appears that much of the activity at the guidance and welfare level must begin in the classroom. Much care must be taken to ensure that the personal help afforded to an individual child or to a group of children is not merely a thinly disguised attempt to deal with those children who do not conform to staff expectations and who do not fit into the social structure of the school. One further difficulty exists and this is caused by the hierarchical nature of the welfare structure within which, for ease of administration, the child is allocated to a tutor and expected to develop a close and personal rapport with this agent. One of the first priorities for a school would seem to be the determination of the degree to which the welfare system they operate is to be child-orientated or authority-orientated.

At present many teachers are seen to be performing a dual role of teacher and counsellor, and incidentally it seems as if most teachers are considered sufficiently expert in welfare/guidance activities not to need any training for their duties. However, if experts in guidance and welfare were available in sufficient numbers in a school, then the role of a teacher would be radically altered to that of organizing learning experiences recommended for the child. In practice, it is suggested, the major part of the teacher's time that is spent upon guidance and welfare activities, is taken up by the routine compilation of records, and this in particular is what teachers might profitably be relieved of.

Within this section documents are presented which examine these issues in greater detail. All are interrelated but are presented separately. They comprise:

1. Pupil welfare

2. Pupil careers guidance

3. Applications for places in further and higher education

4. Pupil records

Initially teachers might like to begin discussion of some of the issues involved by considering whether they would allocate pupil option choices to a curricular or welfare guidance heading. They might also like to consider the more fundamental question:

If it is not possible for a school to discharge its guidance and welfare duties with complete success, then should the school attempt to discharge these activities at all?

A list of suggested further reading is given below for those who may wish to pursue some of the issues in more detail than these documents allow.

Further Reading:

CARTER, M. P. (1969) *Into Work*. Harmondsworth: Penguin.

CLEGG, A. and MEGSON, B. (1968) *Children in Distress*. Harmondsworth: Penguin.

CRAFT, M., RAYNOR, J. and COHEN, L. (edits) (1970) *Linking Home and School*. 2nd edition. London: Longmans.

FURTHER EDUCATION STAFF COLLEGE (1972) 'Guidance,' *Coombe Lodge Report*, 5, 19.

MOORE, B. (1970) *Guidance in Comprehensive Schools*. Slough: NFER.

RICHARDSON, E. (1973) *The Teacher, the School and the Task of Management*. London: Heinemann.

SCHOOLS COUNCIL (1969) *Counselling in Schools*. Working paper No. 15. London.

The Careers Research Advisory Centre (CRAC), Bateman Street, Cambridge, is able to offer advice on most aspects of careers work in schools.

DEFINING WELFARE

Traditionally, class teachers have been expected to exercise both curricular and pastoral responsibility for their pupils. Such responsibility devolved naturally from the position of moral and intellectual superiority held by the teacher over a pupil, reinforced both by the frequency of classroom and probably also by community contact.

The degree to which this expectation was fulfilled in practice might be questioned.

However the size of the large school, as well as the complexity of its curricular and administrative organization, and the rate of staff turnover, are amongst the many features that would make a system based upon such expectations untenable in a large secondary school.

In the large school teacher and pupil do not necessarily interact outside a subject classroom, and subject specialization is likely further to reduce pupil-teacher contact time within a classroom, as well as reducing the possibility of one teacher maintaining contact with a pupil throughout that pupil's secondary school career. The subject teacher is likely to see many pupils but to have a reduced opportunity of knowing any of them well.

Schools anxious to give pupils a sense of identity and to reduce the incidence of problems or of personal unhappiness to a minimum have tended to create separately-organized systems for pupil welfare. In such systems pastoral responsibility is invested in one, or in a group of specially designated teachers. An element of former expectation is retained by formalizing the subject teacher's responsibility for welfare matters, as a house or a year tutor, or by continuing the form teacher tradition. Such a system, overlaying as it does a separate curriculum structure, is sometimes likely to be seen as artificial.

Pupil welfare systems, whilst distinct in many ways from other functioning systems within the school, in practice display interdependence and interrelation with most other aspects of the work of the school.

Welfare processes are organized in many different ways. The three most common seem to be; those located around a house tutor in a vertically organized house reporting to a head of house; those organized around a year tutor, reporting to a head of year in a horizontally organized year system; those located on a form base. All of these may report directly either to the most senior staff in the school or to heads of sections, that is, heads of upper, middle and lower schools. The above outline gives some idea of the possible permutation of systems that prevail since in meeting different problems, schools are found that have adopted to varying extents the types of organization outlined above. A school may have its first year organized on a year basis, year two to five on a house basis, and the sixth form separately organized under a head of sixth year.

In addition to these three main ways of organizing welfare work, most of the schools surveyed had a senior mistress who exercised responsibility for the pastoral problems of girls in the school.

Pupil health and welfare is one of the dominant topics in school administration. It certainly occupies a major proportion of the time of senior staff in the schools studied in the research project and its pervasiveness is such that it will occupy as much time as can be spared for it. Functions which are loosely classified under a welfare umbrella may vary between those which a school has a statutory duty to discharge, those which are composed of a routine clerical component where the gathering and recording of information forms a considerable proportion of the work load, to those which entail intensive face-to-face interaction with single pupils or groups of pupils, some of which may involve considerable trauma for those concerned.

Welfare includes the recording of information, bandaging an injured arm, counselling, co-operation with external agencies, and all matters which occur as a result of the school standing *in loco parentis* to the pupil. The school no longer stands isolated dealing merely with those matters that only appertain to instruction, the outside world continually impinges upon it. It is no longer sufficient to record and punish a child for continually being absent from school, the reasons must be sought and if possible dealt with. Work of this kind, as more and more schools are forced to recognize, begin to take increasing amounts of time and requires considerable organization. The subject teacher has not the time to undertake the concentrated supportive work on top of his normal teaching load, and he lacks the specialist training and insight into a problem that is becoming increasingly pressing.

All of the following are amongst those topics which teachers might undertake, or become involved in during the course of undertaking pupil welfare work.

Would you agree with the content of the list that is presented below? Would you add or subtract any items?

Absence : Consent, Notes, Record, Absence pass, Problem, Book, List, Check, Policy.

Accident : Book, Notes, Report, Arrangements, Procedure.

Attendance Register : Check.

Care : First aid.

Clothing : Maintain, Allowance, New, Pro-forma, Order, List, Money, Check, Theft.

Counsel : Arrangements, Discussion.

Employ : Employment conditions, Part-time, Temporary, Consent, Problem, Testimonial, Record, List.

Health : Medical inspection, Course, Appointment, Pro-forma, List, Record (special tests), Exemptions, Care, Arrange, Correspondence, Problem, Equipment, Meeting.

Lateness : Consent, Notes, Book, Problem, Report, Record.

Meals : Free meals.

Passes : Free bus and train passes.

Theft

Truancy : Problem, Report, Record.

Pupil discipline has not been included in the above list. In your view, should it have been?

Should those staff, do you think, who are responsible for handling welfare problems ever be involved in pupil discipline?

To all Upper School girls
(and to Staff for information)

APPEARANCE

Broadly speaking, one should dress and make-up within the general trend of present day fashion. In no way should a girl stick out like a sore thumb amongst her contemporaries, and yet there should be no need to have to impose a uniform. Indeed, a uniform is undesirable because one particular style of garment, for example, does not suit everybody. For the same reason, no girl should commit herself to a popular gimmick just to be 'with it': it may not suit her and she should make sure on this point before spending her (or her father's!) hard-earned cash.

Another important point is that one's appearance *as a whole* should look just right. A blouse, skirt, tights and shoes might appear nice when studied separately, but put them together and the whole effect could look so horrible that even the most ardent boyfriend would recoil in horror and crawl away to be sick in a corner.

The same remarks could also be said to apply to the choice of cosmetics. For example, if your eyes are inclined to be deep set, there is no point in liberally using eyeshadow just because your popeyed friend does so. She has good reason for her action because she wishes to camouflage a defect: by doing as she does, you are merely accentuating yours. It should be just apparent that you use make-up, *if* you feel you need it to enhance your appearance, but not one of you is so poorly endowed with good looks that she must hide behind the equivalent of a plaster cast of face powder, cream, rouge and lipstick. Leave this sort of thing to those of the much older generation whose features possess cracks, fissures and creases which need to be bunged up before they can be considered presentable to the public gaze.

In short, what I want to see are nice, clean and neat girls, fashionably dressed for work, and—I nearly forgot it—using clear nail varnish or none at all.

Headmaster

September 16th

Should schools attempt to influence their pupils on matters of this sort any more?

WELFARE ORGANIZATION IN THREE SCHOOLS_

Time	Anticipated day	Time	Unanticipated events
		7.25– 7.32	Parent phones up re pupil missing
		8.20– 8.35	Follow up with pupils
8.35– 8.55	Staff meeting		
8.55– 9.10	House assembly		
9.10– 9.30	Filing	9.11– 9.17	Pupil located, phone parent
9.30–10.10	Interview parent	9.17– 9.35	Interview pupil at school
		9.35–10.14	In park, reunite parent and child, discuss child's future with parents
10.15–11.10	Filing and personal entries on pupils	10.14–11.10	Parent/child discussion at school
11.25–12.25	Teach		
12.25– 1.00	House lunch		
1.00– 1.50	Interview 3 pupils	1.05– 1.10	Contact YEO re child's future
1.50– 2.50	Teach		
3.00– 4.00	Pupils' files	3.05– 3.15	Return contact YEO

KEY

░░░	Anticipated day
‖‖‖	Unanticipated events

Where unanticipated events ‖‖‖ clash with the planned activities for the day ░░░, then the planned event is either interrupted or non-occurring.

Case 1: The house system—an unanticipated welfare activity

This example is drawn from a school where pastoral responsibility is organized around six vertical houses. Each housemaster, with a deputy acts autonomously with full responsibility for pastoral activities within his house. The school, which enjoys an adequate provision of resources, ancillary and auxiliary staff, is located in a 'good' urban area, and also serves a rural hinterland. At the time of the events described, the school, with an eight-form entry, had some 1100 pupils and was still in the process of expansion.

In this case, the sequence of activities is relatively simple. A parent contacts a housemaster early in the morning about a child missing from home. The housemaster is quickly able to establish the pupil's whereabouts, and after talking to both parent and pupil separately is able to ascertain the real nature of the problem—it is about the pupil's career—to re-unite parent and child and then to begin the attempt to find the solution to the career difficulties. The housemaster is within the course of a day able to bring the matter to some sort of conclusion.

21

Case 2: The year system

The second case presented represents the flow of activities and personnel involved in another school in undertaking a case of pupil welfare. The activity originally identified as a misdemeanour was a relatively serious one of stealing money and subsequent truancy by two pupils.

An outline of all steps in the activity and their durations and a list of the people involved in Case 2 are attached.

The school concerned is a fully-developed, 11-fe comprehensive with some 1600 pupils; it is located in a small industrial town, and draws pupils from the town itself, a neighbouring forces base, and a large rural area. It is organized internally into upper and lower sections, in each of which there are 3 heads of year who are responsible for pupil welfare, and are themselves responsible to the relevant head of section. At the time that this particular problem occurred, the deputy head was acting head teacher.

Persons involved

1. Acting Head/Deputy Head (DHd)
2. Senior Mistress (SnrM)
3. Head of Lower School
4. Head of Remedial Dept
5. Head of 3rd Year (Hd Yr 3)
6. Head of 2nd Year (Hd Yr 2)
7. Counsellor
8. Form Teacher
9. Pupil(s) (any)
10. Parent(s) (any)
11. Police

WEDNESDAY

Event Numbers	Time	Activity
1	8.50– 8.55	Hd Yr 2 registers for absent form teacher and discovers the absence of Pupil 1 and determines matter should be pursued further.
2	9.20– 9.30	Hd Yr 2 discusses absence with form teacher. An inquiry is started.
3	9.30– 9.40	Hd Yr 2 discusses the case with the counsellor and involves her in the activity.
4	10.30–10.40	Hd Yr 2 talks to form teacher to get more details on pupil.
5	10.40–10.50	Hd Yr 2 interviews pupil's brothers. It transpires that pupil may have run away.
6	11.15–11.30	Hd Yr 2 discusses the case with head of lower school, and brings him into the inquiry.
7	1.15– 1.25	Hd Yr 2, counsellor and head of lower school decide strategy, what action to take.
8	1.30– 1.35	Hd Yr 2 and counsellor decide to interview pupil's mother.

THURSDAY

9	8.40– 8.45	Form teacher reports to Hd Yr 2. Missing pupil has returned.
10	8.55– 9.00	Head of Lower School phones the acting head (D Hd) about an in-school theft of money.
11	9.00– 9.05	Hd Yr 2, counsellor and form teacher discuss the new situation of pupil 1 having returned to school.
12	9.05– 9.15	Counsellor discusses Pupil 1 with parent.
13	9.20– 9.25	Counsellor discusses the stolen money with form teacher. Pupil 1 has admitted to committing theft with Pupil 2. Decision to refer this to acting head (D Hd).
14	9.25– 9.30	Counsellor, head of remedial studies and head of lower school discuss the matter further and discuss possibility of involving police.
15	9.30– 9.40	Head of lower school searches school—confirms that Pupil 2 is missing.
16	9.50– 9.55	Head of lower school reports to counsellor. They decide to search town.

17	10.00–10.25	Counsellor drives round town. Pupil 2 is not found.
18	10.25–10.30	Counsellor reports to head of lower school. They decide (1) to inform police, (2) to visit parents.
19	10.30–10.35	Head of lower school discusses theft with Hd Yr 3 and brings him into the case.
20	10.40–10.45	Hd Yr 3 discusses it with counsellor and brings himself up to date.
21	11.00–11.05	Hd Yr 3 phones the police.
22	11.15–12.00	General discussion with police, Hd Yr 3, head of remedial studies, Pupil 1, form teacher all present at some stage of the proceedings.
23	12.00–12.15	Meeting of head of lower School, counsellor and Hd Yr 3, who reports on police visit. They decide to visit pupils' homes and inform respective parents of imminent police visit.
24	12.15–12.20	Hd Yr 2 is told by form teacher of pupil 2 having been seen at club in his home village.
25	1.55– 2.20	Counsellor discusses case with parents of Pupil 2 at pupil's home, while waiting for CID to call.
26	2.20– 2.40	Counsellor searches the village by herself. She catches a glimpse of Pupil 2, but he runs off across the fields on seeing her.
27	2.45– 3.00	Counsellor reports back to Hd Yr 3 about home visit. Hd Yr 3 decides to report sighting of Pupil 2 to police.
28	3.00– 3.10	Head of lower school discusses the case with the senior mistress.
29	3.50– 4.00	Head of lower school discusses theft with parent of Pupil 2.
30	6.35– 7.15	Counsellor discusses the theft etc. with parents of Pupil 2. The parents are resigned to the pupil's activities and hope he is 'taken into care'.

FRIDAY

31	9.30– 9.40	Head of lower school interviews pupil about his theft and truancy.
32	10.05–10.30	Senior mistress talks over the week's cases with the counsellor.
33	12.30– 1.00	Head of lower school arranges with form teacher that he should visit pupil's homes.

Case 3: The head of middle school and senior mistress

Case 3 is drawn from a fully developed 10 form entry comprehensive school, with some 1600 pupils on roll, and located in a depressed industrial area of a large city. The school is divided into autonomous upper, middle and lower sections, each the responsibility of a head of section none of whom are timetabled to teach.

The case consists of the diary of a senior mistress who is also head of middle school. The diary presented below shows the activities which this particular senior mistress undertook on a day selected for its typicality. In over-viewing the returns made by the senior mistress over her three diary weeks it seems that her activities fall into four major sections. These are:

(1) Timetabling problems for the middle school including daily staff substitution.

(2) Responsibility for general standards of behaviour for all girls in the school.

(3) Responsibility for dealing with exceptional cases of discipline, pupil problems, and referring to the appropriate agencies if necessary.

(4) Any general administrative work specifically appertaining to the middle school.

In the diary presented here it is seen that 14 out of the 22 recorded entries referred to categories 3 and 4 from the above list. It should be pointed out that at this school teaching staff have access to several in-school welfare agents. There is a counsellor, a nurse attends each morning and there is also a full-time campus-based welfare officer as well as the head of department with specific responsibilities for immigrant pupils. The senior mistress liaises constantly with the above people as she also does with other welfare agencies, the educational psychologist, probation officers, social workers, the child guidance clinic and the police.

Case 3: A day's diary for a senior mistress/head of Middle School

Time	Mode	With	Topic
8.45– 9.00	Discuss	Three pupils	Bullying of 3rd yr girl
9.00– 9.15	Phone	D Hd Lower School	Lists of coverages for absent staff
9.15– 9.30		Assembly	
9.30– 9.40	Discuss	Pupils	School uniform, jewellery and hygiene
9.40– 9.50	Discuss	Snr M Upper School	Re above
9.50–10.10	Paying	Middle School staff	Paying out cheques
10.10–10.20	Discuss	Pupils	Not working in CSE course, possibility of withdrawing them
10.20–10.30	Discuss	Teacher	Re above
10.30–11.05	Writing	Self	List of all physically handicapped pupils in school
11.05–11.15	Phone	Headmaster	Pupil caught by police
11.20–11.25	Phone	Welfare Officer	Child whose mother has psychiatric iilness
11.25–12.15	Discuss	Pupils	Lateness, truancy, letters written to parents
12.15–12.30	Supervise	Pupils	Cleaning walls as punishment
12.30– 1.00	Supervise	Self	Dinner duty
1.30– 1.45	Discuss	Pupil	Request for letter from parent to confirm illness
1.50– 2.00	Discuss	Hd of Dept	Impending retirement
2.00– 2.15	Discuss	Snr M Lower School and pupils	Checking registers to check pupils missing lesson although present in school
2.15– 2.55	Discuss	Police	Identification of stolen property
2.55– 3.10	Writing	Secretary	Letters to parents re poor attendance and work
3.10– 3.20	Discuss	Teacher	Assembly
3.20– 3.30	Discuss	Pupils	Continued lateness
3.35– 4.20	Attending	School choir and orchestra	

The three case studies you have just examined are derived from diaries kept by senior teachers in three schools operating different patterns of pupil welfare organization. Members of your group or syndicate are asked to consider the following:

1. Inspect the case studies and identify what you feel to be the strengths and the weaknesses of the systems portrayed.

   (a) Is it a strength of the system that in *Case 1* the head of house concerned does not need to refer to any other member of staff of the school?

   (b) *Case 2.* What do you think is the real function of the counsellor as shown by this example?

   (c) What is the significance to you of the fact that in this example, as more information is collected, the problem is constantly redefined?

(d) Is the sort of work revealed by *Case 3* that which you would expect a senior mistress to undertake?

2. Ascertain how your school organizes pupil welfare concerns, and how it avoids or makes the mistakes you may have noted in the examples above.

THE WORK OF WELFARE STAFF

(1) Duties of welfare staff

(A) THE FORM TUTOR

A large well established secondary comprehensive school convened a working party, drawn from amongst senior staff and form tutors, to re-examine form tutor duties.

The working party reported back to a staff meeting recommending that the meeting adopt the proposals for form tutor duties that are appended below.

Role:

1. To provide leadership, example and care of the individual within the form unit.
2. To establish trusting and friendly relationships with all individuals in the form and to create and maintain loyalty and unity within the form.
3. To act as liaison between child, form, teachers, school.

To carry out this role:

1. The form tutor must be genuinely concerned for the well-being of the individual pupils in his form.
2. He/she must be conversant with the pupils' background and records.
3. He/she will supervise the progress and behaviour of individual pupils and be aware of the difficulties which may lead to behavioural problems.

4. Any child needing disciplinary action in addition to that normally taken by the subject tutor i.e. re behaviour, homework etc. should be referred first to the form tutor. Records of these occasions should be kept by the tutor so that if the need to involve heads of schools should arise the record can be passed to them and the heads are then aware of what steps have already been taken.

5. When a child is having problems either socially or with regard to work the form tutor should convene a meeting with subject teachers to discuss the best means of dealing with the situation.

6. The form tutor may in a free period, with the co-operation of subject teachers, withdraw a pupil for disciplinary or counselling matters.

7. The form tutor should be alert to changes and undercurrents in the form.

8. The form tutor should carry out form administrative duties promptly and efficiently.

9. An experienced form tutor will be attached to a probationer teacher for the period of his/her probation to help him/her to 'learn the ropes'.

10. Unattached members of staff will be attached to one or more forms as a 'Deputy Form Tutor'. They will undertake routine administrative work in the absence of the form tutor and will assist in any way felt to be mutually helpful. It would be advantageous for them to join in any form activities.

Do you agree with the duties that they recommended a form tutor should undertake?

(a) How would you suggest training new and inexperienced staff to be form tutors?

(b) How would you recommend inducting experienced staff into form tutor duties at the school?

How should the school check that the duties are being performed effectively?

(B) DUTIES OF HEADS OF HOUSES AND HOUSE ORGANIZATION (From the handbook of another large secondary comprehensive school)

It is through the house organization that the personal development and welfare of the individual pupil is planned and supervised.

1. *Organization*

   (a) The house is a community of staff and 120 pupils with the house head as leader.

   (b) All staff belong to a house except the members of the executive team. Certain non-teaching staff are also allocated, at least one to each house.

   (c) The house head is the team leader of the staff allocated to the house. The pupils look to the house head as the leader of the house community. The house team assist the house head to carry out the tasks in the house head job description, and are allocated duties by the house head.

   (d) The senior house heads are the team managers. In the upper school a team manager co-ordinates the work of the three house teams in a year. In the lower school the team manager co-ordinates the work of all six house teams. The 6th year head manages the 6th year team.

   (e) The team managers are responsible for seeing that meetings of house staff take place and are conducted satisfactorily by team leaders. Team managers should delegate as much to team leaders as the team leaders are able to accept. Meeting times can be arranged in pastoral care periods by house teams looking after each other's pupils, or at other times outside school.

   (f) The deputy head DP, director of personnel development, is responsible to the head for the house organization.

   (g) Job titles
   6th year head   —Y6
   5th year team manager   —S5
   4th year team manager   —S4
   3rd year team manager   —S3
   Senior master lower school—SL

   (h) Within houses, registration groups may be allocated names 'north, south, east and west.'

2. *Objectives of house organization*

   (a) To ensure that every pupil is known and cared for as an individual—has a school programme appropriate for his or her needs, is being fully developed, is successful in something and recognized as such, and is making a contribution to the school and community in some way.

   (b) To develop home-school links and gain parental understanding, co-operation and contribution.

3. *House periods and registration*

   These periods are timetabled by agreement between house heads and faculty heads. The conduct of these periods is by the house teams, led by the house head who is the team leader, under the overall guidance of the team managers. What goes on in these periods should be planned and recorded in a work book just as in other teaching periods, and team managers are to see that this is done.

4. *Objectives of house periods*

   (a) To ensure that registration is carried out effectively and registers properly kept.

   (b) To develop activities which are not on the school timetable and which may continue outside school.

   (c) To encourage staff and pupils and develop and share mutual interests.

   (d) An opportunity for knowing pupils and counselling in less formal situations.

   (e) An opportunity for pupil participation in the way the school is run.

   (f) To set standards—personal and group—and gain co-operation of pupils.

   (g) To provide extra tuition or continuation work if appropriate.

Pupils may be moved between houses or sub-groups within houses for specific activities. House head is responsible for knowing where every one is.

Room allocation is co-ordinated by senior house heads.

House head—Job description

1. The house head is responsible for the overall development and welfare of the pupils in the House.

2. House heads will normally stay with a group of pupils as the pupils move up through the School. In some cases house heads may be allocated to upper school, or to Lower School, but they must be prepared to accept the house headship of any age group at the discretion of the head of the school and community college.

3. Specifically, the house head's duties include:

   (a) Organizing, conducting and supervising a planned programme of meetings and activities in house periods.

   (b) Getting to know, and be known by, all members of the house.

   (c) At least one face to face contact each year with the parents or guardians of every pupil in the house, either by inviting parents to school or by visiting homes.

   (d) Organizing, helping and supervising the other members of staff who are attached to the house during those parts of the school day which are 'house' times—for example: immediately before and after school, registration, the break, and timetabled house periods.

   (e) Accepting responsibility for the members of the house who remain in school at dinner time, and helping and supervising the staff who volunteer for dinner duties or activities.

   (f) Registration, and the following up of cases of absenteeism and persistent lateness.

   (g) Collating pupils' records, and acting as the co-ordinating agency through which all information about pupils is fed to and from the community team, other staff and outside agencies.

   (h) Recommending to DP* those pupils for whom special help is required.

   (i) Preparing half-yearly reports on all pupils, including information supplied by other members of staff who teach them and making sure that parents have the reports and if possible discussing the content with them. Reports for employers.

   (j) Providing guidance to pupils on careers, and on choices of subjects and courses, agreeing choices with DS†. Proposing or agreeing to timetable changes (all changes must have house head's approval).

* DP: Deputy Head Director of Personnel Development.
† DS: Deputy Head Director of Resources and Services.

B

(k) Where applicable, working closely with the head of careers guidance in providing opportunities for careers talks, consultations and visits.

(l) Representing the house on the Upper or Lower School operations teams.

(m) Continually encouraging pupils to set and maintain high standards of attendance, punctuality, appearance and deportment, care of property and fabric, consideration for others, and school work in all subjects and activities.

Consider the following points:

1. Is there likely to be ambivalence in the roles of heads of houses/years, and even form tutors, because they hold academic as well as welfare responsibility in the school—because they teach, they must assess and they must judge?

   What should they do about ill discipline in the classroom when they are teaching?

2. For the head of house/year, what is the maximum number of pupils he can know and relate to?

3. Should a head of house/year have a tutor group?

4. Should heads of year move up the school with the children or should form tutors stay with the same registration group through the school?

   Alternatively, do first, fifth and sixth years present a special order of problem, such that the staff in charge of these years have an inevitable need to specialize. If this is the case, does the professional development and training of staff present a different order of problem?

5. Should you allow tutors to choose their own groups?

6. If you monitored the work of the head of house/year:
   (a) At what time of the day, the week or the year, does the major part of his work fall?
   (b) What is his busiest time of the day, the week or the year?
   (c) Should lesson time be inviolable?
   (d) Should assembly time be inviolable?

If you ensured that heads of houses/years were never time-tabled during the first two periods of the morning, and were always timetabled within reach of the house/year base, would this begin to resolve some of the dilemmas?

7. (a) What could you learn about how form tutors communicate with their heads of houses/years. Is it likely to be verbal or written communication?
   (b) What does the form tutor communicate upwards and to whom? What does the head of house/year communicate upwards and to whom?

(2) Distribution of welfare posts

The table below shows the distribution of staff to posts in a secondary comprehensive school according to male/female, graduate/non-graduate status, where the staff pupil ratio was to 1 to 18·1.

Post	Graduate (or grad equiv)		Non-graduate		Total
	Male	Female	Male	Female	
Senior post	2	1	–	–	3
Head of Dept	8	1	3	2	14
Welfare post	–	–	6	1	7
Other allowance	2	2	9	10	23
Assistant	1	6	6	7	20
Totals	13	10	24	20	67

Part-time and temporary assistants excluded.

Consider the following points:

1. Does the above table show the distribution of posts that you would anticipate finding in the large secondary comprehensive school?

2. Should a school develop a career structure for welfare staff that presents a viable alternative to the academic career line, which should go at least to the deputy head level?

(3) **Who does what?**

Extract from the *Heads' Tasks Report*

In comparing the work of all males who were heads of houses or heads of years with all females who were heads of houses or years it seemed that the amount of welfare work undertaken does vary and that this is statistically significant at the 5 per cent level. Considerable caution must be used in interpreting these results since the number of females in the sample was extremely small.

However, in comparing the pastoral work, as evinced by diary returns, undertaken by all males who took part in this survey, with the pastoral work undertaken by all females who took part in this survey, then it seemed that this also varies and that the difference is statistically significant at a 1 per cent level. This is an extremely surprising result.

Throughout this survey there has appeared to exist a difference in the admin work undertaken in school by male and female teachers and it is of considerable interest that where welfare activities are concerned this difference proves to be statistically significant.

It has been pointed out in other sections that with reference to male and female teachers completing diary returns, that the women appear to have a wider span of interest and that the male teachers appear to show greater specialization in the administration they undertake in school. Perhaps what is being described is in fact a traditional pattern in which there seem to be tasks undertaken more extensively by women and which perhaps are unconsciously designated as women's work by both sexes. One of our female respondents noted:

'The human and personal approach is considered of paramount importance and paperwork is *not* done for its own sake.'

Thus we see women as dealing particularly with problems in which the quality of the human relationships involved are as important as finding a solution to the problem at hand and are not a means to an end. Perhaps on the other hand in terms of the composition of this sample, those women who are willing to accept senior positions of responsibility in the large secondary comprehensive school are a particularly able, well-motivated and conscientious sample of women teachers who are thus not strictly comparable to a sample of male senior teachers. The differences noted might also account for women teachers being more conscientious in making diary returns.

SOME OF THE CONSEQUENCES_

(1) **How do you ensure that the children (and parents) understand the organization of pupil welfare provision in your school?**

(a) One of the fundamental problems for pupils and parents (and sometimes staff) is to learn how the school is organized and to understand the roles and duties of the staff concerned—to know whom they should contact with a certain sort of query or problem.

The diagram following represents one such attempt at explaining the organization of the school.

What information would you recommend giving to pupils and parents explaining the provision for pupil welfare that exists in the school?

What is the best way to give them this information? How would you recommend checking that the information is being received in the right quarter and understood?

(b) A tendency noted amongst some architects when a developed site is opened is not initially to lay any footpaths, but to wait and see where the public make them. These paths are then laid with proper foundations where the 'flow of traffic' has established them.

Where does the natural flow of welfare problems go in your school?

Organization and pastoral care

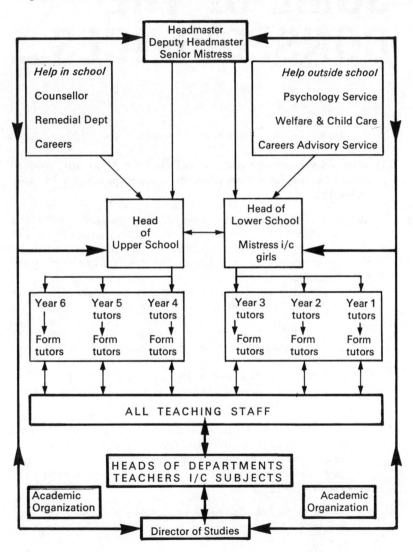

Do they come through group tutors or directly to heads of year or houses; or perhaps even straight to the deputy head?

Why not keep a diary to monitor where the flow of welfare traffic goes, then let the school formalize what the established practice is?

(c) How do children who need help get referred by the staff of the school through the system? In practice does it prove to be no more than a self-referral system? If so, then should schools be appointing 'identified' groups of staff to whom pupils, if they have a problem should refer themselves? If this is the case, then it may well prove that a hierarchically organized system of form tutors, heads of years, heads of sections, and so on, may not only be irrelevant but actually get in the way of the efficient discharge of the system!

Have you ever attempted to find out what pupils and parents think of the welfare/guidance provision your school offers?

(2) **To all staff concerned with PE and games** (and to all other staff and parents for information)

PE, GAMES, and ILL-HEALTH OF PUPILS

1. *A parents' first note* covering a particular indisposition is accepted without question for outdoor work and swimming, but colds do not excuse pupils from gymnasium work automatically. In this case, the teacher decides.

   In general, it is a case of 'NO NOTE—NO EXCUSE', but this would not be made to apply to children who are clearly 'under the weather.'

2. *A parents' second note* for a particular indisposition is also accepted with question, but the child is warned that a doctor's certificate will be required if a further exemption is to be granted.

3. If, after 1 and 2 above, a doctor's certificate is not presented, the child will still be excused, but Mr. Watkinson will be informed and

he will report to the head of school who will arrange for a school welfare department official to call at the child's home.

4. *Doctor's certificates* are accepted without question or comment at all times, and are passed to Mr. Watkinson who will issue to the child an appropriate card which will have to be produced on demand.

5. *Gym shoes.* If a parent prefers that a child shall wear gym shoes in the gym, rather than exercise barefooted, there is no objection.

Headmaster

Do you consider that there is a need in a school for this sort of statement?

If there is, then who should lay down the policy?

(3) The head of maths

A head of maths on the way to his teaching room encountered a group of rowdy third year pupils waiting outside one of the woodwork rooms. They were amusing themselves by throwing stones over the building on to the tennis courts. He promptly quelled the trouble and put two of the most vociferous of the pupils into detention.

A few days later in his mail he received two notes from two housemasters. The notes stated that if he wished to have disciplinary measures taken against pupils in their houses would be in future refer the matter to the house staff concerned for them to deal with.

The head of maths replied that he would save them all the trouble. The next time he would look the other way.

If you were the head teacher of this school how would you resolve this problem?

How do you ensure that there is a uniformity of disciplinary measures in the school?

(4)

MEMORANDUM

From: Head of Remedial Dept   To: Head Teacher

The department now seems to be well established in the school and we have a good staff. It seems an opportune time to look to the future and to think of development.

We might now expand to offer our skills throughout the school. One direction would be to take on coaching for O-Level candidates who have confusions with their spelling, with particular arithmetical processes, etc.

Can I come and have a chat with you?

What should the function of the remedial department be in a school?

Should it ever be thought to be part of the system of welfare provision?

(5) Allocation of resources

How a school allocates its resources is a statement of the policy it implements.

Compared to the classroom contact time expected of teaching staff, time allocated to the discharge of welfare and guidance activities is not very high. (See table following.)

Consequences of this are that urgent welfare matters which press to be recognized will intrude into other ongoing activities, so that other sections of the organization (including the school office) will begin to discharge activities which are not being adequately fulfilled elsewhere.

Time spent by school staff in teaching in a sampled week (Schools arranged in descending order of size)

Staff/ pupil ratio	Number of pupils	Number of periods per week	Av. length of period in mins.	Average number of teaching periods per week for the named post (Figures in brackets denote number of non-teaching periods per week)							
				Head	DHd	Hd Sect	D Hd Sect	Snr Mast	Snr Mist	Hd Hse/Yr	Hd Dept
19.2	2070	40	37.5	0(40)	0(40)	0(40)		24(16)	13(27)		30(10)
19.6	1720	35	40	4(31)	12(23)				16(19)	29(6)	27(8)
16.3	1600	40	37.5	0(40)	7(33)	8(32)	17(23)		10(30)		28(12)
19.3	1593	40	38	Not known	10(30)	15(25)			14(26)	29(11)	33(7)
19.0	1575	40	35	0(40)	1(39)	0(40)					31(9)
19.4	1551	35	40	7(28)	16(19)	11(24)	18(17)		17(18)	26(9)	28(7)
18.1	1502	40	35.6	6(34)	12(28)	23(17)			12(28)	24(16)	28(12)
17.7	1189	35	43	2(33)	13(22)				13(22)	27(8)	29(6)
18.0	1170**	25	59	2(23)	6(19)	14(11)		16(9)		16(9)	18(7)
19.0	1099	40	37	15(25)	17(23)	26(14)	30(10)		23(17)		32(8)
21.6	1050	35	40	19(16)	14(21)					28(7)	31(4)
19.2	1006	35	40	13(22)	22(13)	26(9)	27(8)		18(17)	30(5)	30(5)
18.6	989	35	40	7(28)	19(16)			28(7)	20(15)	30(5)	29(6)
16.2	830	35	40	1(34)	21(14)				21(14)	29(6)	28(7)
15.6	809	40	35	9(31)	16(24)			16(24)		33(7)	31(9)
16.4	733	35	42	9(26)	13(22)	23(12)		25(10)			28(7)

**10 day timetable

Consider the following two records of first aid activities:

1. How can a school best cope with the factors outlined in these two sets of records?

2. From the table showing time spent teaching by school staff in a sampled week what type of welfare activities can staff be expected to undertake in the non-teaching time allocated to them?

(5a) *First aid activities undertaken* (An extract from one day's diary returns of a school secretary)

10 minutes: Pupil with discharging ear—referred to nurse.

5 minutes: Informing parent pupil sent home ill.

5 minutes: Pupil feeling dizzy—taken to nurse.

1 minute: Gave pupil tablet for headache.

5 minutes: Pupil injured in playground—referred to nurse.

5 minutes: Pupil fell downstairs—referred to nurse.

10 minutes: Called ambulance for 2 previous pupils.

5 minutes: Informed parents of above.

10 minutes: Traced sister of pupil to accompany him in ambulance.

5 minutes: Adminster Aspirin and a cup of tea to the Head of Lower School.

The table following was compiled from the first aid book, in which are recorded all occasions, other than entirely trivial ones, on which children required some form of medical attention. The school concerned has some 1700+ pupils, and did not have a matron or nurse. As revealed by the table, the time spent by teaching staff at a large secondary comprehensive school in taking sick or injured pupils to hospital, to the doctor or to the pupil's home in a sampled 47 working days is quite considerable.

(5b) Extract from record book for first aid and sickness

Date	No. of pupils treated	Taken home, to doctor, or hospital	Date	No. of pupils treated	Taken home, to doctor, or hospital
9 Oct.	9	1	18	7	–
10	12	1	19	11	–
13	3	–	20	14	–
14	8	3	21	12	1
15	6	1	24	11	–
16	7	2	25	7	1
17	7	1, and brought back	26	10	–
20	13	5	27	11	1
21	11	3	28	12	3
22	4	1	1 Dec.	20	5
23	11	2	2	9	1
24	4	1	3	13	1
3 Nov.	7	1	4	8	2
4	9	–	5	11	2
5	10	1	8	18	5
6	8	–	9	16	4
7	8	1	10	10	2
10	9	–	11	14	2
11	13	2	12	14	–
12	9	2	15	13	2
13	7	1	16	18	–
14	11	1	17	8	1
17	4	–	18	9	1
			19	4	–

Total number of days considered	= 47
Total number of pupils treated	= 470
Average number treated per day	= 10
Total number taken home, to doctor, or hospital	= 63
Average number per day	= 1.34

You might like to consider the following points:

1. In your view, should schools rigidly control the type of pupil welfare activity they are willing to undertake and refer all other problems to specialist agencies? Do you in fact feel that schools should be involved in pupil welfare at all?

2. Are welfare and guidance concerns in a school part of the educational process in the way that the curriculum is?

3. If the welfare/guidance processes were tailored to the needs and the development of an individual child, it would appear that they would dictate the curriculum that the child should follow. The role of teacher would be drastically redefined and he would become the organizer of the learning experiences that the welfare/guidance processes suggest. Is this the way schools are beginning to develop? Is it the way they should be developing?

4. By what sort of body should the school's welfare/guidance policy be reviewed and developed?
   (a) Who should have the responsibility for determining the allocation of resources to the different sections of the school?
   (b) Where in the hierarchy is the responsibility for the implementation of this policy lodged?
   (c) Who has responsibility for monitoring the work at the grass roots level?

5. Can you together with the members of your study group or syndicate recommend an effective system of pupil welfare organization that will effectively discharge the type of welfare activities that a school is likely to encounter? In doing so, ensure that the pattern of organization you adopt provides solutions to the following questions:

   (a) Is the pattern of delegation unambiguous and are staff clear about operational divisions?
   (b) Does your system of welfare organization clearly indicate its boundaries and can it thus easily relate to other professional welfare workers employed by other organizations?
   (c) Does the organization expose staff to a high level of pressure?
   (d) Does the 'system' you have devised allow sufficient people time to contact each other?
   (e) Does it appear that staff are overloaded in areas of competence and differentiation of work loads?
   (f) Are your staff accessible in an emergency?
   (g) Is there someone accessible to deal with importunate events?
   (h) Does the system you have devised expose staff to a discontinuous pattern of work?
   (i) Have you allowed 'key' staff sufficient non-teaching periods at pressure periods in the day?

   (j) Are lessons likely to be interrupted leading to a net loss of programmed teaching?
   (k) Does your welfare organization allow speedy information dispersal, retrieval, compilation and store, and permit all interested parties to be kept informed without imposing communication strain?
   (l) Can your welfare organization in fact simultaneously handle systems that are concerned with control, record keeping, communication and counselling?
   (m) Does the pattern of delegation impose communication strain?
   (n) Is there a need to appoint staff to posts who will have a full time responsibility for pupil welfare activities, to what scale posts should they be appointed? Would you anticipate that such staff would function as one of a team?
   (o) Can your pastoral staff fulfil your expectations of them? Does your training programme familiarize them with the skills and give the orientation that they will need to discharge their duties?
   (p) Do your staff have adequate office provision—as a base, but also for confidential interviewing?
   (q) Do your staff have access to telephones?
   (r) Can the nature of the task be recognized quickly enough, and is there a maximum duration by which an optimum solution should be sought to any welfare activity?
   (s) Does your system allow a complex event to be sustained from its original identity to its termination?
   (t) Does the pattern of welfare organization pre-determine the way problems are defined and the type of solutions proposed?
   (u) Does your welfare system allow the development of a close rapport between pupils and those with welfare responsibility? Is it client or authority centred?
   (v) Is the system of welfare organization revised at regular intervals to eliminate unintended growth or dysfunction?
   (w) Is there a realistic career structure for those members of staff who hold responsibility for pupil welfare in the school?

Pupil Careers Guidance Programme

CONTENTS

INTRODUCTION___

(This document should be read in conjunction with the chapter relating to the 'Application for Places in Further and Higher Education').

Not so long ago the careers programme in many schools was little more than the production of testimonials, liaison with the Youth Employment Service, and perhaps some direct help for those pupils who might be experiencing difficulty in getting a job.

The focus of attention is now moving from placement of leavers in employment to a *continuous* process of pupil guidance, in which careers guidance is interrelated with most other tasks and with the work of agencies both within and beyond the school. The fundamental problem now seems to be to determine the relationship that should exist between guidance and curricular processes in a school and, in particular, the resources to be allocated to each of them.

Following on from this, it becomes pertinent to ask, since guidance as a term covers the 'personal' ,'academic' •nd 'career' needs of a child, and since the child's personal and academic needs and potentialities should be the basis for developing a programme to prepare the child for his future life as an adult; then, to what degree is the 'careers' aspect of guidance merely a reflection of the other two aspects, or, to what degree should career objectives be the starting point of the whole curricular process for an individual child?

There are many organizational implications following from the resolution of these questions. The determination of priorities and the allocation of a budget have already been referred to. Other factors to be taken note of are: the level in the hierarchy at which responsibility resides and who is to monitor performance of the programme at the grass roots level; the amount of staff time allocated to the programme; the use of 'experts' brought in from outside, and so on.

How have these questions been answered in your school?

Is it likely that the academic staff, or the welfare (and guidance) staff were asked to contribute to the decision?

ONE SCHOOL'S SCHEME

Presented below in the flow diagram, Figure 1, is the careers scheme adopted by one large secondary comprehensive school.

It is not presented here as a model of a careers guidance programme—the intention in presenting the outline is to indicate the complexity of the task and to stimulate discussion.

The bar chart (Figure 2) shows the periods of the year during which each of the steps in the careers programme was undertaken, and the member of staff responsible in each case.

Figure 1: The Pupil Careers Guidance Programme—One School's Scheme

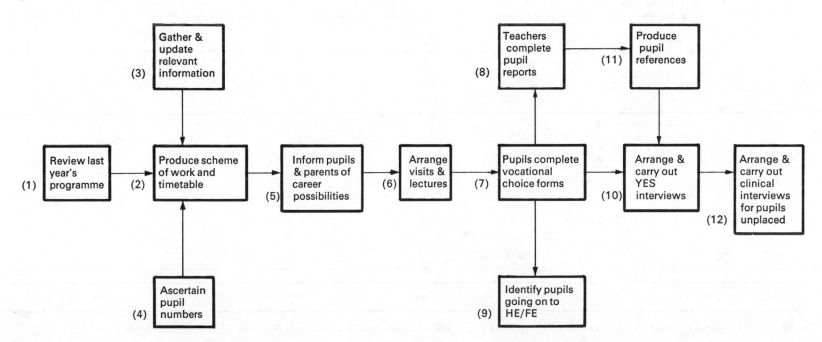

Figure 2: Bar chart to show the time of initiation and termination of each major step in the careers guidance programme

(Numbers relate to event numbers on the flow diagram of the overall strategy)

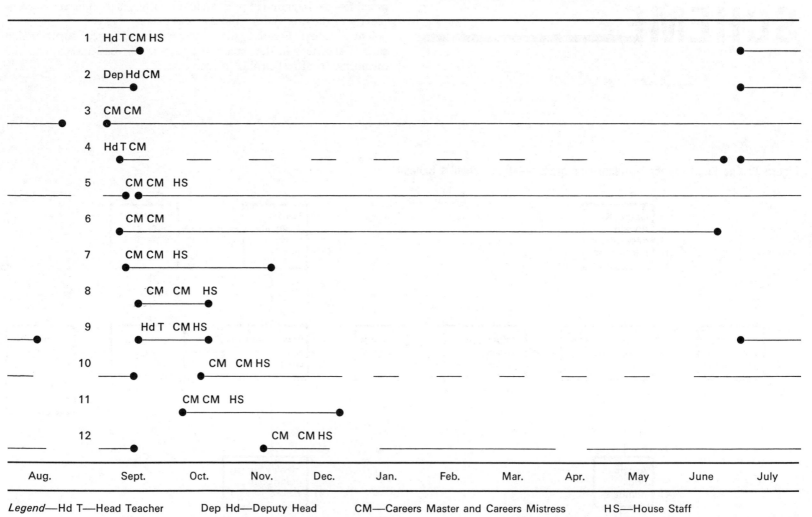

Legend—Hd T—Head Teacher   Dep Hd—Deputy Head   CM—Careers Master and Careers Mistress   HS—House Staff

It is clear that this particular sequence involved some major decisions about the school's objectives and solutions to a number of subsidiary problems also had to be found. Amongst these were:

1. Decisions about the degree to which the school accepts responsibility for helping pupils to obtain employment.

2. The nature of particular crucial deadlines which have to be met.

3. The use to be made of the Youth Employment Service, an evaluation of the sort of help it can offer and the ways in which this might be supplemented by the school.

4. The allocation of responsibility within the school for the careers programme, e.g. is it to be a function of a head of house and house tutor working within the existing in-school welfare system, or should there be one specifically appointed person or even a specifically appointed team to administer the careers programme?

5. The lines of communication to be maintained between those who are likely to know of a pupil's problems and difficulties and those responsible for giving careers guidance to the pupil.

6. The arrangements to be made for a centralized storing of information with regard to a pupil's preferences and difficulties, including responsibility for initiating, contributing to, and updating this store of information, and a feedback of information to those concerned.

7. Any specific LEA directives which might influence the programme.

8. In view of the sensitivity of careers guidance to many other aspects of school life, the stage at which careers guidance should begin.

9. The amount of time, if any, that is to be devoted to careers work with groups of pupils with differing career intentions, e.g. those who wish to go on to higher or further education.

10. The arrangements to be made for special categories of pupils, e.g. those in remedial classes.

11. The type and timing of information given to a pupil as to the career choices that it is felt are suitable for him.

12. The relationship of the careers guidance programme to local schemes that might already be in existence, and the use to be made of visits and work experience in local factories.

13. The first-hand experience that teachers might be encouraged to obtain of conditions in factories, in commerce, etc.

14. The nature of the contacts that should be established and maintained with local firms or professional organizations.

15. The availability of resources such as clerical help, office space for confidential interviewing, storage and display for literature, telephones, etc.

16. The extent to which the placement of pupils in further or higher education is an essential part of the careers programme or separate from it.

17. The extent to which a high national level of unemployment might influence the careers programme.

What other factors could you add to the list?

If one examined whom the careers staff at the school worked with in undertaking the careers programme, the following facts emerge about the time spent:

Contacts with parents amounted to 3 per cent, with potential employers 6 per cent, with the Youth Employment Service 7 per cent, with other teachers in the school 12 per cent, and contacts with pupils accounted for approximately 20 per cent of their time. This leaves a staggering 49 per cent of the careers staff's time spent working alone, that is, undertaking activities which are largely clerical in nature.

ADDITIONAL INFORMATION___

Checklist 1: Fifth year programme

1. This was the brain child of the careers committee, and was conceived with the purpose of giving the 5th year knowledge of the opportunities available to them and the appropriate information to help them decide on a suitable career.

2. The careers counsellor is the co-ordinator of this programme and has mapped out the following plan.

3. Five main areas of occupations are identified:
   - (a) clerical, business, banking and local government.
   - (b) practical work.
   - (c) outdoor and physical.
   - (d) social work.
   - (e) artistic careers.

4. Five weeks are allotted to each section.
   - (a) During the first week visiting speakers address the fifth year. This entails:
     - (i) inviting appropriate speakers, outlining the programme, and explaining to them that their task is not to recruit pupils to their organizations but to give information about employment possibilities.
     - (ii) entertaining and briefing speakers when they arrive.
     - (iii) writing to thank them afterwards.
     - (iv) notifying form teachers of the programme.
     - (v) preparing rooms for the meetings.
     - (vi) generally co-ordinating members of staff who are supervising the careers programme.
       NB—(iv), (v) and (vi) appear at all stages.
   - (b) In the second week pupil organized group discussions take place.
   - (c) Visiting speakers return in the third week to answer any questions raised in the discussion groups.
   - (d) In the fourth week Youth Employment Officers visit the school to fill any gaps in information that might have become apparent.
   - (e) Visits and films are arranged for the fifth week. These involve much organizing, writing letters, telephoning, supervising pupils, and the films themselves have to be collected.

On completion of each stage of the programme pupils are likely to request work experience. Pupils are encouraged to gain this experience where appropriate arrangements can be made.

Checklist 2: Arrangements for Youth Employment Service Interviews

1. Production of pupil lists.
2. Producing/distributing pupil interview forms and informing all respondents of the date by which completed forms are to be returned.
3. Dealing with queries, helping pupils complete interview forms.
4. Producing/distributing teachers' section of pupil interview forms.
5. Chasing dilatory returns.
6. Writing appointment lists of pupils to be interviewed by YES for head teacher: Pupil/parents; Housemasters/Tutors; YES; (Counsellor (where necessary).
7. Completing interview forms and forwarding to YEO at correct time.
8. Answering YEO's queries raised by pupils' careers forms.
9. Checking pupils' attendance at YEO interviews.
10. Arranging second interviews for pupils who were absent for first, or subsequently require a second, interview.

11. Attending YES interviews where necessary.

12. Checking with YES on progress of interviews.

13. Informing house teachers etc. on result of interview.

14. Transferring interview notes onto pupils' record cards.

Checklist 3: Activities occurring throughout the year

Clerical

Filing and cataloguing careers literature.

Keeping careers notice board up-to-date.

Production of announcements *re* applications for various jobs as they become available to the school.

Production and issue of careers forms.

Arranging and notifying pupils/parents/house staff/YES of interviews.

Arranging and notifying pupils/parents/house staff of second interviews should pupil have missed first.

File, store and issue application forms for regular local employers.

Transferring interview notes onto pupils' record cards.

Completing and updating pupils' career record cards.

Keeping records of ex-pupils in employment.

Issue and receipt of careers literature.

Advice to pupils and production of references/testimonials.

Advising pupils and parents *re* careers and further education.

Dealing with special problems, e.g. immigrant pupils, remedial pupils.

Helping pupils complete forms, write suitable letters of application etc.

Production of leaving certificates, references, testimonials.

Giving advice to ex-pupils and preparing references and testimonials for them.

Dealing with Saturday job queries.

Distribution and retrieval of YES (interview) forms.

Discussion amongst colleagues about any aspect of the careers programme, or about any pupil involved in the programme.

Counselling.

Advice to pupils and parents.

Arrangements/availability of grants for FE and HE.

Careers Committee (monthly/fortnightly meetings).

Checklist 4: Liaison and developmental aspect of the careers guidance programme

Liaising with counsellor where personal problems of pupils are brought to light in connection with the careers programme.

Attending YEO/CAO interviews where necessary.

Reporting results of interviews to staff.

Progress chasing as a consequence of dilatory production of pupil records for YES interviews.

Liaising with YEO regarding any queries and difficulties that he may have about pupil interviews.

Arranging vacation courses.

Arranging visits, lectures, interviews with potential employers, also informal interviews with potential employers.

Attending visits, courses, etc. for careers masters, etc.

Review and development of careers programme.

Synopsis of Forms in use in the School

Assessment forms for careers interviews: revised scheme

Division of responsibility

Careers Form No. 1: Personal qualities and health
    House Heads and Third Year Tutors

Careers Form No. 2: Subject assessments
    House Heads and Fourth Year Tutors using 'Teaching Sets Analysis'.

Teaching Set Analysis Forms
    Heads of Department

Form X.7: Bishopston Education Committee: Confidential school report
    House Heads and Fourth Year Tutors using Careers Forms Numbers 1 and 2.

Form X.8 (completed by pupils and parents) will be issued at the beginning of the Fourth Year, and distributed through Tutor Groups. It is suggested that pupils complete their section of the form in Tutor Periods before taking them home to their parents.

Implementation

Form X.7 (this form has severe limitations, but the school is obliged to complete it). Basically it can be sub-divided into two sections:
  (a) *Assessment of personality and health.* This section can be transferred direct from Careers Form No. 1.
  (b) *Subject assessment.* This section can be transferred direct from Careers Form No. 2.

Careers Forms Nos. 1 and 2

These forms are designed to provide a more realistic and standardized assessment than Form X.7. Since X.7 *must* be completed they are set out so that the relevant sections can easily be transferred. They are seen by the careers adviser, but unlike Form X.7 they are retained by the school.

Careers Form No. 1

This form will be issued towards the end of the Fourth Year. It is confidential but it should be noted that Section I is to be transferred on to X.7 which can be seen by parents on request.

Careers Form No. 2

This form will be issued together with the completed Form No. 1 early in the Fifth Year. Fifth Year Tutors will also be issued with the completed Set Analysis to facilitate subject assessment across the whole ability range.

What forms are used for the careers programme in your school? What rationale lies behind them and whose purposes are they serving? Perhaps you could bring examples for your group or syndicate to examine and discuss.

Further comments on careers guidance:

(1) *Careers Guidance: The view of an all through comprehensive school*

The head, his deputy, the senior mistress, the heads of schools, and all heads of departments provide guidance as regards careers and further education.

The heads of departments are specialists in the professions and trades related to the subjects they teach, but the knowledge of the heads of schools, deputy head, senior mistress and head is rather more general and possibly includes a fair detail of the rather more unusual vocations and opportunities for higher education.

Pupils seeking advice of any sort may book interviews, through the secretary, with heads of schools or above. Experience shows that this privilege is extensively used and never abused.

Vocational Guidance Officers of the Youth Employment Service come in regularly to speak to groups and interview and advise individuals. Our links with the YES are happy ones but we have to keep a close ear on what is said to pupils in regard to their subsequent education. For example, one is liable to hear, 'Well you can't go into the Sixth Form unless you have four O levels', (which is untrue) and 'You ought to repeat the fifth year' (which need not be necessary in our set-up). Senior staff have to sit in on these talks and interviews. This used not to be done, but the effects of what was said to pupils (especially girls) were sometimes quite shattering. The YES cannot be blamed entirely for such errors. It is very much understaffed, and staff turnover is enormous. It is believed that only two officers have been there for more than 18 months, and they are so overworked that they just cannot keep abreast of developments in schools. The remainder didn't stay long enough to find out.

The YES puts on careers lectures for sixth formers using a large panel of visiting speakers talking about their jobs, and between them covering just about every aspect of science, technology, commerce, etc., that one could imagine. These are very good and are always much appreciated and well attended.

The 'premature leavers' have a comprehensive programme of industrial and commercial visits, and many are involved in social and welfare work on certain afternoons of the week. For example, some girls provide general help in baby clinics and play centres.

A goodly number of Fifth and Sixth Formers attend short vocation courses in commerce, industry, hospitals, etc. These are popular with our pupils, and so many apply that not all can be found places.

Many organizations make direct approaches to the school when seeking juvenile labour. The College regularly applies to us for Office Staff and laboratory technicians; and the legal, accountancy, insurance and banking professions constantly ask for trainees, both male and female. Such contacts have probably arisen from the fact that an unusually large proportion of the fathers of our pupils belong to the professions or are senior executives.

Headmaster

(2) Careers Guidance

The fourth year pupils had already passed one of the important milestones in their school careers—at the end of the third year they chose, or were chosen, to continue with certain subjects or courses rather than others. This was also the point at which they chose courses leading to various examinations, or, perhaps, to none at all. It was not simply the course that was important to the individual pupil but also its implications for later career prospects. However, during the first term of their fourth year, over half the boys and girls in this study said they had not discussed their careers with any of their teachers, and few had seen someone linked with their intended job, or from the careers guidance office. (What the position might have been one or two terms later, of course, is not known, but with one of the main choice points passed, a proportion as high as one half not having talked to their teachers about careers was obviously undesirably high.)

The facilities provided for giving careers guidance in each school were not directly linked to their size. For example C, a four-form entry school, had a specialist careers teacher and an office set aside for his use. This compared with the large urban school I, where no room was set aside for careers work and the responsibility for advice was shared by the various senior members of staff and the class teachers. It was found that the pupils in schools with good facilities (C, E, H and J) were, on the whole, slightly more satisfied with guidance received than those with poor facilities. On the other hand, a comparison between those schools which gave individual advice to all third-year pupils before fourth year courses were selected and those that did not, showed little difference in levels of pupil satisfaction with advice received. The provision of facilities, therefore, appeared to be more important than whether or not the schools claimed to see all third-year pupils about their career prospects.

(From *Comprehensive Schools in Focus*, J. M. ROSS and G. CHANAN, NFER, Slough, 1972)

POINTS TO CONSIDER———

1. In your view, is the careers programme as described, too separate or not separate enough from the rest of the school?

2. How would you justify the content and the workload of the careers staff at the school?

3. Do you think the basic problem is that the careers programme has been separated from the welfare and curricular processes, thus leaving the careers staff as clerks to both of them?

4. If you use outside experts to give careers guidance to pupils, does this imply that your programme lacks coherence and meaning and will ultimately become inoperable?

5. Can you together with the other members of your syndicate indicate solutions to some of the problems you see in this school's strategy?

CONTENTS

Applications for Places in Further and Higher Education

INTRODUCTION___

formally concerned a child's education is complete when the pupil leaves, although in practice the school is very much aware of the real needs of pupils, and cannot help but continually appraise how it can best help and influence those who are not formally its pupils any longer. Thus is raised whether, or, the degree to which schools are able to absorb feedback from these programmes into their overall direction and into their philosophies.

(This chapter derived from another school's programme should be read in conjunction with the chapter relating to the 'Career's Programme'.)

The programme of application for places in further and higher education is interrelated at many levels with the welfare/guidance programme, with the careers programme, with curricular based programmes, and so on.

Not so very long ago it was possible, in one sense at least, to distinguish clearly between the careers programme and the programme of applications for places in further and higher education. The distinguishing feature lay in the apparent convenience with which a sixth form programme could be separated from the rest of a secondary school's careers programme. Recent changes both in the raising of the school leaving age and in the proposed alterations to the structure of further and higher education suggested in the Government White Paper *Education: a Framework for Expansion** makes this less and less tenable.

Applications for places in higher and further education and the careers programme focus attention upon one of the sensitive areas of a school, that is upon its boundaries. It is here that, in one sense at least, the school's work is judged, as its pupils—its 'output' are considered by potential 'users', either employers or further and higher education establishments. The resources that schools have tended to devote to the latter stages of these programmes emphasizes this sensitivity.

One further point raised by these programmes is that of the continuum of the child's/student's development. As far as the school is

**Education: A Framework for Expansion.* London: HMSO 1972.

ONE SCHOOL'S SCHEME

Presented in the flow diagram, Figure 1, is the programme developed by one large secondary comprehensive school to help pupils in further and higher education choices.

It is not presented as a model programme—the intention in presenting the outline is to indicate the complexity of the task and to stimulate discussion.

The bar chart (Figure 2) shows the periods of the year during which each of the steps in the programme was undertaken, and the member of staff responsible in each case.

It is clear that in devising this particular sequence some major decisions were taken or implied. Many of these decisions replicate the procedure already displayed in the 'Pupil Careers Guidance Programme' but, for convenience, are listed again below. Some, however, are of particular relevance to a sixth form programme. Amongst these are:

1. The degree to which the sixth year programme of applications for places in higher and further education is to be kept separate and distinct from any other pupil careers guidance programme.

2. The degree to which link courses can be forged with local colleges, and the implications to the school of such arrangements.

3. Decisions about whether those pupils who are aiming for a place in higher or further education should participate in a timetabled careers programme (if any), arranged for non-academic sixth year pupils, and the channels of communication to be kept open between those who are responsible for careers up to and including fifth year level and those responsible for a sixth year programme.

4. Decisions as to whether the production of references and counselling of potential 'Oxbridge' pupils is best undertaken within the procedure laid down for other higher and further education applications, or whether it is best made the responsibility of one person, e.g. the headteacher.

Amongst the major decisions upon which the programme would rest which are applicable to the careers guidance programme are:

5. Decisions about the degree to which the school accepts responsibility for helping pupils to obtain employment.

6. The nature of particular crucial deadlines which have to be met.

7. The use to be made of the Youth Employment Service, an evaluation of the sort of help it can offer and the ways in which this might be supplemented by the school.

8. The allocation of responsibility within the school for the programme, e.g. is it a function of a head of house and house tutor working within an existing in-school pastoral system, or should there be one person or a team of people specifically appointed to administer the programme?

9. The lines of communication to be maintained between those who are likely to know of a pupil's problems and difficulties and those responsible for giving careers guidance to the pupil.

10. The arrangements to be made for a centralized storing of information with regard to a pupil's preferences and difficulties, including responsibility for initiating, contributing to, and up-dating this store of information, and a feedback of information to those concerned.

11. Any specific LEA directives which might influence the programme.

12. In view of the sensitivity of careers guidance to many other aspects of school life at what stage should careers guidance begin?

13. The amount of time, if any, that is to be devoted to careers work with groups of pupils with differing career intentions.

14. The arrangements to be made for special categories of pupils, e.g. those in remedial classes.

15. The type and timing of information given to a pupil as to the career choices that it is felt are suitable to him.

Figure 1: Applications for places in higher and further education

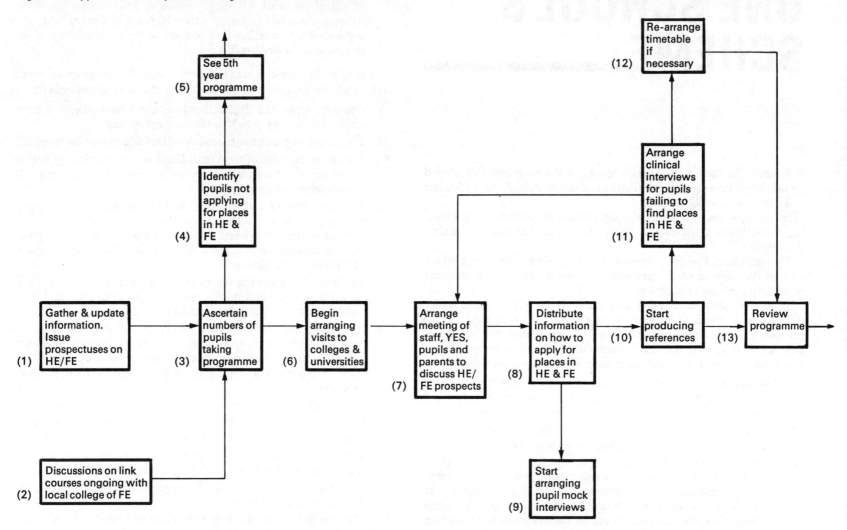

Figure 2: Bar chart to show the time of initiation and termination of each major step in the programme

(Numbers relate to event numbers on the flow diagram of the overall strategy opposite)

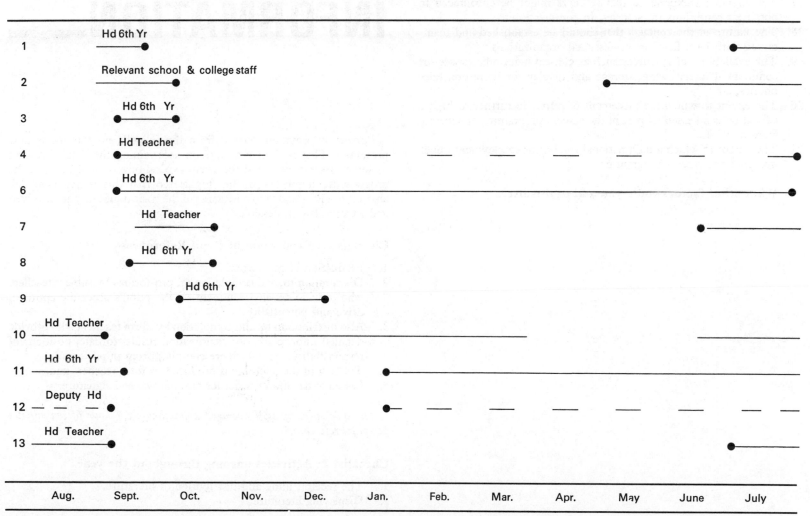

16. The relationship of the careers guidance programme to local schemes that might already be in existence, and the use to be made of visits and work experience in local factories.
17. The first-hand experience that teachers might be encouraged to obtain of conditions in factories, in commerce, etc.
18. The nature of the contacts that should be established and maintained with local firms or professional organizations.
19. The availability of resources such as clerical help, office space for confidential interviewing, storage and display for literature, telephones, etc.
20. The extent to which the placement of pupils in further or higher education is an essential part of the careers programme or separate from it.
21. The extent to which a high national level of unemployment might influence the careers programme.

What other factors could you add to this list?

ADDITIONAL INFORMATION

Further information derived from the school's programme is now presented. This is to give a guide in ascertaining the detail involved in some of the stages, and the likely expenditure of staff time, in the programme. It must again be emphasized that this is not a 'model' answer, but is intended to raise some of the basic issues that are involved and to stimulate discussion.

Checklist 1: Production of Pupil References

1. Production of pro formas.
2. Distribution to, and completion of, pro-formas by subject teachers who provide detailed comment on the pupil's academic aptitude, drive and potentiality;
3. Also distribution to, and completion by, form teachers who provide detailed information on: examination results to date, positions of responsibility, etc. which are compiled from pupil records.
4. The text of the reference is produced by form teachers and,
5. Passed to the head teacher for his approval and signature.

The time spent by staff averaged approximately 1 hour fifteen minutes per pupil reference.

Checklist 2: Activities ongoing throughout the year

1. The receipt, filing and distribution of literature.
2. Displaying literature.

3. Production of pupil references.
4. Updating, filing, checking pupil records (through form teachers).
5. Advice to pupils and parents.
6. Making arrangements for, and discussing availability of grants for higher and further education with pupils and parents.

The school also held 'mock interviews' for pupils during lunch hours. This accounted for, in the sampled period, approximately 42 hours of teaching staff time.

LINKS WITH LOCAL COLLEGES OF FURTHER EDUCATION

Recent proposed changes to the structure and organization of higher and further education, together with the full implications of raising the school leaving age, have resulted in some schools considering much more closely the development of course links with local colleges of further education.

Initially such links appear to confer distinct advantages and a rationalization of resources would certainly favour such proposals. Although advantages are certainly evidenced in such arrangements a school should explore very carefully the full implications of proposals before committing itself.

Amongst the advantages is that the comprehensive school is unlikely to be able to offer the range of courses that a college can. The potential size of the student intake in the college enables it to offer minority subjects which are not 'economically' viable in a school e.g. Advanced Level Latin and Greek might well be taught in colleges of further education. It has been argued that colleges have developed far better links with local industry and commerce than is the case for schools and that their courses are more realistically orientated to local needs. It follows from this that their guidance facilities might be better developed and more able to satisfy student requirements. Links with schools would certainly work to the benefit of the colleges in that a firmer base to their budgeting could be provided and would reduce to some extent at least the entrepreneurial nature of their course development. Since many of the staff employed in colleges are in fact ex-school teachers the links would confer mutual advantages that would also be of immediate benefit to students.

Disadvantages however also exist although some of them might prove more apparent than real. Institutions working together would need to plan to some extent at least their joint future. This has implications for resource allocation for curricular discussion (which has at least one output in joint timetabling) and there is also the possibility of participating institutions suffering a loss of freedom. In addition the consultation necessary between staff of the co-operating institutions is an extra workload.

Other factors become more problematic since they are likely to involve personal attitudes. It is likely that the college might have a much more attractive image to dissident school children, and that the school might as a consequence feel its disciplinary procedures undermined. Both institutions might have a residual interest in retaining the best students; certainly, some school teachers see their *raison d'être* in the teaching of their A-level students—hence proposed changes might be viewed as an undermining of their personal status. The raising of the school leaving age has compelled pupils to stay at school who, prior to RoSLA, would have attended the college. The potential conflict may be further exacerbated through the salaries of principals and heads of departments in colleges being tied to the numbers of students they can attract, as is the case of course for head teachers whose salaries are related to the numbers of pupils in their sixth forms.

The discussion of factors such as these begins to raise wider issues about the extent to which the whole of the education of the 14 to 19 age group should in fact be firmly laid down by the LEA itself.

POINTS TO CONSIDER____

1. Recent years have seen considerable change in higher and further education. How would you advise a school to keep abreast:

   (a) of the implications of these changes,
   (b) of the attitudes of pupils towards the efficacy of full or part-time courses in further or higher education,
   (c) of changes in the concept of continuing education,
   (d) of employment possibilities, both locally and nationally,

   in order to give its pupils the soundest possible advice before entering HE or FE?

2. (a) Is it in fact the job of one man in the school to determine and interpret these trends, on the one hand to the staff of the school, and on the other to its pupils, and to advise on course development to suite these trends; or

   (b) Should this agent be based in the LEA where he would be in a position to advise and co-ordinate provision at the wider LEA level; or

   (c) Is this a task for a national agency?

3. Is the dissemination of information to pupils effective? How do you check that this is so?

4. What information would you look to for feedback into the programme?

5. The production of 'references' is a time-absorbing and costly process. How best can a school handle this? What is the experience of the members of your group or syndicate on this point?

Pupil Records

CONTENTS

INTRODUCTION____

This document seeks to explore twin dilemmas which a school must contend with in designing, and using its pupil records. A school needs to collect information on its pupils, but in orientation and potential use:

does this information need to be so exclusively pupil centred; or

should its format enable it to serve other organizational purposes;

and:

can a school get by with a whole series of disparate and incomplete sets of records; or

should it aim for one complete unitary information system of which pupil records forms an important part?

This discussion document seeks to explore these dilemmas and is intended to provide the basis for work in groups (or syndicates). Tutors should ensure that groups meet in plenary session to compare view points at regular intervals.

Teachers should be encouraged to bring samples of the pupil records that are in current use in their own schools. This will not only facilitate discussion by providing practical examples related to the individual teachers own experience, but will automatically provide a basis for the comparison of practice adopted by different schools.

Section 1 of this chapter raises some of the more fundamental issues which are then discussed in greater detail in subsequent sections. In doing this it goes well beyond the point that would be a normal concern for most schools and it might appear to be overwhelming in its claims. Perhaps the real point is that the school must take its stance on that to which it must accommodate, that which it must at least be ever aware of, and that which it can safely choose to ignore.

SECTION 1

1.1 Why should one keep records?

Pupil records are an integral part of the total information system of the school in which the pupil record card and the pupil report occupy crucial roles. They reflect processes ongoing at a particular moment of time and occupy a central position in a school's administrative procedure. Their very existence, however, disguises some of the more fundamental dilemmas and problems which a school must contend with for information on a record card, in providing a basis for action, may neatly sidestep the evaluative status of the information itself, and the subjective basis of its compilation.

To a school the case for a unified record system might under some circumstances appear overwhelming. A properly kept set of records with standardized, easily accessible information, could provide data for all of the following administrative tasks: admittance and induction of first year children, subject choices, careers, HE and FE guidance, budgeting, stocktaking, statistical returns, requisitions, staffing and staff development, arrangements for student teaching practice, time-tabling, arrangements for internal and external examinations, parents' meetings, the production of the school calendar and so on; there are many other administrative tasks that could be added to this list. It would also be a ready source of information to all sorts of 'populations' who wish, quite properly, to use such information for their purposes.

You might care to make a list of all these interest groups, based both in and outside school, whose demands may at some stage call upon the information contained in pupil records.

Thus the attraction to a school of a body of organized data which will immediately lend itself to a whole range of requirements is obvious. Although the cost might be enormous, is it in fact feasible to expect one record system to satisfy aims as diverse as those listed above, as diverse, for example, as:

Doing counts of generalized categories if it so desires?

The Secretary to make a list of all children with speech impediments?

The school to compile DES Form 7 (schools), and so on.

The opposing view would claim that in the case of pupil records, for example, welfare requirements are not of the same order as curricular requirements, and in the gathering processing, storing and so forth of such information, very fundamental ideological issues are being raised.

The size of the campus and the speed at which information may be needed, are also factors mitigating against the case for a unified record system, plus of course the serious lack of clerical help to undertake filing in a school. A 'unified' record system is not a practicable possibility. It is also the case that many teachers feel hostile towards the keeping of confidential information. Too much of this is not a good thing, in their view. Here there exists the basis of a conflict between those whose needs are to run the organization, and those who see themselves in a school primarily to teach.

A school may well find itself in the position of holding a whole series of incomplete records. But does this matter?

What, in fact, is the minimum amount of information a school needs to store for each of the different aspects of its work? How should it supplement this information should this prove necessary? The most common way appears to be for an individual member of staff to go and collect it. The implication of this appears to be that this is less costly than storing all information, and, that pupil time is cheap. Does it also follow that staff time is cheap?

If pupil records are to be regarded as a series of essentially separate systems then the task of the top management of the school would appear to be:

to design a structure which will enable co-ordination and liaison to proceed most effectively between the different sides of the school all of whom collect and store information on pupils for their own purposes—and:

to reconcile the potentially different positions of those who 'hold' and those who want to 'use' the information.

SURNAME	CHRISTIAN NAMES	DATE OF BIRTH

SURNAME EVANS

CHRISTIAN NAMES TRACY

DATE OF BIRTH 2nd Sept. 1962

ADDRESS
11 Higher Rd.
Bishopston

FATHER'S NAME WILLIAM EVANS

OCCUPATIONS AND PLACES OF EMPLOYMENT
FATHER Merchant seaman
MOTHER Office Cleaner

PREVIOUS SCHOOL(S)

ADMISSION No. 73/189/F

CHANGE OF ADDRESS
10 WALLUM AVE.
BISHOPSTON

SPECIAL NOTES
PREVIOUS EDUCATION

INFORMATION RECEIVED

DATE OF ADMISSION 14th Sept. 73

LEFT/RIGHT HANDED
HEALTH, etc.

CAREER INTERESTS

DATE OF LEAVING 19th Oct. 74

CHANGE OF ADDRESS
19 BERKELEY PLACE
BISHOPSTON

HOME CIRCUMSTANCES

EMPLOYMENT

Photograph

SUBJECTS
M E   DATES   COURSE

TUTORS COMMENTS

HOUSE Willard

STAY

OFFICES, SOCIETIES, GAMES, INTERESTS

YEAR 1

YEAR 2

YEAR 3

YEAR 4

INSIDE: NOTES OF INTERVIEWS, ETC.

SUBJECT	YEAR 1		YEAR 2		YEAR 3		YEAR 4		YEAR 5		YEAR 6		YEAR 7	
	Exam %	Class Ave.	Exam %	Class Ave.	Exam %	Class Ave.	Exam %	Class Ave.	Exam %	Class Ave.	Exam %	Class Ave.	Exam %	Class Ave.
ENGLISH 1	35	48												
ENGLISH 2	42	47												
FRENCH														
LATIN														
HISTORY	40	44												
GEOGRAPHY	53	51												
MATHS	21	39												
SCIENCE 1 Dic.														
SCIENCE 2 Che.	27	41												
SCIENCE 3 Phy.														
RELIGIOUS ED.	38	46												
MUSIC	⁓	⁓												
ART/CRAFT	60	50												
NEEDLEWORK/~~WOODWORK~~	65	47												
DOM. SCIENCE/~~METALWORK~~														
TECH. DRG.														

In your view are the problems of pupil records really no more than completing the top copy of a 'no carbon required' pro-forma and forwarding the copies made to the office, one for their own files, and the others for dispatch to the required destinations.

1.2 What is the minimum amount of information required?

The attached photocopy of a record card relating to a transferring pupil has been sent to you by the pupil's last secondary school.

Does it provide a sufficient basis for you to admit the pupil and to allocate her to pastoral and teaching groups?

If not,
  (a) what other information will you seek?
  (b) will you interview the pupil and her parents? Do you do this as a matter of course for all pupils?
  (c) what will your next action be?

Do you consider that there should be standardized record cards that all schools should use?

1.3 Location and accessibility of records

The location of records always seems to be a ready source of friction since at the time they are needed they inevitably seem to be locked inaccessibly in someone's office.

In your opinion should a school hold both central and operational files? There rarely seems to be a central agency for putting the records together.

1.4 Does the weight of paper grind you down?

It would seem obvious that a pupil record should be both continuous (that is, a continual compilation over a child's complete schooling) and cumulative. This should reduce the unnecessary duplication of effort on the part of many different teachers who set out to collect the same information time and time again. It should make available data which might otherwise prove difficult to obtain, and it should ensure that information required for any task is at hand whenever it is needed. The gathering of essential information is therefore reduced to a minimum and times of contact with pupils and parents can be more profitably utilized.

Is this really the case? Consider the following:

The pupil record is a cumulative document, but do the aims of the organization change as a child is processed through the school? Is the information collected at earlier stages of a pupil's career therefore of any use at all?

If 95 per cent of all records were to be thrown away each year, what would you recommend keeping, and on what grounds would you justify your choice?

Is there any point in hanging on to information in case it is asked for? You lack resources, space, filing cabinets, filing clerks, and paper is expensive. You need to be hard on yourself to be fair to yourself.

Would a decision of this sort be easier to make if the records system was not quite so overtly geared to the child?

Should it be so child-centred in your view?

Does your school make a sufficient distinction between 'permanent' information, and, 'temporary' information? What are those items of permanent information regarding a pupil that the school simply cannot do without?

In designing a pupil record system each piece of information collected should be absolutely vital. The compilers should see the need for all the information that is asked for.

Are there more empty spaces on the records your school holds than completed ones? Why?

A record system, however well designed, has to depend upon the willingness of the compilers to fill the records in adequately. It seems that so many records have acres of empty space and contain information rarely used anywhere with the result that they lose all credibility with the compiler. He might ask himself the questions: Is the record reliable? What will happen if I don't fill it in, will the school really grind to a halt?

Some questions

1. Has the pupil record card outgrown the purpose for which it was originally conceived?

2. In your view can a large complex organization such as a secondary comprehensive school use the information pupil records contain to service its many aims and functions? and:

3. Is the traditional pupil record flexible enough for this purpose?

4. (a) What kinds of demands for information most frequently come up in practice? and,

   (b) Is it possible to categorize them for system design and decision making?

5. (a) What are the information needs of the different sides of the school?

   (b) How does the school arbitrate between competing claims on staff time, they after all, are the ones who provide the information in the first place?

6. To view a school as an organization concerned with maintaining its boundaries provides a useful stance in explaining a school's concern with its records, their timing, accuracy and content. The principal concern will thus be at the times the pupil crosses major boundaries: e.g. on entry to the school, option choices, at entry to the sixth year, when the pupil is leaving.

   Do you agree?

   Can you add to the list?

7. How long does it take, on average, to extract the information from a record to compile, for example, a reference for a pupil?

8. What kinds of pupil records should a school keep in its own defence?

9. The only way that the subjective basis of record compilation may be overcome is for the school to 'know' the compiler, and presumably make the necessary allowances. Do you agree?

10. Do you consider that it is possible for there to be an omnibus, unitary record covering all manner of needs? How many different sections would such a system contain? How does it show up if the school hasn't such a record system? What would a pupil record look like that was designed with the needs of a wider information system in mind? What stance does your school adopt on this issue?

11. With the other members of your group, produce a list of what you think to be the most important criteria that should be taken into account when designing pupil records. Use this as a check list, when you look at the rest of this document.

SECTION 2_____

2.1 What record systems are available?

If one of the arguments advanced in Section 1 were to be adopted, that is that the schools pupil records should be made up of sets of separately held files, perhaps relating to one central file held in the school office, then, what would this system look like? What would its parts consist of?

It would appear that the information stored in the various files should be determined by:

> The use made of the files in the different parts of the school;
> the frequency of this use;
> an analysis of the pitfalls and of the elements that cause breakdowns and require information to be separately collected;

The whole should then be costed.

Did your school do this in designing its pupil record system?

It is a large task but you might like to consider attempting it!

Whilst on the one hand the appeal of computer based information systems is immediate, cost will almost inevitably prohibit their use by all but the richest schools, and of course, the question of confidentiality of information becomes acute. Edge punch cards provide a cheaper alternative that proves in practice to be adaptable and durable, and there are of course countless variations upon the folder/pocket type of record, one example of which is provided at the front of this document.

More sophisticated versions of these simple pockets are available, and some allow the making of a number of copies from one compilation.

Your working party (or syndicate) might like to set itself the task of establishing what record systems are available. Many commercial firms offer such for sale, some of which might suit school use, and one might learn from local industries what (personnel) record systems they favour. Other educational establishments have 'problems' similar to those of schools: contacts with local polytechnics, colleges and universities might prove fruitful; as may, of course, an examination of what other schools use.

2.2 How many sets of pupil records might exist in a school?

Records will be kept on a pupil by those staff responsible for pupil welfare; the careers staff; the academic staff; all of whom will of necessity keep formal records but will almost certainly keep private records for their own convenience.

The administrative side of the school will require information for its own processes and also to supply the needs of other users, for example, exam boards, the LEA, the DES.

The school has a statutory requirement to keep certain legal documents, the class register being such a document.

The timetable is another sort of record which (should) allow the school to answer the question, 'Where can I find pupil "X" at a given time?'

Pupil reports represent another sort of record, and so on.

You might care to add to the list.

2.3 Should you encourage or discourage private record keeping?

It seems inevitable that the subject teacher particularly will keep two sorts of records. One, compiled on a day-to-day basis for his own personal use in assessing the pupil, and the more formal record which is periodically entered on to the pupil's record card. Many staff will of course keep private records sometimes as an aid to identification—we all know the sort of thing involved—'Form 3A, Jennie Smith, red hair and glasses, sits at front, good orally but shocking written work.' It is interesting to speculate whether information contained in private records is ever exchanged between teaching staff and the degree to which there may be a growing sensitivity about committing opinion to record cards, and, whether discrepancies might be found to exist between the information forming the basis of reports about a pupil to external agencies, other schools, educational institutions, parents and so on, and the information contained on the formal record card.

SECTION 3

3.1 Assessment and the ideological basis of records

The existence of information on the somewhat mundane record card blurs the distinction that exists between simple factual data, name, age, form, address and so on, and information which is evaluative.

Is it really the case that they provide the same factual basis for action, for:

a fundamental question is being posed when a child is being measured against a (sometimes unwittingly arbitrary) set of standards.

What is the reliability and dependence that is to be placed upon class or subject teacher assessments?

In terms of all that is now beginning to be known about marks awarded by examiners, how many schools retest for reliability? What in fact is the meaning of 60 out of a possible 80 marks, does it have any meaning? What do grades A to E mean; to the class teacher; the subject teacher; the pupil; the parent; the pupil's elder brother; yourself; is there any social or academic consensus of meaning to be found—are you prepared to use such grades as a basis for action in a school? Can a school afford the time to standardize its procedures?

3.2 Are records labels?

Is there a danger in your view of the assessments made about children, partcularly in writing, becoming an excuse for lazy thinking, in fact becoming labels. Thus, judgements that such and such a child is bright, a slow learner, a CSE child, are perpetuated, and become known *to the child himself*. The original assessment has become a self fulfilling prophecy. It is not so much the formal record that may bring about this state of affairs as the cues the child may pick up and interpret from the behaviour of his teachers and peers.

3.3 How long should a school leave information on a record?

A head teacher has been asked to provide a reference for a pupil in the fifth year at his school. On consulting the pupil's file he discovers that he had been caught taking money from a coat pocket in the cloakroom, information recorded during the pupil's first year.

If you were the head teacher what would you do? Can you recommend a code of practice for a school to follow?

3.4 Is there information which shouldn't be kept, at least in a written form? The problems of confidentiality and security.

A tension exists between the school's need to see to its own defence, and to cope with the special problems of children who are at risk. Has the school in fact any responsibility for diagnosing the situation of these children and using this information as a predictor of behaviour?

For children who are 'most at risk' the need for full records is overwhelming—you cannot have enough information. Is this really the case?

What does the school do with the information that Jimmy Smith's dad has gone to jail again? Can it really cope with it?

Is the following practice to be adopted?

Where the school collects information on a pupil of a highly confidential nature, this will most probably be locked away in the head teacher's desk and will not be available for general circulation. However, if this is the case, it seems likely that unofficial methods of learning of the existence and contents of these additional records, and the dissemination of information based on 'hearsay', could be a possible consequence.

Or is the following?

MEMORANDUM

From: Head   *To:* All Staff

The school is concerned to hear of pupils whose work may be affected by unfortunate occurrences, illness, etc. When staff are dealing with these pupils, they are asked to give them special consideration.

Mr. Bramwell has agreed to put up on the main staffroom notice board information about these pupils, and to remove it by 3.55 p.m. each day.

Should a school carry a 'register of risk' and if so, for whose purposes does it carry this register?

3.5 In whose interests does the school act?

It seems as the school moves away from the more traditionally expected areas of behaviour associated with curriculum, pupil discipline and other academic concerns, and begins to act in areas served by other professionally staffed agencies, there begins to be increasing uncertainty about its actions. This uncertainty is reflected in the school itself, for it becomes more and more difficult to determine for whose purposes the school may be acting. A school presents a ready target to many organizations whose staff may often be quite unable to understand why (pupil) information is not more readily available, and why the school should so often appear to be unwilling to pass matters over into their hands—'we have all the good of the pupil at heart haven't we?' For example, for whose purposes does the school collect medical information? For its own purposes, or those of the medical officer of health? Whichever, it is clearly to the pupils' own benefit.

However, some people may get very hot under the collar about such an issue.

The whole question of the school's working together with other organizations and supplying them with pupil information, ostensibly for the pupil's benefit, raises many contentious issues.

You might like to discuss with your group examples with which you are personally acquainted, and see if you can, within the confines of the group, suggest guidelines for action which could be adopted by a school and help in determining its policy and its stance.

Questions

Is there any reason why a child should not be shown his own record?

Could pupils profitably be employed in undertaking clerical work on pupil record cards?

SECTION 4————

4.1 Are the needs of users and compilers necessarily identical? Do they act in harmony?

'We must teach ourselves to put more into writing.'
—Head Teacher, large secondary comprehensive school

'In obtaining a servant's character it is not well to be guided by a written one from some unknown quarter; but it is better to have an interview if at all possible with the former mistress. By this means you will be assisted in your decision of the suitableness of the servant for your place from the appearance of the lady and the state of her house.'★
—*Beetons Book of Household Management*, 1861, p.7.

Pupil records traditionally contain information about a child's intellectual ability and curricular progress, and also information of a personal nature about the child, his home and circumstances, and so on, insofar as the school ostensibly considers this information necessary to throw light upon the child's curricular progress. However, this raises questions of an ideological nature, possibly clashing with the professional stance of some members of staff, concerning the invasion of a pupil's privacy, and raises serious problems too about the practicality of collecting the information.

For records to fulfil their purpose they must be complete and up to date. All organizations need a foolproof way of updating their information, and in a school this responsibility devolves on to a teacher and principally a form teacher or tutor. Thus those furthest from the consequential use of the information are those responsible for its compilation.

★ I am grateful to Neil Porter for bringing this quotation to my attention.

4.2 Do you need training for record compilation?

The collection and compilation of different types of information from numerous sources is a complex process which certain curricular and pastoral patterns of organization are likely to complicate still further. It is unlikely that enough time is ever made available for staff of a school, who are principally recruited to teach, adequately to compile records. The very fact that they are required to be responsible for this type of reporting seems to be based upon a further assumption, namely, that once trained by a professional institution teachers are able and willing to undertake the confidential interviewing and counselling that seems to go hand in hand with certain types of record compilation, and, in addition, that they are able to observe and record accurately all the relevant facts. It would seem more realistic to question this supposed willingness on the part of all teachers and to suggest that before undertaking work of this type they will need an adequate training.

What in your view would comprise an adequate training programme?

Before you make your decision, consult the information given in the document 'Pupil Pastoral Welfare Concerns', duties of the form tutor.

You might like to discuss in your group (or syndicate) what you would consider to be the essential outlines of a training programme.

Imagine you are a head teacher interviewing a candidate for a teaching post:

If the candidate refused to undertake pastoral tutorial duties,

or, If he asked for written guidelines that delineated his sphere of operations,

or, if he asked for the school to train him in skills necessary for performing the task, particularly confidential interviewing, the recognition of personality disorders and objective reporting,

or, if he suggested that there should be a well defined limit beyond which the school should not intrude into an individual's private life,

Would you:

   (a) Compliment him on his perspicacity?

   (b) Remind him of the professional nature of the occupation he has chosen?

   (c) Recommend him to try elsewhere for employment?

4.3 Instructions on record compilation

Does a document such as the following, which is taken from a School's Handbook for Teaching Staff, represent from your point of view, sufficient information and instruction to staff in the compilation of records? If your answer is no, how would you improve on these instructions?

From a School Handbook—Instructions to Staff

PREPARATION OF REPORTS & RECORD CARDS

1. *These must always be written in blue or black ink.*

2. *New Reports*
   Form Teachers should be responsible for the preparation of **new** report books.
   (a) *The Cover* Surname first in block capitals, followed by the Christian names in script.
   (b) *Inside Page* Full details—name, address, date of birth, date of admission, admission number (obtained from secretary or from record cards).

3. *Form Teacher's Entry*
   (a) *Before circulating to subject teachers*
   Full name, term (Autumn, Autumn/Spring, Spring/Summer), year, form, date of beginning of next term.
   (b) *After completion by subject teachers*
   Form teacher's comments, check that all subject teachers have completed them, and fill in the school positions section. (Form teachers should try to include here any useful information about special school offices held, duties performed, attendance on residential courses, school journeys, school societies, etc.)

(c) *Merit and Demerit Marks and Times Absent*

These should be completed for the period up to the date set.

(d) *Headmaster's or Year Tutor's signing*

Form teachers should bring these to the headmaster or year tutor at the time stated, after they have checked that the reports are complete in all respects.

4. *Subject Teachers*

(a) *Grade Letter*

The Grade column will be filled in each time with a letter for the term work for the period under review:

A = Excellent or very good
B = Good
C = Satisfactory
D = Poor
E = Very unsatisfactory

This 5 letter scale is quite satisfactory without the addition of plus or minus marks. It applies to the spread in the form, set or group.

Staff should apportion these letters so that approximately:

A = 0–10% of form, set or group (0–3 of a form of 35)
B = 10–20%   ,,   (3–7   ,,   )
C = 40%   ,,   (14–20   ,,   )
D = 10–20%   ,,   (3–7   ,,   )
E = 0–10%   ,,   (0–3   ,,   )

This is approximate. A slow set or poor group may have no As or Bs, and more Ds and Es than is shown, but each form or set should be judged against its own spread and potential.

The grade letter is given for attainment only for the half year, not for effort or attitude. Reference to effort, attitude, or a wish to warn or encourage, can be covered in remarks.

(b) *The Percentage*

This should state the percentage in an exam, taking 45 per cent as a pass or a C, and be geared where possible to GCE or CSE for the forms aiming for that examination.

(c) *Exam Position*

This should indicate the position in the form, group or set. If the number in the group or set is not the same as the number in the form the position should be given as a fraction,

e.g. the eleventh in a 'set' or group of 29 would be 11/29.

(d) *Remarks*

These should be made as full and particular as possible. Try to avoid the single word such as 'Fair' or 'Satisfactory'.

Please remember that for parents these remarks are often the most useful part of the report. Remarks should always be initialled.

(e) *Subject Designations*

Where there is a dual designation, the one which does not apply should be crossed out.

Blank sections can be used for subjects not designated.

Two subjects should never be placed in one section.

(f) *Sets*

Where a subject is 'setted' under the subject title should be written 'A set' or 'B set'.

5. *At no times should reports be carried by pupils or left in classroom.*

6. *Sending out and collection of reports*

(a) Form teachers will ensure that each report has an envelope with the name and address of the parent clearly indicated in ink.

(b) Reports will be taken home by pupils at the time stated, to be read and signed by parents. This may be at the end of a term, half term, or at the end of a week. Pupils must be reminded to return them, properly signed, at the beginning of the next term, after the half term, or on the following Monday.

(c) Form Teachers will then check that they are signed, and *when all are returned* place them in form list order and return them to the secretary who will store them. Losses must be reported at once to the year tutor.

(d) Reports for pupils who are absent when they are to be taken home must be returned to the secretary who will post them or keep them until the pupil returns.

7. *Record Cards*

These are kept by year tutors, will be handed out by and returned to them. They must never be carried by pupils nor left lying about in the class or common rooms. Care must be taken to see that insert papers do not fall out of the cards.

Form Teachers will be responsible for completing the following sections of these by the end of term:

(a) *Attainment Record Assessment of Ability*

Transfer the term grade letter for the second half year from the report book to the grid for each subject taken, placing name of form in first column.

(b) *General Personality*

The form teacher will attempt to sum up fairly in both columns 'Attitude towards self and others' and 'Attitude towards work', a comment which covers both his or her impression of the pupil through his school year and also the general impression of staff as reflected in the report.

Use the appropriate line, e.g. for a pupil in 4A1 or 4L2, a comment will be placed in the line Year 4 although the three above will be blank.

(c) Below also on the appropriate year line place any positions held, significant membership of school societies (including drama, magazine committee, orchestra, choir), membership of school teams, visits abroad or school courses.

(d) It is appreciated that form teachers do not always teach members of their forms, but it should be remembered that in entering comments on record cards and reports they are *summarizing the views of their colleagues* and are giving their own opinions.

8. *Report Books*

These go out to parents at the following times:

1st & 2nd years	(i) December	(ii) July
3rd & 4th years	(i) February	(ii) July
5th year	At the end of Spring Term	
6th year	(i) January	(ii) July

9. *Internal Reports*

Form teachers circulate form lists to subject teachers, the columns in the grills headed by appropriate subject titles. Each subject teacher places against each pupil he teaches a grade letter for attainment (A: good, B: satisfactory, average for the group, C: below average, needing discussion).

Times for completion (approximate, can be adjusted slightly each term):

Autumn Term	Years 1 & 2	End of October
	Years 3–6	Mid-November
Spring Term	Forms 1 & 2	Early March

10. *Progress*

Subject teachers will complete sheets and pass them to form teachers. Form teachers will examine them with year tutors and a selection will be made of pupils whose work or effort is generally poor.

All these pupils will then be considered individually by the year tutor or heads of schools.

4.4 Memo to form tutor

MEMORANDUM

From: Head of Swallow House   *To:* D. T. Ayres
                                     (Form Tutor 4TC)

It seems from reports I have received that Dianne Windsor in your group is being bothersome again. I saw her late the other night with some young men I took to be from the RAF station.

Will you talk to her and see what you can find out?

Role play this interview: One of you take the part of the young PE master and the other the girl concerned.

If you were the young PE man, how much did you in fact manage to learn about the girl's behaviour?

As it transpired, whom else would you have need to contact?

What information have you collected that can go on the record card?

What conclusions do you draw?

In urgent circumstances the school might for an individual child set out to collect all the information again—at least it should ensure that the information is up to date.

But does this imply a breakdown in the record system?

4.5 Monitoring compilation

(a) *How is the school to maintain the effectiveness with which its pupil records are kept?*

Does the following represent this effectiveness?

MEMORANDUM

From : Head   *To :* All Heads of Houses

Will you make a point of checking with each of your tutors one pupil record card that they have updated this week. The points I wish you specially to emphasize are the import- ance of up to date information and the completeness of the record in the file—and that they are legible!

Or does this?

Test the record system by seeing what knowledge it can produce on a pupil, e.g.:

When he wants a careers reference;

When he wants to attend school camp but says he can't pay;

When he wants to change to French Option 2.

Have you retrieved sufficient information to enable you to take a decision?

Does it seem more sensible to give one person overall responsibility for monitoring the 'truthfulness' of the records that are kept?

(b) *How frequently do you think records should be updated?*
Perhaps a deliberate 'organizational' ploy should be introduced to ensure that records are updated:

every year, or
every term, or
every six months, and so on.

How does your school check that:
a child's change of address;
change of timetable;
change of tutor; and so on.
are promptly entered into the files.

How does your school monitor the effectiveness with which your pupil records are kept?

4.6 How do you collate all the information that is available?

The way schools seem to work implies the existence of (at least) two modes of retrieving information.

One mode depends upon already 'processed' information and this is available from the pupil's record. It will include simple factual information—name, age, form, timetable, photograph, address, where mother and father are to be contacted, and so on.

The other method relates to information which is more confidential in nature and possibly includes opinion or subjective judgement. This information is available in school but is not collected unless determined by some specific circumstance and is totally dependent upon a rapid means for its retrieval existing. In practice, this type of information is usually collected by a senior member of staff and presupposes the dis- tribution of resources which will allow senior staff the time to collect and collate the available information.

That procedures of this sort continue to be tenable is based upon the knowledge that staff have of individual pupils, and of each other. But in schools of more than 1000 pupils, and where staff turnover of at least 10 per cent per annum should be anticipated, it becomes less and less likely that this can be the case.

How do you in the large school mobilize this information and channel it in one 'usable' direction?

SECTION 5

5.1 Does the rest of the educational system act in concert with you?

MEMORANDUM

From: Head of Lower School   *To:* All Heads of Houses

8th June

Can I have your lists of new pupils with physical disabilities, and those who had poor primary attendance records—by the end of the week please?

Your freedom of action might have been constrained by the beliefs, the needs, and the actions of those who work outside your school. It could have been, for example, primary schools, the LEA itself, or one of a whole host of agencies external to the school, who nevertheless work with the school, and upon whom the school has to rely for the provision of information at the relevant time.

What do you do in such circumstances?

What do you consider the main organizational failings that would result in a head of lower school sending out a memo such as the one above?

What are the experiences of those in your syndicate on this point?

5.2 Memo from the careers master

MEMORANDUM

From: Careers Master   *To:* Head

The Careers Officers doing the interviewing are constantly complaining that the information we give them is skimped and out of date. It takes all my energy to get this much out of the staff—I daren't ask for more.

Should we ignore their complaint? Their officers seem to change every few months anyway.

What should a head teacher learn about the school's record system from this memo?

If you were this head teacher what would your next action be?

5.3 How do you collect and use the information which others who may be interested in your pupils may have?

The macro system—social services, probation officers, and so on, may have all sorts of information on a child.

Is it possible to pass this information on to the school in a form usable to the teacher?

Should such information in fact be passed on?

Social services hold 'case conferences' in which different members of a team representing different experiences, specialisms and interests, perhaps even representing different branches of the welfare service meet together pooling their information and points of view to determine how best to handle a particular case.

Can this technique be profitably applied by a school do you think?

Is it in your view likely to be the most effective way of collecting (and disseminating) information on a pupil?

SECTION 6
DO YOU USE YOUR RECORDS FOR FORECASTING____

If one examines most pupil records it appears that the contents relate to things which have already happened. But consider the needs that schools have to forecast trends, to allow the school to see what happens next.

Can rapid summaries be made of the information contained in the records your school holds?

How do you process and interpret the information contained in pupil records as a link to action?

Will the record system in your school allow Heads of Departments to reply quickly to the following memo: and

Do you think that it should in the first place?

MEMORANDUM

From : Deputy Head   *To :* All Heads of Departments

1st March

Can you give me some provisional estimate of the numbers you expect for the various 3rd year options so that I can put together a preliminary timetable.

Imagine for your school a situation where pupil option choices are being considered, and 31 pupils have indicated interest in an option that only has space for 30 pupils. Since each child will be considered on his or her merits, how and from where do all of the following, in helping make the decision, obtain their information:

(a) the academic staff, at faculty and department level.

(b) the pastoral staff.

(c) the careers staff.

(d) the head of section concerned.

(e) the director of studies.

Do you consider this an effective use of manpower?

Has your school made an effective use of the information it possesses for forecasting its future needs?

What, in your view, should happen?

SECTION 7
PUPIL REPORTS

Pupil reports are an integral part of the pupil record system and a school often takes considerable trouble to ensure that the report is delivered safely into the parents' hands.

The reports have cost many hundreds of hours of work to the school.

What does a school expect to happen once the report has reached the parent? Do you agree with the following viewpoint?

Conversation with a Head Teacher

'Pupil reports are one of the most important ways for the school to reach the community. For this reason it is most important that a "good image" is presented. Since all staff are not equally strong in their spelling and use of English, I consider it imperative that I see and check all reports before they are issued.'

Make a list in order of importance of what you consider to be the priorities in issuing a report to parents.

Did you include that the report forms part of the 'feedback' system?

What determines the date at which a report is presented to a parent?

What should determine the date at which a report is presented to a parent?

SECTION 8
THE OBJECTIVES
OF A PUPIL
RECORD SYSTEM

'What is called into question and should be more emphasized is the matching of records to purposes—the requirement for any kind of record to be justified in terms of the purposes to which it will be put.'

'Is it possible in a large organization such as a comprehensive school for there to be a set of uniquely determined and legitimated set of objectives for a pupil record system?'

Set up a committee meeting which has the following items on the agenda:

1. Standardization of entries.

2. Information retrieval from records.

3. Determination of how the school ensures that records are effectively kept.

4. Frequency of review of procedures and weight given to feedback of information.

5. Costing of the operation.

Who would you invite to sit on the committee?

Present to this committee meeting a brief that represents the views of a class teacher; a form tutor; a head of department; a head of faculty; a head of year or house; a head of section; the school nurse; the school counsellor; the bursar and school secretaries; the senior mistress; the deputy head(s) organization and curriculum; and the head teacher.

Give advice to the meeting as to how it should seek the views of outside bodies who may make a regular use of pupil records, e.g. the careers service, the LEA, social services, the EWO, and so on. Should governors, parents and pupils be invited to give their opinions?

WHERE DO WE GO FROM HERE?__

It was suggested at the beginning of this document that a school is exposed to twin dilemmas which by their nature appear to be irreconcilable.

In practice a school will *most probably* operate a pupil centred system —justification for which will *most probably* lie in specified traditional needs:

One set of pupil records will satisfy immediate requirements of identifying and locating a pupil as well as sparing the organization the embarrassment of being unable to do this, and, there is in addition, a legal requirement that certain information is collected and retained. Further to this, the school principally needs the information to form the basis of reports to parents, and for references and testimonials.

In practice this situation leads to disparate collection, use, and store of information.

However some centralization will occur. The secretarial office will hold a basic pupil file and can inform the user which part of the school to turn to for other information. Thus 'careers', 'subject teachers', 'subject departments', 'the welfare system', and so forth, all set out to produce and keep their own pupil records, passing this information on to the central file in the school office once their immediate use of it is satisfied. The office thereby becomes a storehouse of obsolete and obsolescent information. But such practice does no more than magnify the existing problems for the fundamental problems remain and, as the school copes with system maintenance the *ad hoc* nature of decisions made becomes more apparent; the creaks in the structure begin to signal imminent collapse.

What is to be done about: a register of risk; confidentiality; location and access; about the subjective basis of compilation and assessment and the disguising of the real nature of the school's practice that this allows; about the need to standardize; about persuading and training staff to alter practice; about intrusions into privacy; the lack of time and pressures upon overworked staff, about not enough or no clerical help; spiralling costs; inefficiency that allows pupils to slip through the screening process; about ever increasing demands from outside agencies; the inter-linking of one set of information with another; the duplication of effort, where in fact does one draw the line?

At some stage it must appear overwhelmingly attractive to a school to cry 'enough' and begin the attempt to rationalize and standardize the process, for it cannot continue to go on in this piecemeal fashion, can it?

But unfortunately the value bases underlying the process, the problems referred to above are all still there. In fact it might prove infinitely more expensive to attempt to build a complete information system than to carry on as before.

It is a cruel dilemma.

But examining the problem and adopting a point of view is at least one stage further. Such a stance enables the school to do that which it must, to be always on the alert for other factors, and to choose carefully those items which it can safely ignore. Some schools no doubt have already made significant steps in this direction.

Transfer, Induction and Allocation

of First-Year Children to Classes

INTRODUCTION — TRANSFER OF PUPILS

As a consequence of the patterns of educational organization that have emerged in the last few years, the very relationships which existed between institutions, the roles and responsibilities of the staff of the schools, and the patterns of curricular organization must be re-appraised. The necessity for schools to work together as part of the larger educational system challenges the prevailing sense of autonomy; for it is vital that close working relationships are forged between co-operating schools. This should not lead to a feeling that the junior high school is being squeezed between the interests of primary and senior schools, or that the primary school is dictated to by the large secondary comprehensive. Constant liaison is necessary to ensure that staff are sufficiently sensitized to each other's problems and are adapting to new demands. Although whether the co-operation on curriculum and pedagogy should lead to the demand that transferring pupils should know this or that, is an open question.

With the transference of pupils to the secondary school one is looking at the beginning of the educational cycle, a process which, once started, will prove difficult to restructure. It would therefore seem self-evident that the 'educational design' should be on a right foundation from the start. A high turnover of teaching staff is a hindrance to its smooth operation, based as it is on close co-operation between institutions. It will also prove a disruption to the confidence that pupils, parents and teaching staff must share when a decision on which course to take and which school to go to may profoundly affect a pupil's career. Such a decision should be taken with the knowledge of the potentialities of the system in operation and with the all-round development of the pupil in mind.

The outlines presented below show schemes operating where transfer is (i) at 11+, between primary school and secondary comprehensive, and (ii) at 13+, where the transfer is viewed from the standpoint of a junior and senior high school—this is in fact a simplified outline, for in practice pupils at the junior high school were allowed the choice of three senior schools, and the senior school dealt with several junior high schools.

The task imposes a significant amount of work of a clerical nature. It is not unusual for a large secondary comprehensive school to be recruiting pupils from more than 50 contributory primary schools. The research on which this document is based indicated that to cope with these time-absorbing and specialized tasks a head of a lower school is often given the specific responsibility of maintaining and developing the programme. Considerable efforts are made to ensure the free flow of information between all the participants. It appears to be customary to spread the tasks over a full twelve month period prior to the pupils' arrival, and also, to use at least the first term of the first year as a diagnostic term before more permanent pupil allocation to classes is finalised.

This task presents a number of distinguishing features characteristic of major administrative tasks including a dependence upon external agencies for the provision of information to undertake the task, and the need to complete the work before a deadline—in this case the beginning of the new academic year.

The two outlines which follow are not presented as model programmes—the intention is to indicate the complexity of the task and to stimulate discussion.

Figure 1 : Transfer of pupils at 11+, from Primary to Secondary Comprehensive School and their Allocation to Classes

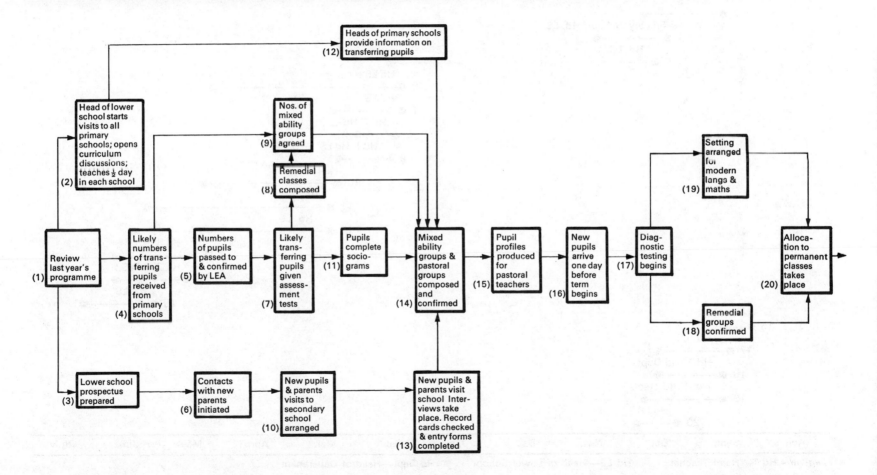

Figure 2: Bar chart to show time of initiation and termination of each major step in the programme

(Numbers relate to event numbers on the flow diagram of the overall strategy opposite)

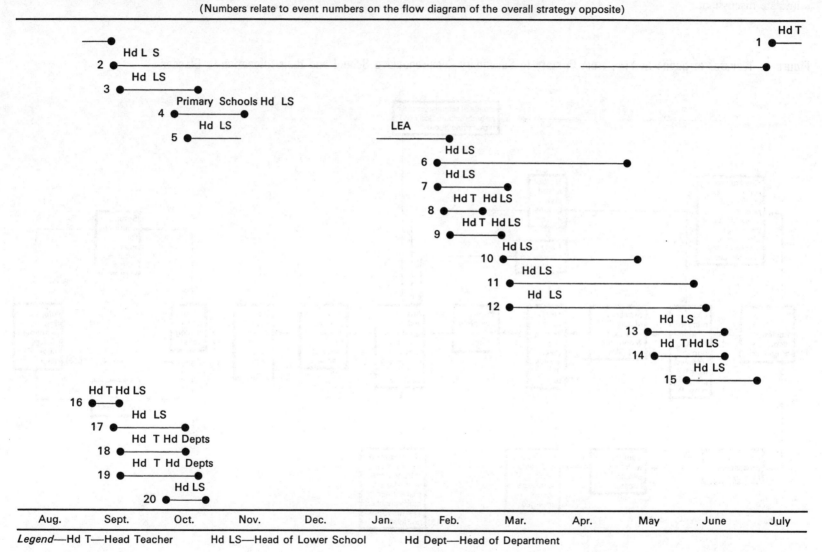

Legend—Hd T—Head Teacher   Hd LS—Head of Lower School   Hd Dept—Head of Department

Transfer at 11+

The bar chart on the previous page shows the periods of the year during which each of the steps in the programme was undertaken, the member of staff who was responsible for initiating each step of the task and the member of staff responsible for maintaining the progress of each of the steps. The flow diagram illustrates the sequence of steps in the programme and it is clear that in devising this sequence of action some major decisions were taken. Amongst the more fundamental decisions are those concerned with long range planning and will probably have involved:

(1) Policy decisions likely to influence the type and pattern of secondary provision.
(2) Estimates of potential school population and consequent building requirements and possibility of expansion.
(3) Determination of the ultimate size of the school.
(4) Determination of catchment areas.

Amongst other decisions are:

(1) Determination of the nature of the first year in a secondary school.
(2) Determination of the type of information to be given to pupils and parents and the timing of the dissemination of this information.
(3) Whether to hold discussions on record compilation and the transfer of information with contributory primary schools.
(4) Whether to hold discussions on curricular matters with contributory primary schools.
(5) Whether staff of the secondary school might be timetabled to teach in contributory schools.
(6) Whether equipment might be loaned to contributory schools.
(7) Determination of the latest possible date at which items of essential information must reach the secondary school in order for other essential processes to take place.
(8) Determination of the curricular and pastoral policy to be applied by each teaching department and each pastoral unit in providing for the needs of first year pupils.

Are there other factors which you might wish to add to this list?

(ii) Transfer of pupils between a junior high school and a senior high school (at 13+)

AUTUMN TERM

Actions involving Junior high school	Actions involving senior high school	Internal arrangements of senior high school
1. Policy re transfer from jnr high to snr high established		
2. Letters to parents re pupil transfer		
3. Pupil transfer forms sent by snr high to deputy hd of jnr high		
4. Meeting of snr high deputy hd with deputy hd of jnr high to explain procedure		
5. Pupil transfer forms given to transferring pupils		
6. Arrangements made for parents of transferring pupils to meet with staff of snr high and jnr high		
7. Deputy hd of snr high to jnr high to meet parents, answer queries re curriculum, banding, etc. Hd of snr high addresses parents. Also YEO and Careers Advisory Officer present. Parents split into smaller groups with staff of jnr high		
8. Further discussion with individual parents and pupils re transfer begins		
9. Arrangements made for pupils from jnr high to visit snr high		
10. All 3rd year pupils of jnr high visit snr high one evening		
11. Pupil transfer forms filled in		

Autumn Term—continued

Actions involving junior high school	Actions involving senior high school	Internal arrangements of senior high school
12. Provisional numbers of transferring pupils sent to LEA		
13. Informal contact allows provisional list of intending pupils to be sent by jnr high to snr high		
14. Estimated potential of pupils by subject rated and sent to LEA		

SPRING TERM

Actions involving junior high school	Actions involving senior high school	Internal arrangements of senior high school
15. Further details about transfer (prospectus, option forms) provided by snr high to jnr high for potential pupils		1. Deputy hd submits suggested form teachers to head teacher for approval
16. Pupils given information re subject choices and careers		2. Appointment of year tutors
17. Subject choices discussed with parents and pupils		3. Prospective form teachers informed
18. Undecided pupils from jnr high visit snr high again		
19. Option forms completed and returned by jnr high to snr high		4. Preliminary timetabling begins
	20. Official list of intending pupils received from LEA with names, addresses, dates of birth, and subject potential rated by jnr high	

SUMMER TERM

Actions involving junior high school	Actions involving senior high school	Internal arrangements of senior high school
21. Head teacher of snr high has general discussion with head teacher of jnr high		5. Briefing meeting for staff
22. Pupil friendship forms constructed by snr high, sent to jnr high, completed and returned to snr high		6. Construction of sociograms
	23. PTA committee meeting to discuss arrangements for new parents evening	7. Collection into registration groups and houses
	24. New parents sent documents re school, etc.	8. Option choices totalled
	25. Careers advisory officer briefed about new parents meeting	9. Pupils placed into 3 bands
	26. New parents visit school, meet teachers, etc.	10. Preparation of lists showing option plans for individual forms
	27. New pupils visit school. Interviewed by prospective house heads and form teachers. Curricular choices further discussed, and re-arranged if necessary. Pupils informed re social organization of school	11. Briefing session for staff attending new parents evening
	28. Travel arrangements finalized	12. Dept heads informed of option choices, and setting begins
	29. Claims for clothing and maintenance grants passed to LEA	13. New pupil forms into teachers' files
		14. Discussion of option choices with form teachers. Attention drawn to over-subscribed subjects
		15. Re-allocation of pupil options if necessary
		16. Timetable finalized
		17. Arrangements for 1st day of term finalized

ADDITIONAL INFORMATION———

Further information in the form of diagrams, forms-in-use in the schools and documentation on factors relating to the programme of transfer and induction of first year children is presented below. It must again be emphasized that this does not represent a 'model' answer, but is intended to help with the design of your own programme by stimulating discussion about the nature and sequence of actions that are required.

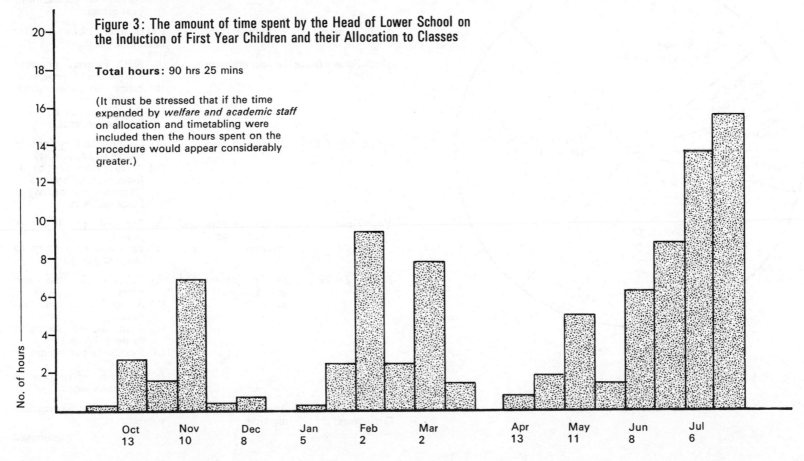

Figure 3: The amount of time spent by the Head of Lower School on the Induction of First Year Children and their Allocation to Classes

Total hours: 90 hrs 25 mins

(It must be stressed that if the time expended by *welfare and academic staff* on allocation and timetabling were included then the hours spent on the procedure would appear considerably greater.)

No. of hours

Figure 4:
Percentage of total time
spent with the named
persons

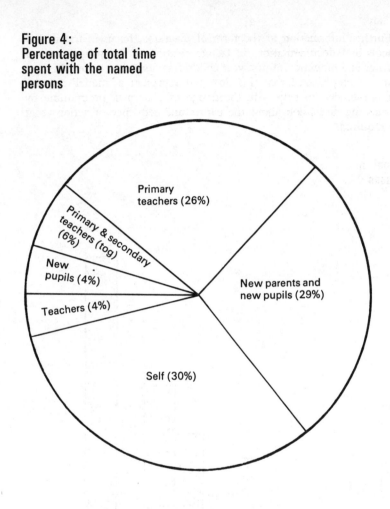

Primary
teachers (26%)

Primary & secondary
teachers (tog)
(6%)

New
pupils (4%)

Teachers (4%)

New parents and
new pupils (29%)

Self (30%)

(1) Information for parents of new pupils

WHOM TO SEE, WHEN, ABOUT WHAT

Headmaster or, in his absence, *Deputy Head*	By appointment, or at year meetings, etc.	(a) Matters of concern to whole school. (b) Temporarily, careers and sixth form entry. Advice to certain fifth year groups.
Senior Master	By appointment	Particulars about public examinations
Sixth Form Master	By appointment	(a) Sixth formers' personal progress and prospects. (b) Entry to universities, colleges, etc. (c) Admission to sixth form for new entrants.
Hd Middle School	By appointment	(a) Courses and options in fourth and fifth years. (b) Admission to third, fourth and fifth years. (c) Removal, and placing in future schools.
Year Tutors	By appointment, and at annual year meeting	(a) Personal problems of pupils. (b) Problems of concern to the year group.
Head of Lower School	By appointment, and at annual year meeting	(a) Courses in first two years. (b) Admission to first two years. (c) Removal, and placing in future schools. (d) Personal problems of pupils. (e) Problems of concern to first two years.
Heads of Department	At annual year meeting	Progress in a particular subject

continued

Tutors		Routine notes—absence, dress, homework, etc.
Bursar	By telephone or appointment	Uniform, finances, grants, expenses.

If you are still not sure, try the most likely and we will do the rest.

Please understand that a matter addressed to the Headmaster which is within the responsibility of a member of staff will be passed on to him; so try the most direct route!

If there is a real emergency, just phone or come.

(2) Form to be completed by parents of new pupils

BISHOPSTON HIGH SCHOOL

Dear Parent,

Please complete this page; the information asked for is very necessary for our records. If any information given changes at a future date, please notify the high school without delay.

1. CHILD'S SURNAME ....
   CHRISTIAN NAMES ....
   ADDRESS ....

2. Please enter here where you may be contacted during school hours in emergency.

   FATHER'S INITIALS .... MOTHER'S INITIALS ....
   ADDRESS .... ADDRESS ....

   Tel. No. .... Tel. No. ....

3. I wish my child to have dinner at school each day. (YES or NO)

4. My child has certificate of cycling proficiency. (YES or NO)

5. If your child's home is more than 3 miles from school (by shortest route), your child will be entitled to free bus travel. Do you wish application forms to be sent to you? (YES or NO)

6. Name of child's primary school ....

7. Does your child suffer from any illness or disability at the present time? (YES or NO)

8. Does your child wear glasses, hearing aid or any other medical aid? My child wears ....

9. Has your child suffered from asthma, rheumatism, polio or any allergy? ....

10. Do you have any particular religious preferences that might occasion your wishing to withdraw your child from school worship? (YES or NO)

    ....

11. Please enter here any other information which the school should know:

    Signed .... (Parent)
    Date ....

Please return this form to the headteacher of the primary school your child attends at present.

(3) Letter inviting parents of new pupils for interview

BISHOPSTON HIGH SCHOOL

Dear Parents,

Your child will be entering this school in September. I invite you to meet your son's/daughter's year master, to have outlined to you our organization and intentions, and to give you an opportunity to forge the first link in a good parent/school relationship which will be helpful to us all in the future. Would you please indicate the day and time you find most convenient to come to School.

Yours sincerely,
Head of Lower School

Choosing a school: A parent's reactions

Interviewer : 'Did you have any choice as to which secondary school he went to?'

Parent : 'Not really. I was asked which of the schools nearby I would like him to go to but I wasn't told anything about choosing one.'

Interviewer : 'So what did you do?'

Parent : 'Well, I was told to give three alternatives and I gave them three schools nearby that I knew the names of. Then I got a letter to say which one he was going to.'

Interviewer : 'Did you try and find out anything about the schools in the area, by visiting them, for example?'

Parent : 'Not really. I had heard a neighbour talking about one which she said was very rough, so I didn't put that down. It never occurred to me that I could go and visit them, and even if I'd known I don't think I'd have gone. I'd be scared to, I had enough of schools when I was a kid.'

Interviewer : 'If you had tried to find out about the schools, what sort of things would you have wanted to know?'

Parent : 'I don't know really. I've never thought about . . . I suppose . . . I think lots of schools don't bother with discipline any more. I'd have liked to know that they were going to teach him to be well behaved and things like that, and also that they were going to teach him sensible subjects like English and arithmetic. I can't understand the use of half the things they seem to teach kids these days. And if they'd do much about helping him to get a job.'

What forms and documentation does your school use for new pupil allocation and induction? Bring some of the forms to your syndicate or group to illustrate your school's procedures.

Do you think that they might overwhelm or serve to confuse parents?

Which are the best forms your group has examined? Why do you think this is so?

Constructing a sociogram*

1. *Obtaining the information*

   (i) Ask pupils to choose the three pupils in the class with whom they would most like

   (a) to sit next to in class and/or
   (b) to play with in the playground and/or
   (c) to work with on a project.

   Each of these constitutes a distinct dimension of choice, and requires to be plotted on a separate sociogram.

   (ii) If possible, make the choice *meaningful*, i.e. implement their choices as far as possible.

   (iii) Among younger children a single dimension of choice may suffice in indicating the nature of a group's structure. The choices of older children tend to be more functionally specific, and two or more

* I am grateful to Dr. W. Taylor B.Sc. (Econ.), PhD for his permission to use this paper.

choice situations may need to be offered in order to obtain a complete picture.

(iv) Choices should be written on slips of paper and pupils assured of 'secrecy'.

2. Recording the results

(i) Before a sociogram can be constructed, the choices need to be classified in a usable form. A chart such as that below is suitable for this purpose.

Chosen	Brown	Smith	Jones	Roberts	etc.
Chooser					
Brown		2		1	
Smith	1		2	3	
Jones	2		1		
Roberts	1		3	2	
etc.				etc.,	etc.
Totals 1st					
2nd					
3rd					

(ii) From the *totals* line at the bottom of the chart some idea of the centrality of members of the group can be obtained—some individuals will have many choices, others may not be chosen at all. This is a useful guide in constructing the sociogram, and can sometimes be of value in itself as indicating the social isolates.

3. Constructing the sociogram

(i) Use a large sheet of paper, and start by entering the symbols for those individuals who have received the largest number of choices. If the class is a mixed one use, for example, triangles for the boys and circles for the girls. Even if the class is not mixed, however, triangles, circles, squares and so on can often be introduced to indicate 'objective' differences that may be relevant to the sociogram, such as different primary schools attended, residential locality and so on. Numbers written within the area of the symbol can be used to identify the child concerned.

(ii) Indicate the direction of choice by means of a straight line with an arrowhead, thus

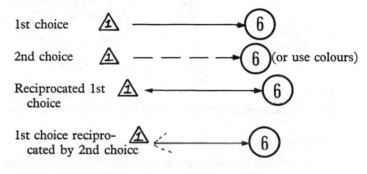

(iii) In the first instance, plot only 1st and 2nd choices, for otherwise the sociogram becomes too complicated.

(iv) Keep lines to the minimum length (i.e., keep members of a sub-group close together), and pay particular attention to reciprocated choices.

(v) Enter symbols and choices on the sociogram from the date chart, and cross out each choice on the chart as it is entered.

(vi) When the first draft is completed, you will probably find that you have positioned a number of symbols wrongly, i.e., long choice lines lead from or to the other side of the sociogram. It is generally necessary to redraw the sociogram, emphasizing the sub-group structure and constellations of choices by placing them in appropriate positions.

(vii) The final result might look something like this

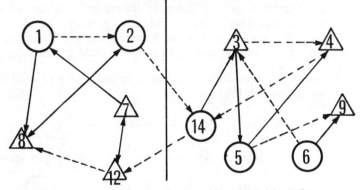

There is clearly a split within the class, and considerable differences between the numbers of choices received by different individuals.

4. *Interpreting the sociogram*

(i) Sociograms do *not* constitute answers to social problems. We need *not* consider it imperative to take action on the basis of what a sociogram reveals (e.g., placing the three 'different' pupils in the form, who choose each other, together in a work group). People cannot be reduced to lines and symbols.

(ii) The sociogram serves:

1. To make clear to us, as students, the existence of group structures.

2. To provide a framework in terms of which questions can be asked, and, possibly, answered, with respect to the structure of the group.

(iii) Some questions to ask:

1. Why are the social isolates *not* chosen? This, and many other questions, can only be answered if we possess a prior knowledge of the group and its members. If we do not have such knowledge, we must use our time with the class to look for possible answers.

2. Certain individuals appear to be chosen very frequently. Why? What type of values do these pupils represent, e.g., conformity or rebellion. What can this tell us about the general attitude of the class?

3. There are fairly definite splits between sub-groups in the class. What is the basis of these—previous primary school, residential factors, intelligence and attainment differences, social class, classroom seating arrangements, etc.

4. Two new boys joined the class this term. One now appears to be very well integrated, the other is an isolate. Why is this the case, and what does it tell us about the two boys and the form?

5. The sociogram yields results which differ greatly from our own prior judgment of the situation. Why is there such a discrepancy? On what factors has our own assessment of the situation been based?

6. How specific are the children's choices, i.e., do they choose according to the functional value of the person to their group, or on a simple basis of 'liking'? (This can only be found out by providing several dimensions of choice).

5. *Conclusions*

(i) This is merely a very over-simplified introduction to the use of sociograms. If you are interested in the technique, there are a number of books which contain references to it and examples of its use.

(ii) References

FLEMING, C. M. (1963) *Social Psychology of Adolescence*. London: Routledge and Kegan Paul.

FLEMING, C. M. (1968) *Teaching—A psychological analysis*. London: Methuen.

NORTHWAY, M. L. (1969) *A Primer of Sociometry*. University of Toronto Press.

JENNINGS, H. H. (1972) *Sociometry in Group relations*. Greenwood Press.

MORENO, J. L. (1953) *Who shall survive*. NY: Beacon House.

PUPIL-LEAVING PROCEDURE

POINTS TO CONSIDER

In concentrating upon the induction and allocation of new pupils it might be overlooked that the pupil leaving process calls for a considerable effort of organization.

Below is the procedure adopted by one school.

BISHOPSTON HIGH SCHOOL—LEAVERS' PROCEDURE

When a pupil states his intention of leaving school the following procedure will be adopted:

(1) Pupil will report to his form teacher and bring a supporting letter from his parent or guardian.

(2) This letter will be sent to HoS.

(3) HoS will notify form teacher of his decision by sending DRO slip to him and another to the deputy head.

(4) Form teacher will send pupil to secretary for a leavers clearance slip and assist him in completing it.
Subjects requiring clearance will be ticked.
The pupil's present address will be written at the bottom of the slip.

(5) HoS will send pupil's folders with record card to HM.

(6) Record card will be completed by HM and file cleared.

(7) Secretary will put record card into the left pupils' drawer.

(8) Deputy head will publish DRO and enter details in leavers' books.

Headmaster

(1) Do you agree that an overriding consequence of both of the programmes outlined above of transfer between junior and senior high school and transfer between primary and secondary school is likely to be a particularly disruptive effect upon the pupils of the contributory schools?

(2) One of the weakest parts of the strategies outlined in this document is the dependence that the secondary comprehensive school has to place upon information supplied by others.
In the schemes you have devised, how do you recommend

  (i) reducing the duplication of effort?

  (ii) best approaching

    (a) parents
    (b) pupils
    (c) the contributory schools
    (d) the LEA

  for the information that you need, in the form that you can use it in at the time that you need it?

(3) The induction process initiates a three to eight year cycle for your pupils, depending on the age of transfer and the age of leaving school. Is it in fact possible to restructure this process once it has started?

(4) What are the implications you find in:

    (i) the massive clerical workload which the schemes suggest?

    (ii) the problems posed to communications?

    (iii) the rank of staff involved in the task?

(5) (a) Because of the contacts which have to be forged and the specialist knowledge that the task implies, is it best to make one person only responsible for the allocation and induction of new pupils?

    (b) What are the implications of your answer to the professional training and development of staff?

(6) Since forewarned is forearmed, a considerable amount of effort can be saved if problem pupils are rapidly identified. Every attempt should be made to gain from contributory schools detailed records of transferring pupils. A useful, but no more than crude index for identifying a problem pupil is his absence rate. Would you recommend schools using a pupils absence rate as a means of an identification of problem pupils?

(7) Solutions to the problems displayed in the schemes outlined above are such that one school cannot hope to resolve them. The only hope of a rational solution is to tackle the problem at LEA level. Do you agree?

Pupil Subject Options

CONTENTS

INTRODUCTION___

Pupil subject options are closely related to several other aspects of a school's administrative work. The links with 'curricular formation' and 'timetabling', with staffing and staff recruitment, and also with the pupil welfare and guidance system are obvious. Option choices, therefore, in no way constitute an isolated process.

It is apparent therefore, that there are in existence, some extremely complex factors which reflect fundamental decisions taken by the school—decisions about what it considers its priorities to be, and the allocation of its resources. At the most rudimentary level then the question becomes: Is the pastoral/guidance system in the school more important than the teaching curricular process, and to which of these does the school attach the greater priority and, what are the real implications for the support services necessary to maintain these processes? Are pupil option choices part of the academic or the pastoral guidance system in your school? Does this indicate the way in which priorities may have been determined? Was this decision taken after due deliberation and consultation? It is suggested that, in practice, decisions such as these are often not *taken*— they 'slip off the table' as it were.

Pupil options present a series of logistic problems to a school. If the school permits pupils to exercise open choices, then immediately it has the task of finding teachers to cover the choices. If, on the other hand, the school exercises constraints upon choices, then it has to produce the rules by which these constraints are exercised, to set up a panel to consider appeals, to retrieve unsuitable choices, and so on. In either of these two situations, it is highly unlikely that homogeneous teaching groups will have been formed. In practice, smaller comprehensive schools, in attempting to resolve some of these dilemmas, often find that they have produced a standard curriculum for their pupils.

It seems that the typical 11–18+ secondary comprehensive school uses the first two years of the pupil's time in the school for general diagnostic purposes and to teach basic core subjects. At the end of the second year, the pupil makes the first of his option choices for entry into the third year.

The range of options made available reflects the extant philosophy of the school, although it is immediately apparent that pupil option choices may be constrained or enhanced by factors other than subject availability.

Amongst factors affecting the potentiality of choice are those which relate to resources, administrative processes and social expectation. The recent history of a school, its physical and curricular organization, pupil, staff and parental attitudes will all, in conferring high or low approval on respective choices, exert an influence. For one of the functions of a school is to socialize children into their 'expected' career patterns.

The decisions may equally have been influenced by other factors such as the image the school wishes to project and the proportion of pupils thought necessary to fit the desired projection; adequate assessment of a pupil is also vital, as is the possibility of flexibility within choice and therefore the opportunity of retrieving 'unsuitable' choices. Other considerations include whether an outline timetable is produced before option choices are made or vice versa; who is to ensure that a pupil has a balanced curriculum and what is to constitute this balance?

You might care to add to the list.

If a limited number of pupils are able to choose a course, by what priorities should they be selected and who is to counsel those who are rejected in their choice? What do you recommend?

Make a list of all those in the school who appear eligible to help the pupil in his option choices.

Make a list of all the different sectors of the school's 'admin' processes that are likely to be involved.

If a 'panel' is to recommend allocation to option choices, who would you include on the panel? Would parents and pupils be represented?

Who should be the final arbiter in disputes about choices?

The compilation and co-ordination of records upon which a judgement can be made are likely to prove most important and particularly so in the large secondary school where there may be a sizeable staff turnover. (See for comparison the section on 'Pupil Records'.)

One way that schools might resolve the dilemmas presented here, and they may in fact already be taking steps in this direction, is for them to regard themselves as twin planks composed of firstly welfare, counselling and guidance functions relating to pupils, and secondly the organization of resources (including staff).

Teachers thus become responsible for the organization of learning experiences for the children 'according to the recommendations of those who counsel and give guidance' and the head teacher clearly has the responsibility for manipulating the two main streams.

Do you think there would be a function for the director of studies in schools organized in this way?

Whatever the solutions proposed to the dilemmas which have been outlined, this is an area of school life where administrative convenience should not be allowed to prevail. In matters where a pupil's future career is so fundamentally affected by the subject options he chooses, decisions should be based upon the proper criteria and not upon the dictates of administrative tidiness.

The problem effectively becomes that of ascertaining what is happening in practice. Does that which is occurring reflect the stated policy of the school, and, if not, then what are the implications in organizational terms?

How do you find out what is happening?

How do you overcome the organizational limitations you may find?

How do you identify the children as individuals?

For those who may wish to pursue further some of the issues raised above, a list of further reading is attached at the end of this chapter.

PUPIL OPTION CHOICES - ONE SCHOOL'S SCHEME

The following scheme represents the organization of pupil subject option choices at one large secondary comprehensive school. It must be emphasized that this is not presented as a 'model' scheme. It is the intention in presenting this outline to indicate the complexity of the task and to stimulate discussion.

Dear Parent,

GROUP CHOICES FOR 3A-E

It is the custom for all pupils in the above forms to take English, mathematics, history, geography, music, scripture, physics, chemistry, biology, PE, games and to choose *three* more subjects from the attached sheet. Choosing subjects now does not guarantee that your child will eventually enter one of these forms; such a decision is made at the end of the year and is based on the year's work and examinations.

These options are designed to allow pupils to develop their particular interests in languages and craft subjects. German and technical drawing will be 'new' subjects to all pupils and all subjects are open to pupils of both sexes throughout the school.

(1) A modern language is still useful for university entrance, although

these days it is not compulsory for many courses or colleges. However for some subjects such as English or history at university it provides candidates with an opportunity to choose between more universities and for would-be science graduates it provides the necessary reading knowledge for foreign periodicals. Do not cease to study a foreign language unless you feel completely out of your depth.

(2) Latin is not needed for medical careers but still is required by a few (but by no means all) universities for arts degrees in English, history and modern languages.

(3) Technical drawing should ideally be linked with either woodwork or metalwork. These subjects lead in the upper school to ordinary level design or metalwork and/or technical drawing. Design is a workshop based subject involving creative practical and artistic skills of a high order and is useful, for example, for potential engineers or architects. But a good education and proficiency in mathematics and physics is just as valuable for someone not absolutely certain that he/she wishes to enter these fields.

(4) Under current arrangements in Form 4 all subjects except mathematics, English and physical education become optional and pupils study up to nine for GCE/CSE examinations, the subjects, number and level being determined by progress and ability.

Each pupil will have an opportunity to discuss these choices with his/her form tutor and subject teachers. If there is any major difficulty please make an appointment to see your child's form tutor or the year tutor. *Serious* difficulties should be referred to me.

The school reserves the right at this planning stage to make alteration to the range of subjects offered and all pupils should be aware that they may be asked to reconsider their choice.

In all subjects, especially those requiring practical rooms, classes will be limited in size for safety reasons and to ensure adequate individual supervision.

Please return the attached form by MONDAY, MAY 14th to your child's form tutor.

Yours sincerely,

Director of Studies

Make a note here of your choices for reference:

A	*B*	*C*

GROUP CHOICES FOR 3A-E

Choose one subject from each column. You must not pick the same subject more than once. Indicate your choice by placing a tick in the space provided.

SURNAME .... CHRISTIAN NAMES............................

PRESENT FORM ....

A	*B*	*C*
FRENCH	FRENCH	FRENCH
WELSH	WELSH	LATIN
GERMAN	GERMAN	GERMAN
WOODWORK	WOODWORK	WOODWORK
TECH. DRAWING	TECH. DRAWING	METALWORK
METALWORK	ART	ART
NEEDLEWORK	COOKERY	COOKERY
		NEEDLEWORK

Please return to your form tutor by Monday 14th May.

Parent's Signature ....

28th March

Dear Parents,

GROUP CHOICES FOR FORMS 4A-F

Next year many subjects become optional and pupils are given a wide choice in the construction of their courses of study. The subjects listed lead, together with compulsory English language, English literature and mathematics to certificate examinations in two years time. They offer as wide a choice as possible and are repeated so that pupils can choose a combination to suit their own interests and abilities. In addition to these all pupils take PE, games and a lesson each of general Scripture, music and careers. This information is supplied on the assumption that your child will enter one of these forms but does not commit the school to such an event. The school also reserves the right to alter these arrangements if staffing or other reasons make necessary a change.

The following notes may help you in your choice.

1. Interest in a subject is as important as the results already achieved in it.

2. No language is compulsory but anyone who has the interest and ability can take more than one. German and Welsh are only available for those pupils already studying them.

3. A balanced selection of subjects is desirable for all pupils but especially for those unsure as yet of their future career. No choice should be made which heavily weights the combination towards either 'arts' or 'science' subjects and which will prevent a future change of emphasis to suit later choices of career.

4. Pupils will take nine subjects which could lead to certificate examinations. Those who feel that this will be too much should opt for liberal studies in Line F to lighten their load. Pupils may not be presented for examination in all nine subjects; this will depend on their progress. Those not entering for any examination will continue with the subject as part of their general education. They will not be granted 'free time'.

5. Pupils should consult their form tutors and subject teachers about their choices. Parents will have an opportunity to meet teachers on May 15–16 at school. Details of this meeting will be issued separately. *Serious* difficulties over these choices should be referred to me.

6. WJEC examination regulations do not allow pupils to sit both biology and human biology.

New Subjects

1. Technical drawing is a form of graphic communication which requires original ideas and copies of existing plans to be presented by means of sketching, pictorial views and plane and solid geometry. Ideally it should be linked with either metalwork or design. It requires the ability to produce tidy drawings.

2. Design (Three dimensional studies—crafts design) is a workshop based subject in which the pupil is encouraged to think creatively and solve problems through the use of wood, metal, plastic and other materials. It requires the ability to draw and sketch and to turn these plans into articles in the woodwork and metalwork rooms. It therefore combines manual skills with artistic and creative ability in a demanding course of study.

3. Commerce deals with the ways in which people earn and spend their incomes and thus includes the main commercial and economic institutions of the country, e.g. banks, retailers, trade unions. It is an academic subject and does not contain any practical book-keeping or typing.

IN ALL SUBJECTS, BUT ESPECIALLY THOSE REQUIRING LABORATORY OR PRACTICAL ROOM SPACE, IT MAY BE NECESSARY TO LIMIT NUMBERS FOR SAFETY'S SAKE AND TO ASK SOME PUPILS TO RECONSIDER THEIR CHOICES.

Please ensure that your son or daughter returns the attached sheet to the form tutor by Monday May 21st.

Yours sincerely,

Director of Studies

Write a copy of your choice here for reference:

A   *B*   *C*   *D*   *E*   *F*

D

GROUP CHOICES, 4A-F

Pupil's Name (in full) .... Present Form ....

Instructions Choose a different subject from each group *A-F*. Tick your choices in the spaces provided in pencil, having read the notes on the attached sheet and discussed them with your form tutor and subject teachers and parents.

RETURN TO YOUR FORM TUTOR BY MONDAY 21st MAY

Ordinary Levels: some pupils may be transferred to CSE classes later if their results prove this to be necessary

A	B	C	D	E	F
Chemistry	Chemistry	Chemistry	Welsh	Scripture	Music
Physics	Physics	Physics	Tech. Drawing	Metalwork	Tech. Drawing
Biology	Biology	Biology	Commerce	German	Human Biology
Needlwork	History	Design	Cookery	Cookery	Design
French	French	Latin	French	French	French
Geography	Geography	Geography	Geography	Geography	History
Art	German	Art	History	History	Liberal Studies (non-examination)

Possible career, if known:

Parents Signature ....

28th March

Dear Parent,

GROUP CHOICES FOR FORMS 4G-K

Next year many subjects become optional and pupils are given a wide choice in the construction of their courses of study. The subjects listed lead, together with compulsory English, mathematics and arithmetic, to certificate examinations in two years time. They offer as wide a choice as possible and are repeated so that pupils can choose a combination to suit their own interests and abilities. In addition to these all pupils take PE, games and a lesson each of general scripture and careers. This information is supplied on the assumption that your child will enter one of these forms but does not commit the school to such an event.

The school also reserves the right to alter these arrangements if staffing or other reasons make necessary a change.

The following notes may help you in your choice.

1. Interest in a subject is as important as the results already achieved in it.

2. A balanced selection of subjects is desirable for all pupils but especially for those unsure as yet of their future career. No choice should be made which heavily weights the combination towards either 'practical' or 'academic' subjects and which will prevent a future change of emphasis to suit later choices of career.

3. Pupils will take eight subjects which could lead to certificate examinations in ten subjects. (English can become English and English literature and mathematics also includes an arithmetic certificate.) Pupils need not be presented for final examinations in

GROUP CHOICES, 4G-K

Pupil's Name (in full) .... Present Form ....

Instructions   Choose a different subject from each group A-F. Tick your choices in the spaces provided in pencil, having read the notes on the attached sheet and discussed them with your form tutor and subject teachers and parents.

RETURN TO YOUR FORM TUTOR BY MONDAY 21st MAY

CSE examinations: some pupils may be transferred to O-Level classes later if their results justify it

A	B	C	D	E	F
Chemistry	Chemistry	Biology	Rural Science	Scripture	Human Biology
History	Physics	Physics	History	Cookery	Music
Geography	History	Geography	Geography	Geography	Needlework
French	Art	Art	Tech. Drawing	French	Tech. Drawing
Commercial Studies Typing	Commercial Studies Office Practice	Scripture	Cookery	Commercial Studies Typing	Commercial Studies Office Practice
Needlework	Metalwork	Metalwork	Woodwork	Woodwork	Art

Possible career, if known:

Parents Signature ....

---

all subjects; this will depend on their progress. Those not entering for a particular examination will continue with the subject as part of their general education. They will not be granted 'free time'.

4.   It is possible for some pupils to be transferred to Ordinary Level classes in some subjects if their progress warrants it and they will eventually sit a mixture of CSE and O-Level examinations.

5.   Pupils should consult their form tutors and subject teachers about their choices. Parents will have an opportunity to meet teachers on May 15–16 at school. Details of this meeting will be announced separately. *Serious* difficulties over these choices should be referred to me.

6.   WJEC examination regulations do not allow pupils to sit both biology and human biology.

New Subjects

1.   Rural science is a course involving study of plants, the soil, animals and greenhouse work. It contains practical and theoretical aspects and is designed to foster an interest in the culture of plants and the care of animals.

2.   Commercial studies involves two options, either office practice or typing. The former is a theoretical study of office organization and

the latter is practical in nature. Numbers will have to be limited to ensure satisfactory arrangements for practice in typing.

3. Technical drawing is a form of graphic communication which requires original ideas and copies of existing plans to be presented by means of sketching, pictoral views and plane and solid geometry. It should be linked with either metalwork or woodwork and it requires the ability to produce tidy drawings.

> IN ALL SUBJECTS, BUT ESPECIALLY THOSE REQUIRING LABORATORY OR PRACTICAL ROOM SPACE, IT MAY BE NECESSARY TO LIMIT NUMBERS FOR SAFETY'S SAKE AND TO ASK SOME PUPILS TO RECONSIDER THEIR CHOICES.

Please ensure that your son or daughter returns the attached sheet to the form tutor by Monday May 21st.

Yours sincerely,

Director of Studies

Write a copy of your choice here for reference:

A   B   C   D   E   F

To Pupils in the Fifth Form and their Parents

BEYOND THE FIFTH YEAR

This summary is for parents and pupils to ensure that everyone in Form 5 is thinking and acting constructively towards a target for next September.

There are two main courses of action open to fifth form pupils:

(A) to leave school to take up employment, or a full-time course at a college or another form of training;

(B) to remain at school for either one, two or three more years.

(A) *Leaving School*

You should have seen a careers advisory officer by now who will have talked to you about jobs and courses. If you have not done so you must see the careers master as a matter of urgency. The director of studies and heads of departments will also give advice if asked. It is essential that everyone has been helped into a job or course before they leave in July.

(B) *Remaining in School*

There will be three main ways of continuing your studies at school.

1. *Lower sixth remove*

This is the form for pupils who wish to take Ordinary Levels having completed a CSE course. The subjects likely to be available are shown below. All pupils in this form must take English, maths and one of each of the alternatives and follow a full timetable. They will sit Ordinary Levels (not necessarily in all the subjects they are studying) in summer and can then proceed to L6 arts or sciences if they wish.

> English, mathematics, chemistry/art, physics/ human biology, art/TD, metalwork/needlework /French, geography/history, history/geography/ scripture, cookery/woodwork/physics, games.

2. *Lower sixth general*

(a) This form will cater for those pupils who need to resit a range of Ordinary Level subjects. The following classes are likely to be available: mathematics 'O'/general maths, English Language and Literature 'O'/general English, games, geography 'O', history 'O', French 'O', physics 'O', general science, human biology CSE. Other subjects can be resat under special arrangements. No Advanced Level work can be done by pupils in this form.

Pupils wishing to resit O-Levels will follow a timetable containing at least 30 periods a week tuition, made up if necessary by new subjects and general lessons from the commerce course arrangements shown below.

Pupils are advised that they should whenever possible delay resitting subjects until summer. Even if some subjects are resat in November—the WJEC allows a maximum of three—pupils must continue with these subjects as an integral part of their course until summer. It is not possible to resit subjects in November and commence A-Level work in January; this places too much strain on existing A-Level classes and teachers and especially on the pupils who have to catch up lost ground.

(b) Commerce Course. This is designed as a one-year course containing the following subjects: general English, general maths, games, economics 'O', British constitution 'O', commerce 'O', economic and social geography, typing CSE, homecraft 'O', craft lettering 'O'. Parts of this course can be taken together with O-Level resits but pupils will be expected to receive at least 30 periods of tuition a week throughout the year.

3. *Lower sixth arts and science*

Entry is dependent on a good performance this June and on gaining the correct number and grades at O-Level or CSE. No exact figure can be put on this as the requirements vary from course to course in the sixth form. A good general rule would be 4 or 5 passes at O-Level or CSE Grade 1 in appropriate subjects, but it must be emphasized that each case is considered on its merits. Only in exceptional circumstances will pupils enter these forms for A-Level work when they still have O-Level resits to take. The subjects available next year are likely to be: English, French, German, history, geography, Welsh, scripture, geology, economics, engineering science, physics, chemistry, biology, woodwork or metalwork, art, geometrical drawing, mathematics, pure maths, applied maths, music and some extra O-Levels.

Pupils normally sit three A-Levels but arrangements can sometimes be made to sit only two. If in doubt it is better to start with three and reduce later; the reverse process is not possible. Possible combinations of subjects are shown on the attached form. Even in a large school the choices cannot be unlimited, and the arrangements cater for as many ideal combination of subjects as possible.

Open Afternoon Heads of Departments will be available for consultation by pupils and/or parents. Pupils and parents are asked to assemble in the Upper School Hall at 2.00 p.m. on Monday 9th July.

End of Holiday The Director of Studies and volunteer staff will be available at school on Tuesday–Thursday 28th–30th August from 9.30 a.m.–1.00 p.m. and 2.30 p.m.–4.30 p.m. for consultation on all aspects of sixth form admission.

NB—All pupils who return to school for a sixth year will be expected to follow a balanced timetable and a suitable number of courses. Those who expect to return to resit one or two subjects only, involving perhaps just 4 or 6 lessons a week and who see the possibilities of much leisure time in or out of school, would be better advised to find a job and to sit their subjects externally at a technical college through evening classes or day release schemes.

Director of Studies

BEYOND THE FIFTH YEAR

This form is designed to record the provisional choices of all members of the present fifth form. Please complete it as accurately as possible, discussing your choices with your parents, form tutor, subject teachers and heads of departments. Many subjects are quite different at Advanced Level compared with Ordinary Level, others are new. You will have more opportunities to find out about this:

(1) *Open Afternoon:* For parents and/or pupils to consult heads of departments. Please assemble in the Upper School Hall at 2.00 p.m., Monday 9th July.

(2) *End of Summer Holiday:* The Director of Studies and volunteer staff will be available at school on Tuesday–Thursday, 28th–30th August, from 9.30 a.m.–1.00 p.m. and 2.30 p.m.–4.30 p.m. for consultation on all aspects of sixth form admission.

Your provisional decisions are required now to help in planning next year's arrangements.

Director of Studies

NAME .... PRESENT FORM ....

Most of the following questions require a simple YES/NO:

1. Are you definitely leaving school?...............................

2. If YES, to what job or course are you hoping to proceed?...............

....

3. Are you hoping to remain at school?............................

   If YES, to which form do you hope to gain entry?

   (a) L.6 Arts or L6 Science...................................

   (b) L6 General, 1 year Commerce Course ....

   (c) L6 Remove—CSE conversion to O-Level ....

4. If your O-Level results are unsatisfactory would you want to return to L6 General to repeat some of them?.........................

5. Have you any career in mind? ....

6. Have you any higher, further or professional education course in mind? Give as many details as you can. ....

....

To those wishing to enter L6 arts or science

Pupils aiming for these forms should indicate their *provisional* choices by underlining *ONE* subject from each column. Pupils normally study three A-Levels, but it is possible to take two only.

I	II	III
English	English	English
French	German	Geology
Geography	Economics	History
History	Geography	Economics
Domestic Subjects	Scripture	Welsh
Engineering Science	Music	Art
Maths & Statistics	Geometric Drawing	Applied Maths
Metalwork/Woodwork	Pure Maths	
Physics	Chemistry	Pure & Applied Maths
Chemistry	Physics	Biology

(a) The last two lines are the usual science combinations but these subjects may be combined with others to produce sensible courses of study.

(b) Those taking chemistry, physics, biology also take additional O-Level maths.

(c) Other O-Level subjects available in combination with 2 or 3 A-Levels are listed below. Underline one only *if you wish*.

'O' German
Italian
Spanish
Craft Lettering

Director of Studies

To Pupils in Lower Sixth Remove and their Parents

This summary is for parents and pupils to ensure that everyone in Lower Sixth Remove is thinking and acting constructively towards a target for next September.

There are two main ways of remaining in school:

1. *Lower Sixth General*
  (a) This form will cater for those pupils who need to resit a range of Ordinary Level subjects. The following classes are likely to be available: Mathematics, 'O'/General Maths, English Language and Literature, 'O'/General English, Games, Geography 'O', History 'O', French 'O', Physics 'O', General Science, Human Biology CSE. Other subjects can be resat under special arrangements. No Advanced Level work can be done by pupils in this form.

Pupils wishing to resit O-Levels will follow a timetable containing at least 30 periods a week tuition, made up if necessary by new subjects and general lessons from the Commerce course—arrangements shown below. Pupils are advised that they should whenever possible delay resitting subjects until Summer. Even if some subjects are resat in November—the WJEC allows a maximum of three—pupils must continue with these subjects as an integral part of their course until Summer. It is not possible to resit subjects in November and commence A-Level work in January; this places too much strain on existing A-Level classes and teachers and especially on the pupils who have to catch up lost ground.

  (b) Commerce course. This is designed as a one year course containing the following subjects: General English, General Maths, Games, Economics 'O', British Constitution 'O', Commerce 'O', Economic and Social Geography, Typing CSE, Homecraft 'O', Craft Lettering 'O'. Parts of this course can be taken together with 'O' Level resits but pupils will be expected to receive at least 30 periods of tuition a week throughout the year.

2. *Lower Sixth Arts and Science*

  Entry is dependent on a good performance this June and on gaining the correct number and grades at O-Level or CSE. No exact figure can be put on this as the requirements vary from course to course in the Sixth Form. A good general rule would be 4 or 5 passes at 'O' Level or CSE Grade 1 in appropriate subjects, but it must be emphasised that each case is considered on its merits. Only in exceptional circumstances will pupils enter these forms for A-Level work when they still have O-Level resits to take.

The subjects available next year are likely to be English, French, German, history, geography, Welsh, scripture, geology, economics, engineering science, physics, chemistry, biology, woodwork or metalwork, art, geometrical drawing, mathematics, pure maths, applied maths, music and some extra O-Levels.

NB—All pupils who return to school for a seventh year will be expected to follow a balanced timetable and a suitable number of courses. Those who expect to return to resit one or two subjects only, involving perhaps just 4 or 6 lessons a week, and who see the possibilities of much leisure time in or out of school, would be better advised to find a job and to sit their subjects externally at a technical college through evening classes, or day release schemes.

If you intend to leave school to seek employment or to take a further education course at a technical college you should seek an interview with a careers advisory officer or with the careers master or the director of studies. It is essential to settle your choice as soon as possible.

There will be two opportunities to consult staff about a choice of course for next year:

(1) *Open Afternoon*: for parents and/or pupils to consult heads of departments. Please assemble in the Upper School Hall at 2 p.m. on Monday 9th July.

(2) *End of Summer Holiday*: The director of studies and volunteer staff will be available at school on Tuesday–Thursday, 28th–30th August, from 9.30 a.m.–1.00 p.m. and 2.30 p.m.–4.30 p.m. for consultation on all aspects of sixth form admission.

Director of Studies

To pupils in Lower Sixth Remove

Your provisional decisions are required now to help in planning next year's arrangements.

NAME .... PRESENT FORM ....

1. Are you definitely leaving school? ....
   If YES, to what job or course are you hoping to proceed? ....
   ....

2. Are you hoping to remain at school? ....
   If YES, to which form do you hope to gain entry?
   (a) L6 Arts or Science ....
   (b) L6 General, 1 year Commerce Course ....

3. If your O-Levels are unsatisfactory, would you want to return to L6 General to repeat some of them? ....

To those wishing to enter L6 arts or science

Pupils aiming for these forms should indicate their *provisional* choices by underlining the subjects they wish to take to A-Level. You can only choose one subject in each column. Pupils may take either two or three subjects. Many of these subjects, e.g. languages, English, mathematics, are quite different at A-Level and you should seek full advice from your teachers.

I	II	III
English	English	English
French	German	Geology
Geography	Economics	History
History	Geography	Economics
Domestic Subjects	Scripture	Welsh
Engineering Science	Music	Art
Maths & Statistics	Geometric Drawing	Applied Maths
Metalwork/Woodwork	Pure Maths	
Physics	Chemistry	Pure & Applied Maths
Chemistry	Physics	Biology

(a) The last two lines are the usual science combinations but these subjects may be combined with others to produce sensible courses of study.

(b) Those taking chemistry, physics, biology also take Additional O-Level maths.

(c) Other O-Level subjects available in combination with 2 or 3 A-Levels are listed below. Underline one only *if you wish.*

'O' German
Italian
Spanish
Craft Lettering

Director of Studies

POINTS FOR DISCUSSION___

SUGGESTED FURTHER READING___

Third year options

(1) What are the implications of this scheme on options for subjects not shown on the choices sheet?

(2) In the circumstances of an option being oversubscribed then who will determine the final pupil allocation? Upon what criteria is this decision likely to be based?

(3) Do you think the letter sent to the parents serves its purpose? If you are dissatisfied with it, how would you change it?

Fourth year options

(1) Look at point 2 in the letter. Compare this to the letter sent to third year parents to help in their option choices.

(2) Look at the allocation sheet. Is it possible that pupils might be subsequently allocated into teaching groups to ensure that the groups are of a similar level of ability?

(3) Is the provision of sciences and languages reduced do you think? What is to take their place?

(4) What mechanisms should schools develop to help pupils overcome the consequences of 'unsuitable' option choices?

Fifth and sixth year options

(1) What happens to those children who wish to stay in a non-examination sixth form? What is the process for counselling these children out? Do you think schools could tolerate a remedial group in the sixth form?

HARGREAVES, David (1967) *Social Relations in a Secondary School.* London: Routledge and Kegan Paul.

HOLT, John (1965) *How children fail.* New York: Pitman. (also Penguin, 1969)

LACEY, Colin (1968) *Hightown Grammar: the school as a social system.* Manchester University Press.

Curricular Activities

CONTENTS

INTRODUCTION

It is not the intention in this chapter to suggest strategies which would allow curricular evaluation, renewal or development to take place more effectively in the large secondary school, but rather to put forward for discussion those curricular activities which were monitored by a research project* concerned with the non-teaching admin. work of senior teachers in a sample of large secondary comprehensive schools, and to consider their organizational implications.

That curricular activities represent extremely complex processes is self-evident and for those who might wish to pursue the topic in more detail some suggestions for further reading are attached at the end of this document.

* LYONS, G. *Op. Cit.*

WHAT ARE CURRICULAR ACTIVITIES?

Throughout this document* 'curricular activities' is taken as a general heading under which all of the following are included: The Curriculum; staff record books; field courses; homework; inspection of teaching; professional literature; school magazine; teaching methods; pupil progress; special tuition; school visits.

'Pupil Option Choices' and 'Timetabling' have been regarded separately.

Do you agree with the topics included in this list?

If you don't, then what would you include, or what would you exclude?

Do these activities raise in your mind any implications about the interrelationship of the different aspects of the 'admin' work of the large school?

The time staff spend on curricular activities

There is some strong feeling to suggest that the proper realm of activity for staff within a school should be concerned with curricular matters. It is evident that the majority of 'teaching' staff spend the

* For the purposes of the research on which this document was based teaching, marking, lesson preparation and supervisory duties were excluded to allow a greater focus of attention upon teachers' 'admin' work.

greater part of their scheduled time upon teaching, marking, lesson preparation, supervisory duties, etc., but if one examines the other (i.e. 'admin') work undertaken by staff, then it becomes apparent that curricular activities represent by no means a major portion of this time.

The table below shows the percentage of time spent by senior staff in 16 large comprehensive schools upon the stated administrative work, and upon teaching, marking and lesson preparation.

	Administrative work				Teaching, marking & lesson prep'n
	Curricular activities	Timetabling	Equipment	Other administration	
	(%)	(%)	(%)	(%)	(%)
Head teacher	9	3	2	77	9
Deputy head	7	12	1	58	22
Senior mistress	5	3	2	63	27
Head of section	9	3	1	61	26
Deputy hd section	6	2	2	48	42
Male hse/Yr hd	5	2	1	39	53
Female hse/Yr hd	5	1	1	49	44
Male hd dept	6	2	5	33	54
Female hd dept	5	2	5	35	53

Does this table show the distribution of time that you would have anticipated?

Can you justify the distribution of time you see in this table?

It would seem, on the face of it at least, that the anticipated common core of curricular matters in a school is not a coherent whole but is made up of a series of diffuse bits and pieces, loosely associated under a generalized heading 'curricular activities'. Further, it transpires that much of this work is, in the level of performance required, at a relatively minor system maintenance level, thus ensuring that the organization continues next year. Substantial inputs upon curriculum renewal or development, the identification of staff needs for future development and training, all seem to be conspicuous by the small amounts of time spent upon them.

Should there in fact be a common core of curricular activity in a school, and if there isn't, then is this a fault of poor organization?

If there is to be such a core of curricular activity, then:

Where should it be located? and

Who should have overall responsibility for it?

Consider once again the list of topics included under the general heading 'curricular activities'. Assuming that one person or 'committee' is given responsibility for all of them, then how should such a body relate to the person or persons who determine the overall policy structure of the school?

What do you think are the likely organizational implications for the allocation and use of staff time? Some sort of support structure is necessary to ensure that work in this area is cultivated at the grass roots level and that the operational stages can be effectively monitored.

Is the answer to these problems to appoint a deputy head curriculum (director of studies)?

Write a job description of a deputy head curriculum (director of studies).

THE DEPARTMENT___

It has been suggested that the department is the proper place for curricular discussion within a school, as the unit is a relatively small one and therefore likely to provide an atmosphere which will be conducive to the genuine exchange of views. However, in practice, such curricular discussion will probably take place within each individual department and there will be fewer exchanges between departments.

But is the department the place where future curricular policy can be formulated, or is it more likely that the department will become overburdened with the routine maintenance of procedures?

At one large comprehensive school eight heads of departments volunteered to keep a diary record of their departmental meetings during a Spring Term. Thirty-six meetings were recorded, of which half were attended by all departmental staff and half were sub-departmental meetings, e.g. the head of science holding a meeting for the physics staff.

The spread of meetings showed that few occurred during the first week of term, none during the following two weeks, and then a steady increase occurred in the number, with the majority of meetings (25 out of the 36) taking place in the last five weeks of the term. The reason became obvious when the topics are noted—preliminary plans for the following year, curriculum options, and allocation of pupils to sets were recurring topics; additionally, stock taking, requisition and examination arrangements were also featured. The number of times each topic arose in departmental meetings is shown in the table below.

Topics recorded in Spring Term departmental meetings

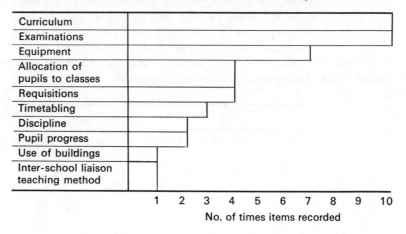

No. of times items recorded

The department as an agency for transmission of information—a function discharged particularly through meetings

Several different types of meeting were identified:

(1) Formal meetings: those which had been arranged in advance, agenda prepared and circulated, and a decision reached, even if this meant passing information on to another higher committee. All staff were expected to attend these meetings.

(2) Informal meetings: all staff were present but a social occasion was made of the event and no formal minutes were taken. For example, the English Department met in a public house.

(3) Sub-departmental meetings:
   (a) meetings which took place with reference to a particular subject, e.g. Science sub-divided into physics, chemistry, etc.
   (b) meetings when all members of the department were not necessarily present.

(4) Casual meetings: e.g. those which occurred because a group of people met together, possibly for another purpose, over coffee or on the way to lunch.

(5) Meetings of individual members of the departmental staff with the Head of Department.

(6) Departmental meetings to which parents were invited in order to discuss teaching techniques.

Heads of departments drew attention to the fact that many spontaneous meetings take place, where a casual conversation over coffee can lead to problems being raised and dealt with. In home economics, the staff met daily over coffee, thus obviating the need for formally organized meetings.

Duration of meetings

Meetings could be as short as five minutes or as long as 75 minutes. Short meetings tended to deal with emergency matters needing immediate action. Longer meetings took place when policy formulation and other important long term decisions were necessary. Departments varied in how long their meetings lasted; contrary to expectations, the length of meeting seemed to bear no direct relationship to the frequency with which meetings were held.

What do you think?

In practice, what do departments do in school?

In your opinion, what should they be doing?

Why is it, do you think, that departments seem to involve themselves with the level of detail that they do? Shouldn't this be someone else's job?

But whose job could it be?

Is it likely that organizational changes are necessary in order to bring about the functions that you are recommending for the department?

What status should a school give to a departmental meeting?

Is it possible to define the department's place in the overall structure of the school as the agency which will move ideas upwards through the school's hierarchy, and will effectively see the downward transmission and implementation of policy determined at the top of the school? Do the changes you recommend guarantee that upward and downward transmission of information will now be facilitated?

Will a faculty structure resolve some of the difficulties you have indicated? Will it, for example, facilitate cross departmental working within and between faculties?

What should be the criteria for judging the effectiveness of the courses a department offers?

Curriculum development—the Science Faculty

It seems that curriculum development in the large secondary school is unlikely to be a continuous programme of curriculum appraisal and renewal but rather a problem-solving response, that is, a response to a situation where it is seen that something has gone wrong.

The following is such an example:

Various members of the science departments of one large comprehensive school felt that the courses they were teaching were not suited to the needs of pupils of lower ability, particularly in the first two years. Independently, chemistry, physics and biology staff were coming to realize that they were suffering from similar problems and that really their courses were a legacy from the pre-comprehensive grammar school days. The retirement of the head of science and the promotion of one of the heads of department to the vacant science post provided the necessary catalyst for action.

The science staff included both men and women of proven experience and high qualifications as well as those who were new comers to the profession. In addition there were two female technicians.

The school was contained in two buildings on separate sites, the upper and lower schools. The lower school consisted of all pupils in the first three years, allocated into two bands with one remedial class. Apart from minor modification, little change was possible to the buildings. Separate laboratories equipped to meet the needs of the different sciences were in existence on the lower school site as well as one newly built multi-purpose laboratory, and these were judged as sufficient for the anticipated needs of lower school pupils.

A meeting for the heads of all the science departments was held which had the brief of outlining the problem and seeing whether a common strategy could be adopted in the pursuit of courses to meet the needs of pupils of lower ability in the first two years. It should by no means be assumed that there was necessarily unanimity of approach amongst the heads of departments, but one factor, subsequently to prove of importance, was that one of them, a man whose opinion was held in high esteem in the staff room, had become persuaded of the need for change.

The first step for the heads of science departments in their initial meeting was to outline various background factors which would prove to be major restraints on available courses of action. The following proved to be the most important:

(i) There had already been expressed by the cabinet of the school an interest in all first year forms sharing a common curriculum.

(ii) The chances of receiving extra teaching, ancillary or auxiliary staff were non-existent.

(iii) There was a need for all the members of the different science departments to be in favour, and

(iv) There was a need to accommodate the different backgrounds and orientation of the various members of the science staff.

As a result of this meeting it appeared that certain courses of action were open to the science department. These were:

(a) to make further modifications of existing courses;

(b) to develop entirely new courses in the separate sciences;

(c) to adopt a published course of 'combined' or 'integrated' science;

(d) to write a new 'integrated' science course.

The advantages of (a) were that minimal organizational changes would be necessary, and that the staff concerned would be able to meet the difficulties as and when they occurred. The disadvantages seemed to be that no-one really believed that existing problems would not re-emerge and that the teachers facing the most acute difficulties were those least equipped to remedy them alone. It thus seemed likely that solution (a) would not materially improve the situation. Solution (b) was open to arguments similar to those offered for and against solution (a) and co-ordination would be a considerable problem. Once again it seemed likely that any such change would be more apparent than real. The choice thus seemed to lie between solutions (c) and (d).

The decision finally taken was that a ready made course suitable for pupils of lower ability should be bought. The immediate question raised was whether money could be made available to cover the initial capital purchase of such a course. At this stage the role of the LEA science adviser became particularly crucial, and he was a useful ally in discussions with the head teacher. Since additional money was not available from central LEA sources, he gave considerable support to the case for the capital sum to come from the school's capitation allowance.

Once the head teacher and senior staff had given their approval in principle to the purchase of a course, there began a period of discussion in which members of the science departments were asked to consider the relative merits of the available published materials. The amount of time to be allowed by the timetable would be that formerly available to the individual sciences.

A course was finally chosen and purchased.

It rapidly became apparent that the role of the technicians was crucial to the scheme's success. Their day-to-day involvement in the implementation of the new course was greater than that of anyone else. Their view of it was also more objective. Soon they became acknowledged experts on the syllabus content, the equipment, and even the teaching approach. Upon their goodwill depended the smooth running of individual lessons and of the introduction of the whole course. It was essential that the demands made upon them by teaching staff should be reasonable, consistent and submitted in such a way that an even flow of work could be maintained.

Although all members of the science staff were not involved in teaching the course to low ability children in Years 1 and 2, all were involved in assessing its effectiveness. It worked so well that a suggestion was put forward that all children in the first two years should follow this course. Accordingly another round of consultation was begun.

Each member of the science staff was approached by the head of science and asked for their opinions and reactions. Individual heads of departments were won over and a meeting convened at which it was determined to give the course a try on a watch and see basis. Before each of the 15 units of the course was taught for the first time a full discussion was held to review any problems which had arisen and to iron out any problems which were foreseeable.

The course has now been successfully adopted.

As a result of introducing this course, various spin-off effects have become apparent to the science staff:

(a) The science department has become a more cohesive body and is now capable of working as a unit.

(b) Worksheets for the original course are being rewritten to suit the school's purposes more closely.

(c) Co-operation was easier to forge in the RoSLA area.

(d) Greater flexibility in teaching methods has become a possibility; experiments are beginning with team teaching.

(e) Informal contacts amongst staff have led to a more sympathetic response to those members of the staff who are known to be experiencing difficulties, difficulties easily appreciated by other scientists, and help on a co-operative basis is therefore made available.

(f) The staff are now in a better position to tackle the consequent questions of the third year curriculum.

But above anything it has become apparent that:

The adoption of a new curriculum by one department in the school, even one as self-contained as science, cannot take place without there being some considerable impact upon the rest of the school, both at curricular and organizational levels.

CURRICULAR PLANNING

A major reorganization by a local education authority of primary and secondary education into first, middle and upper schools allowed one head teacher the opportunity of fundamental curricular revision. His existing school, 'an all-through' 11–18+ comprehensive, was to become one of the new upper schools by the simple expedient of gradually cutting off the 11-year-old intake and substituting, in the course of time, a 13-year-old intake. The head teacher kept a diary recording the progress of curricular planning for the new Upper School, and this is appended on the next page.

CURRICULUM PLANNING FOR NEW UPPER SCHOOL

DATE	WITH	TOPIC	OUTCOME
Oct. '67–Mar. '68	LEA, Deputy Head, Governors, Other schools	Proposal of 3-tier system	Decision to start Sept. 1970
Oct. '67	Self	5-year plan for curriculum	Curricular plotting '68–73 set out
Mar. '68–Sept. '69	LEA and architects	5-year plan for buildings	Buildings phased to curriculum
Mar. '68	Lower school staff & Upper school HoDs	Curriculum for 1970 intake	Curriculum compared with donor schools
Aug./Sept. '69	Self	Plans for accommodation regarding curriculum	Curriculum phased to buildings
6th Sept. '69	Self	Curriculum 1970–71	Agenda for planning meeting
8th Sept. '69	Deputy Head, some HoDs	Curriculum 1970–71	Additions to agenda
9th Sept. '69	Head of Middle school	Curriculum 1970–71	Planning meeting, topics and views
9th Sept. '69	HoDs	Curriculum 1970–71	Planning meeting: study groups set up
15th Sept.—69	Bursar	Intake numbers 1970–71	Circular letter to check for primary schools
15th–21st Sept. '69	Self	Feasibility of curriculum 1970–71	Feasible timetable constructed
15th–21st Sept. '69	Self	Flexibility of curriculum 1970–71	Preliminary staffing analysis
30th Sept. '69	HoDs	Dept study groups working notes	Received
6th Oct. '69	Head of 6th Form	Lower 6th non A-level curriculum	Understanding of requests
20th Oct. '69	Self	Circulation of factual information for curriculum plans	Lists of numbers, rooms, groups etc.
4th Nov. '69	Dept Study Group	Requests for 1970–71 curriculum	Problems identified
11th Nov. '69	HoDs	Problem for 1970–71	Possible solutions
15th–16th Nov. '69	Self	Feasibility of requests	Modifications to timetable and staffing analysis
24th Nov. '69	Head of 6th Form	Lower 6th curriculum	Further requests understood
28th Nov. '69	Self	Staffing needs 1970–71	Forms to LEA
29th Dec. '69	Head-designate of Middle School (start '71)	1st year curriculum and continuity	Agreement on curriculum
9th Jan. '70	Self	Curriculum 1970–71	Summary of last term's conclusions
13th Jan. '70	HoDs	Curriculum 1970–71	Problems discussed
14th–19th Jan. '70	5th Year pupils	Careers and 6th Form courses	Agreement on desired courses
22nd Jan. '70	Lower school 12–13 year olds' parents	Pupils to be transferred Sept. '70	Agreement on grouping and integration
6th Feb. '70	Head of Middle School	4th Year options 1970–71	Procedure and timing for option choices
6th Feb. '70	Commerce teacher and Head of business studies and tertiary education	Careers and commerce course	Decision to expand commerce course
17th Feb. '70	Parents	Careers and commerce course	Exploration and discussion
13th Mar. '70	Self	Lower 6th form courses	Analysis of desired courses
14th Apr. '70	HoDs and relevant staff	4th year options 1970–71	Finalize arrangements
29th Apr. '70	Deputy head	First 3 years curriculum	Understanding of timetable implications

DATE	WITH	TOPIC	OUTCOME
6th May '70	County science adviser and HoDs	Nuffield Science courses	Decision to adopt
12th May '70	Head-designate of middle school	1st year curriculum and continuity	Agreement on problems
16th June '70	HoDs and section heads	Curriculum planning 1971–73	Dates agreed
30th June '70	Head-designate of neighbouring upper school	General curricular policy problems of upper school	Agreement on curriculum and staffing
30th June '70	HoDs and section heads	Curriculum planning 1971–73	Procedural framework agreed
1st–8th July '70	Self	Curriculum planning 1971–73	Provisional plan to check against dept findings

The two examples you have been given of curriculum formation are both in response to a crisis of some sort. Change had to take place. It seems so often as if curricular change occurs as a reaction to a crisis.

Why do you think this is so?

In the two examples given is it likely that the organization of the schools may have changed sufficiently for a review and development process to be permanently ongoing and, in your view, would this be a desirable state of affairs?

If one of these schools is more likely to have brought about a permanent state of curriculum renewal than the other, which one is it?

What do you think is the scope for a head teacher to bring about curricular change in his school?

In the example provided by the head teacher's diary, can you justify the pattern of work and the time this head teacher spent upon curricular formation? If in your view the head teacher should not have been undertaking this work, then who should?

Is it likely that one type of organizational structure may facilitate change whereas another type may hinder it? What sort of organizational structure is this likely to be? Compare the information given in the chapter 'Organization'.

Since such a proportion of the work of one or two members of senior staff is taken up by relief timetabling, why not make a virtue out of necessity. Ensure that the head teacher and deputy head have no teaching responsibilities but each day let them act as first relief on the timetable. This would allow ample opportunity of finding out what is happening in classes. It might also have a marked effect on attendance.

What conclusions have you reached about curriculum formation in the large secondary comprehensive school?

SUGGESTIONS FOR FURTHER READING ___

GROSS, N., GIACQUINTA, J. B. and BERNSTEIN, M. (1971) *Implementing Organizational Innovations*. Harper & Row and Open University Press.

HOOPER, R. (edit.) (1971) *The Curriculum: context, design and development*. Oliver & Boyd and Open University Press.

WHEELER, D. K. (1967) *Curriculum Process*. University of London Press.

WISEMAN, S. and PIDGEON, D. (1970) *Curriculum Evaluation*. Slough: NFER.

The Schools Council Information Section, Great Portland Street, London, W1N 6LL, is also a useful source of information.

Procedures for Mounting Internal and External Examinations

CONTENTS_____

INTRODUCTION___

In one sense the setting of examinations represents a culmination to those processes directed at a child whilst he is in school and permits, whether intentionally or unintentionally, some measurement of output. To raise this one issue, however, is automatically to raise many others, all of which are involved in the question of examinations in schools—what reliability can be attributed to the results? How can they be standardized to make comparison possible? What weight should be given to the results? How can feedback from assessment best be interpreted and incorporated into curriculum development? Is the examination process a reflection of educational objectives or the other way round? And so on. One further important point is whether the process is such that it needs to be entirely in the hands of a very senior member of staff, or, whether sections of it, or all of it even, can be safely delegated—to the bursar possibly?

Since examination arrangements are spread over a full academic year they make particularly heavy inroads into staff 'admin' time. In an attempt to overcome this, the schools examined in the research project had adopted a number of different approaches. At one school the deputy head has responsibility for all A-Level GCE exams and the head of middle school looked after all O-Level GCE and CSE exams. In another school, one teacher was responsible for all exam timetabling, another teacher was in charge of exam stationery and a third was in charge of exam returns and official documentation: all three received special responsibility allowances for their work. At a further school, the whole of the strategy was planned through an examinations committee chaired by the deputy head, with individual committee members undertaking the sub-components of the task and meetings being held regularly throughout the year in order to co-ordinate the work. This method, at least in theory, allows quite junior members of staff to participate in the work of the examinations committee, and thus gain experience of school administration procedures.

One further aspect of internal and external examination arrangements in the large secondary comprehensive school is that the procedure contains some of the features which distinguish major administrative tasks from more routine and everyday aspects of school administration. Amongst these features are that the dates of inception and termination of the task, as well as several of the intervening stages, are constrained by external agencies—in this case the examination boards. Also, that large and relatively self-contained areas of the task are delegated to a designated member of staff.

An inspection of the processes by which examination work is undertaken, immediately makes apparent the extent to which the task operations are of a clerical nature.

ONE SCHOOL'S SCHEME

Presented in the flow diagram, Figure 1, is the programme adopted by one large secondary comprehensive school for mounting its external examinations.

It is not presented here as a model programme—the intention in presenting the outline is to indicate the complexity of the task and to stimulate discussion.

The school's strategy for mounting internal examinations is given under 'Additional Information' Checklist 1 on page 112.

Figure 1: The procedure for mounting external examinations—One school's scheme

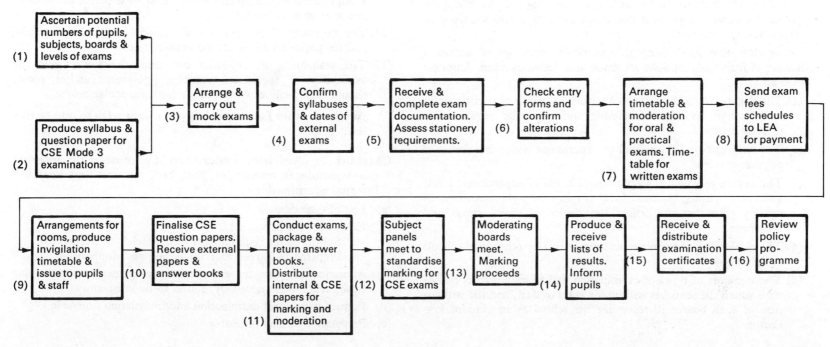

ADDITIONAL INFORMATION___

Further information in the form of checklists and documentation on factors relating to the mounting of internal and external examinations is presented below. It must again be emphasized that this is not a 'model' answer, but intended to help with the design of your own programme by stimulating discussion about the nature and sequence of actions that are required.

It is clear that in devising this particular sequence of actions a number of major assumptions are made and decisions taken. Amongst these are:

(1) The degree to which the school wishes its pupils to participate in examinations and the timetabling and curricular requirements thereby involved.

(2) The willingness of the school to experiment with other forms of pupil assessment.

(3) The degree to which the opinions of heads of department, LEA, governors, pupils, parents, local employers, and institutions of tertiary education will affect the choice of examinations and syllabuses.

(4) The availability of examination courses run by other local schools or colleges.

(5) The numbers of types of examination and of examination boards with which the school is willing (or able) to deal; and the willingness of such boards to recognize the school as an examinations centre.

(6) The willingness and availability of staff to act on subject and moderating panels.

(7) The policy of the LEA with regard to the payment of fees.

(8) The nature of particular crucial deadlines which may have to be met.

(9) The availability of resources such as clerical help and office space both for initial planning and the production and storage of literature and examination papers.

(10) The conditions upon which pupils are allowed entry to examination courses and the extent to which pupils are counselled on such choices, particularly where the availability of places is restricted, or where choices are likely to link unusual combinations of subjects.

(11) The determination of who has the final responsibility for whether a pupil takes an examination—the head of department, head of house or year, or head of school.

(12) The necessity of arrangements for special categories of pupils, and for pupils unable to attend examinations.

(13) The availability of staff who can teach the subject and the availability of specialized teaching equipment and/or rooms should such facilities be necessary for a particular course.

Are there other factors which you might wish to add to this list?

Checklist 1: Activities undertaken by master i/c internal examinations to mount 1st, 2nd, 3rd, 4th and first year 6th internal examinations

(a) List of candidates

(b) Exam question papers set
   (i) Subject to the requirements of the Heads of Department.
   (ii) Prepared by agreed date for typing and duplicating.

(c) Allocation of room for exams and arrangements for installing equipment (where necessary) found to be satisfactory

(d) Prepare provisional examination and invigilation timetable

(e) Preparation of final timetable

(f) Timetables—distributed to staff and pupils
(g) Exam stationery distributed as appropriate
(h) Briefing of pupils
(i) Preparation of exam rooms completed
(j) Check pupils are present
(k) Check invigilators are present
(l) After exam, collection of answer papers and distribute to appropriate member of staff
(m) Collection of spare exam stationery
(n) Clearing of exam rooms
(o) Ensure marking of exam answer papers follows agreed method in use of headmaster's five point scale
(p) Make and present a report for the exam committee

Checklist 2: Sequence of activities to produce external examination returns

(a) Pupils inform form teachers of subjects they wish to take who in turn check with subject teachers
(b) Information passed to deputy head for A-levels and head of middle school for CSE and O-levels
(c) These are checked against mock exam results or other appropriate exams, careers or further education plans, and subject load in general
(d) Adjustments are made and provisional entry list drawn out
(e) Entry lists sent to exam board
(f) Exam estimates made
(g) Deputy head deals with exam fees
(h) Subject teachers and pupils complete forms for deputy head or head of middle school to check that they have been entered for the correct exams
(i) Information is posted on weekly notice sheet

Checklist 3: Finalization of all examination preparations

(a) Receive exam timetables from exam boards
(b) Provisional school exam timetable drawn up

(c) Arrangements made with village hall to hold exams there
(d) Any timetable problems dealt with, rooms checked, final timetable posted up
(e) Any individual examination clashes with pupils dealt with
(f) Pupils and staff absent, kept up-to-date
(g) Timetables of invigilators drawn up
(h) Pupils and staff briefed
(i) Pupils issued with individual timetables
(j) Information posted on weekly notice sheet

Checklist 4: Practical arrangements for examination day

(a) Making exam number cards
(b) Checking equipment for practical exams
(c) Checking exam stationery
(d) Checking number of exam papers
(e) Checking physical condition of room, heating, ventilation
(f) Removing chairs and desks to village hall
(g) Arranging the rooms
(h) Informing the kitchen of special meals arrangements
(i) Packing up and returning exam scripts to exam board
(j) Cleaning room

During Exam

(1) Check invigilators' presence
(2) Check pupils' presence
(3) Check up on reasons for pupils' absence

Checklist 5: The results sequence

(a) Receive results
(b) Circulate to staff for information
(c) Inform pupils
(d) Check any queries

Checklist 6:

Write report reviewing procedure for exam committee.

Some of the objectives of another school in mounting an internal and external examination programme

EXAMINING, ASSESSING AND REPORTING

1.1 Classroom lessons are not enough. There must be:

Feedback
to the children
to the parents
to subject teachers

for effective feedback can motivate children who like to know how they are doing.

1.2 Careful assessment can also improve our own teaching ability.

1.3 Purposeful reporting can enlist the co-operation of parents.

1.4 The examining, assessing and reporting system is designed to achieve these ends. It is conceived on the following principles:

(a) Children to know how they are doing and to be encouraged to improve on their own performance rather than compare themselves with their neighbours.

(b) Subject teachers to keep detailed mark books (children listed in house groups) so that continuous assessment is possible.

(c) Communicating comment on work to be done on individual slips to ensure as much objectivity as possible.

(d) Tutors to regard academic control as an important aspect of their work.

(e) Reports to be issued to parents personally—ensuring maximum parental involvement.

FEWER EXAMS, NOT MORE

We may shortly move towards a common examination structure at age sixteen. This will be of no significance. Whatever develops within that structure may be. More important, however, will be the opportunity to evaluate not one or other system of examining, but the very basis of examinations as we can envisage them today.

Each year, I sign documents which show the total paid in examination fees for candidates from my school. Something in the order of £2,000 is involved. This is more than the entire money available to one of my contributory middle schools for books, stationery, furniture, apparatus and equipment, for all its pupils for a whole year. It is as much as the allowance would be for two years of nursery education for the whole of my catchment area. Are our priorities right?

In my own school, the summer term is buried in public examinations: the changes in organization required make severe inroads into the courses of all pupils, not just those about to complete their examinations; for the latter, the summer term is removed and practice runs have dominated half the preceding term; internal examinations have tended towards the patterns for which they too are seen as a preparation; our courses are in some measure built round the examination; as teachers we accept it as a necessary objective.

Pupils accept or reject the objective, and accordingly accept or reject the content of their work and the school which encourages it. In terms of pupil and teacher time, we may be spending about £100 a head on the examination itself as distinct from the learning content.

Yet I am confident that teachers' assessments of a pupil's ability to manage each course are already more valid than the results of public examinations, and that without the existence of the latter, each school's assessments would be more professionally handled than now. This is not just an utterance of faith: in advising pupils, parents, and employers, or in deciding whether a pupil can manage a sixth-form course, all the significant decisions are taken on internal evidence before the examination is sat, let alone the results known.

Is it not appalling, then, to allow this examination objective to engage the minds and the time of pupils and their teachers, rather than to foster the pursuit of knowledge, the acquisition of learning techniques, the development of self understanding and mutual understanding, the preparation for adult life which is, presumably, what education and schools are all about?

—John SAYER

Times Educational Supplement, 26th June 1972.

(Published by permission of Times Newspapers Limited)

MEMORANDUM

October 14th

From: Head   *To:* Deputy Head

I've received a letter this morning from the Chief Education Officer that has been sent to all secondary schools. It tells us that: 'due to the current financial situation, we are to cut back on external examination entries by 10 per cent.'

If you were the head teacher what would your next action be?

Set up a committee or working party to discuss guidelines for the school to follow in making the required 10 per cent reduction in entries.

Who would you invite to serve on the committee or working party?

Does your school offer advice to staff on examination procedures? Perhaps this is contained in the staff handbook. Bring examples to your group or syndicate for consideration.

POINTS TO CONSIDER _____

(1) Is it inevitable that a school's examination procedures should be in the hands of one of the most senior members of the staff even though most of this work is of a routine clerical nature?

(2) Who should have control over examination processes in a school— the pupil welfare and guidance side, or its academic side?

(3) Is the existence of an examinations advisory committee desirable? Amongst the functions of such a committee might be the following:

   (a) to deal with all cases that present difficulties to the existing system, e.g. a pupil wishing to take an exam but who is on a non-examination course;

   (b) to recognize and comment upon cases which arise due to faults in the system;

   (c) to be in a position to ensure that all problems are systematically treated and not dealt with arbitrarily;

   (d) to recommend the future examination policy of the school.

   What should the membership of such a committee be? Who should the advisory committee report to?

(4) (a) The subject of examinations presents 'departure issues' to the

organization. This is in the sense that pupils are transferring either to next year's classes or are leaving the school.

Why is it do you think that schools become particularly sensitive at such times? Is it because there is some measurement possible of the degree to which a school is meeting its objectives?

(b) The information which is available to a school at this time could constitute an important 'feedback' cycle to the organization.

How would you recommend a school to interpret and incorporate this feedback into its organization and curricular processes?

Production of a Timetable

CONTENTS

INTRODUCTION

The production of a timetable appears to fall into at least two sections, one section relates to those processes that decide the curricular plan for a school, the other to the complex procedure by which those decisions are implemented to produce the document that is usually referred to as 'the timetable'. In a large comprehensive school, this document could well fill the wall space in the room of one of the senior members of staff.

The task involves a considerable number of man hours work. The need for the timetable to be completed by the beginning of the new academic year, and the comparatively late stage in the programme at which the available information is assembled, before which the jigsaw puzzle element cannot be begun, impose severe restraints. External examination results, published during the summer vacation, and failures in staff recruitment, may so seriously upset a projected time-table that the process may have to continue throughout the summer vacation. In these circumstances the 'running in' of the timetable at the beginning of the new term becomes a major exercise.

In outlining the operational phases of timetable production, several key issues are identifiable. One problem that seems to arise is establishing the extent to which timetabling is a 'high level' or a 'routine' process. The difficulty a school may have in allocating timetabling to one or other level is related to the fact that timetabling is clearly a time-consuming process. It may be that the problem is to identify where 'control' resides, that the head is responsible for the process, but that the technician carries it out. However, in practice, it seems that if I, as a teacher, object to being timetabled to a particular class, then it is to the head or to the deputy head that I would turn for a decision, and would expect one of them to act as final arbiter. Such factors, together with the need to produce a daily absence or relief timetable in which the rapid co-ordination of information is essential, almost inevitably mean that someone of 'high level' status in the organization undertakes a largely routine process.

There are a large number of methods by which a school may form its timetable. It may follow a traditional approach; it may adopt a faculty timetable which the deputy head can write in half an hour on the back of an envelope on the beach at Benidorm; it may have totally individuated timetables for each pupil; or it may have a self-choice timetable where, for example, one puts up a blank board with all the periods that need to be covered and asks teachers to stick their own pins in where they want to teach.

Whichever operates, it is difficult to discern whether the planning and determining of curricular policy precedes or goes hand in hand with the jigsaw puzzle stage of timetable production. Is a timetable to be started at departmental level and then co-ordinated further up the institution, or is it imposed downwards from the top and does one have a committee structure involved with timetabling so that consultative and participative procedures, or at least co-ordinating procedures, are brought into play? A further complication here is that there may be a necessity for external links, i.e. if linked courses with further education colleges exist, then the timetable will then be a forcible expression of external policy as well.

Whichever method a school adopts, all make assumptions about the relative roles of the head, the deputy heads, heads of faculty, heads of departments, etc. within the organization.

The essential feature underlying timetable production is to ensure that a school offers the very best education that it can to each child. In order to do this effectively, it is suggested that two processes must permanently interact and be in tension with each other. For example: Firstly, the individual needs of each child at differing stages of that child's development must be determined. The question to be satisfied then is whether the courses offered by the school suit a particular child and are useful and effective courses.

Those who are likely to produce courses in a school do so reflecting the skills and philosophies of the teaching staff of that school together with other resources that may be available. But the production of courses is not a task that can be undertaken in isolation, it can only be undertaken in relation to those who are likely to be the buyers or users.

They must be the judge of what is appropriate. But the users cannot act without reference to the suppliers any more than the suppliers can act without reference to the users. They must enter into permanent negotiation with each other.

The users are those teachers who represent the guidance welfare/counselling side of the school's organization; they will probably share some similarity of duties with heads of years, as we now know them. The suppliers are heads of the faculties that the bargaining process has determined should exist. It is likely that each of these sides of the school's organization will be represented in the school cabinet by a deputy head, as well as having their own representation upon the academic board.

This form of organization is usually referred to as a matrix and further information about it can be found in the chapter 'Organization' (page 203).

One other aspect of a timetable which is worth noting is whether the timetable might be used as a planning tool to test the degree to which certain objectives, which the school may wish to set for itself, are in fact realistic targets.

For those who may wish to pursue this topic of timetabling in greater detail, suggestions for further reading can be found at the end of this document.

WHAT ARE THE CONSTRAINTS?___

The freedom or restriction which the school has to follow its educational and curricular policy is manifested in a number of key decisions, modified by resource availability. Amongst these are:

Time

Total number of available periods
Number of days on which the timetable is based
Normal unit of time
Timing of pre-determined events, e.g. swimming, TV programmes

Teachers

Total number
Sex balance
Main subject coverage
Subsidiary subject coverage
Conscientious, physical or competence restraints
Part-time or supply teacher availability
Non-teaching periods
Sabbatical leave
Special requirements of probationary and possibly student teachers

Organizational Characteristics

The pattern of administrative organization in existence in the school and the determination of the amount of non-timetabled time to be allocated to senior staff.

The pattern of welfare organization in existence in the school and the determination of the amount of non-timetabled time to be allocated to pastoral staff.

Desirability to free subject or pastoral staff for staff meetings.

Premises

Site factors (e.g. split site, bottlenecks, etc.)
Total number of teaching spaces available
Availability of specialist facilities (labs, craft rooms, drama team teaching, etc.)
Form/house/tutor group bases
Classroom size

Pupils

Total numbers
Numbers per age group
Age and ability range
Type of pupil grouping, streaming, mixed ability, banding, setting, single sex groups

Subjects

High frequency short duration subjects
Low frequency long duration subjects
Specialist facilities and requirements
Broadcasts
Desirability of work off school premises
Noise factors
Examination policy
Subject/option choices and their relation to examination requirements
Timing of option/subject choices
Balancing of individual head of department requirements
Need to balance/co-ordinate each pupil's curriculum to match

(a) school curricular policy, and

(b) the potentiality of each pupil

Teaching methods

Joint curricular schemes with local colleges or other schools

Extra-Curricular Activities

Other factors conditioning timetable construction could be provided by:

(a) the desirability of curriculum change

(b) pressures from agencies external to the school, e.g. parents, local industry

(c) policy changes due to the influence of the LEA, its advisers or from HMIs.

Perhaps members of the syndicate would wish to suggest additional factors under the headings given, or to add new headings to those already listed.

The following three diaries are presented as examples of timetable involvement on the part of senior teaching staff.

Deputy head's diary. First day of the school year

Start of Task	Termin-ation of task	Mode	With	Outcome	*	Topic	Where	As a result of information passed to you by	Communicated by you to	Form of document if any
8.30	8.45	Phone and Writing		Reorganization of staff teaching	✓	Substitution for staff absent				
9.10	9.20	Discussion	Staff member	Decision	✓	Photograph				
9.25	9.35	Discussion	Head of science	Amendment to timetable	✓	6th Form science timetable	Physics Lab	Head of Science	Staff	Timetable
9.55	10.10	Discussion	Head of geography	Decision	✓	3rd Form geography timetable				
10.10	10.15	Discussion	Headmaster	Decision	✓	Prefects	Head's study		Head	
10.20	10.25	Discussion	Senior mistress. PE master	Boy's leg treated. Accident report requested	PR	Boy scratched by dog on games field				
10.50	11.00	Discussion	Several staff	Classes re-roomed	✓	Classroom accommodation	Several places	Head of English	Several staff and class of 4th form	Timetable
11.05	11.10	Discussion	Head of history	Decision	✓	5th year pupil				
11.15	11.35	Discussion	Senior mistress	Dates arranged	✓	Dental inspections				
11.35	11.50	Phone	Manager, Provincial Bus Company	Bus company to correct	✓	School bus taking wrong route leaving children stranded	Own study	Head of 1st year	Manager, Bus Co.	
12.50	1.05	Discussion	Head of 4th year	Decision	✓	Common room fund	Own study	Head of 4th year	Staff	Notice
1.35	1.45	Writing		Notice sent round		Common room meeting				
1.50	2.10	Writing		Decision partially implemented	PR	Prefect's duties	Own study			List begun
3.35	4.00	Writing		Prefect's duty list	✓	Prefect's duties				

Deputy head's diary. First day of the school year (Continued)

Start of Task	Termination of task	Mode	With	Outcome	*	Topic	Where	As a result of information passed to you by	Communicated by you to	Form of document if any
4.00	4.30	Discussion	Headmaster	Decision— another meeting arranged	PR	School administration				
4.30	4.50	Discussion	Area Fire Officer	Fire precautions for new classrooms	✓	New classrooms—fire precaution	On site	Fire Officer	Head	

Deputy head's diary of timetabling activities

Start of task	Termination of task	Topic	Outcome	*	With	Mode	Where	Communicated By	To	Form of document
Date 1.45	2nd June 3.00	House staff and room/allocation	List	PR	Senior mistress	Discussion	SM's room	Self/SM	Staff	List
Date 11.15	4th June 11.30	Maths project	Memo	✓	Head of maths	Discussion	DH's room	Head of maths	Head of maths	
2.00	2.45	Integrated studies project	Memos	PR	Head of geography	Discussion	DH's room	Heads of geog/hist	Heads of geog/hist	
Date 3.15	5th June 4.00	Next year's 4th year option sets	Memos	PR	Heads of senior houses	Discussion	DH's room	HoDs and HoHs		Lists
Date 3.30	10th June 3.45	Allocation of maths staff	Memo	✓	Head of maths	Discussion	DH's room	Head of maths	Head of maths	
Date 10.00	13th June 12.15	1st to 3rd year subject allocation	Lists	✓	Senior mistress	Discussion/ Writing	SM's room	Self/SM		Lists
Date 11.15	17th June 12.15	Art/Tech Drawing/ Metalwork requirements	Memos	PR	Heads of depts	Discussion/ Writing	DH's room	Self	HoDs	Lists
Date 10.00	18th June 11.00	HEc./RE requirements	Memos	PR	Heads of depts	Discussion/ Writing	DH's room	Self	HoDs	Lists
Date 11.20	19th June 12.20	Allocation of form teachers	List	PR	Senior mistress	Discussion/ Writing	SM's room	Self/SM	HoH	Lists
Date 11.45	20th June 2.00	Allocation of English staff	Memo		Head of English	Discussion/ Writing	DH's room	Head of English		List

* Was the objective: achieved? ✓ partially reached? PR not achieved? X

Senior mistress' diary of timetabling activities

Start of task	Termin-ation of task	Topic	Outcome	*	With	Mode	Where	Communicated By	Communicated To	Form of document
Date 11.15–8 p.m.	2nd June 12.30–9 p.m.	Staff/dept for next year	List of staff in depts with time allocation and symbol	✓	Self	Writing, thinking	Own office and home	Self	Dep Hd	
Date 1.45	2nd June 3.00	House staff (esp. new house)	List in houses with rooms allocated	✓	Dep Hd	Writing and thinking discussion	Own office	Self	Headmaster	
Date 10.00	3rd June 11.00	Staff/class pattern	Lists prepared to receive information from heads of departments	✓	Self	Writing	Own office	Self		
Date 11.15	3rd June 12.00	Groups for games	Lists of boys and girls groups with possible numbers involved	✓	Self	Writing	Own office	Self	Heads of PE	Attendance list from sec
Date 12.00	3rd June 12.30	Groups for games	Memo on which classes to join for games	X	Heads of PE (Boys & Girls)	Discussion	Own office	Self	Dep Hd	
Date 10.00	4th June 10.45	Requirements for geog dept teaching	List of periods to be taught by each teacher	✓	Head of geog	Discussion	Own office	Self		Last years allocation and present list of staff
Date 10.00	5th June 11.00	Staff to forms and form rooms	List for discussion at later date		Self	Writing, thinking	Own office	Self	Head of houses	
Date 1.35	6th June 3.00	Estimates for no. of teaching periods per subject	List of dept's requirements	PR	Self	Writing	Own office	Self	Dep Hd	Last year's TT
Date 10.00	9th June 10.35	Staff/subject allocation	3 charts for 1st, 2nd and 3rd years to be filled in later	✓	Self	Writing	Own office	Self	Dep Hd	Last year's TT
Date 10.00	13th June 10.55	Course patterns for year 1–3	3rd year subject/period chart prepared	✓	Dep Hd	Writing and discussion	Own office	Self	Dep Hd	Last year's TT

* Was the objective: achieved? ✓ partially reached? PR not achieved? X

SOME QUESTIONS

1. Do the diaries show the distribution and level of involvement by these senior members of staff that you would (a) expect and (b) be prepared to justify?

2. Would you agree with the following comment made by a head of department?

   'The curriculum pattern of the school for the following academic year, including the number of periods allocated to each subject and each form, ought to be decided late in the Autumn Term.

   The whole staff should have the opportunity of discussing the allocation of resources and the curriculum model well in advance of the actual timetable being made. The head of department can then allocate his staff to forms by February and can have an individual discussion with the timetabler regarding the disposition of periods.'

   OR

   Would you agree that since there are clear disadvantages, in fact impracticalities, in starting the timetable too early, the major part of the work must fall in the months of July and August?

3. The large secondary comprehensive school needs to balance the participation of staff in democratic decision-making, on the one hand, with their allocation of priorities, on the other. Do you agree that the 'staff allocation sheet' is an excellent way of achieving this balance in the case of timetabling?

4. Perhaps you could in your group or syndicate, produce a flow diagram of timetable production either for a hypothetical school or for your own school.

   Can you justify—the priorities your flow diagram reveals and the underlying value bases of your strategy?

   At which stages does feedback take place in your strategy?

SUGGESTIONS FOR FURTHER READING

DAVIES, T. I. (1969) *School Organization: a new synthesis*. London: Pergamon.

RICHARDSON, E. (1973) *The Teacher, the School and the Task of Management*. London: Heinemann.

WALTON, J. (edit.) (1972) *The Secondary School Timetable*. Ward Lock Educational.

Budget, Capitation and Requisition Procedures

CONTENTS

INTRODUCTION___

Statements of finance are statements of the desire to implement certain policies. Statements of policy are no more than vague expressions of organizational intentions until they are expressed in budgetary terms. However it is a fundamental organizational flaw to separate budget and policy—whatever organizational pattern is in existence, there must be a continuous to and fro between the two.

Traditionally in schools, development of policy and its implementation in budgetary terms were both invested in the position occupied by the head teacher. The money allocated to the school has therefore in the past proved a subject of considerable mystique. Its oversight and sometimes the day to day administration of the allowance rested solely in the hands of the head; the distribution of the allowance was possibly not shared between departments, or even within departments, and thus the head teacher remained the only person with an overall picture.

The size and the complexity of the aims of the large secondary comprehensive school make this practice more and more difficult to discharge effectively, until there comes a point when the need to involve others in the process both at the level of policy determination and in its implementation is crucial. It would seem that there are profound implications for the role of the head teacher involved in this change.

Another factor which makes it difficult for the head teacher alone to retain financial control is the appearance in large secondary comprehensive schools of bursars. (It is in fact also likely that schools with a bursar will enjoy a better relationship with the LEA on finance than was previously the case, if only because the bursar is able to follow up some of the details more closely than time formerly permitted.)

Budgetary control relates to a number of headings. It relates to expenditure upon capital and equipment, but should also relate to expenditure upon staffing. To have control over a budget entails that decisions can be made in all three of these areas separately, and also for each one related to the others.

State schools in England and Wales rarely have this freedom, although the situation is changing and there always have been considerable variations between LEAs. Generally speaking, financial control is tightly retained by the LEA. The most forward looking of them are relaxing the rigidity of their control and giving powers of virement to their schools. This facility to 'vire' between headings gives to a school far greater control over its own development.

The situation which most commonly prevails is that the principal source of revenue for a school is its capitation allowance, and for staff, the extent of their involvement is likely to be restricted to heads of departments who spend this money on requisitions.

The actual sum of money allocated to a school is computed according to a scale laid down by the LEA, based upon pupil numbers weighted according to age. However, variations in the scales are likely to be found between LEAs.

Although the capitation allowance is the principal source of income to a school, there is provision for making claims to the LEA under special headings, and most schools are also involved in their own fund-raising activities. Generally, in England and Wales, state schools are not responsible for the provision and upkeep of their buildings—this is usually the direct responsibility of the local education authority.

Budgets and estimates, and capitation systems are essentially incrementalist in concept. Unless the 'system' is founded upon a sound basis it is bound to be inconsistent and inequitable, and in need of corrective action of one sort or another. Inevitably problems in management will arise.

BUDGETARY PROCEDURES

Presented below are two entirely different strategies by which two large secondary comprehensive schools undertake their budgeting and requisitions procedures.

The two strategies are not presented as model ways of doing work—the intention is to indicate the complexity of the task and to stimulate discussion.

List of steps in the requisition procedure of one large comprehensive school

(1) Staff informed of requisition procedure
(2) Head teacher produces draft allocation list
(3) Consultation between and within departments
(4) Consultation between head teacher and heads of departments
(5) Cases made out for special allowances
(6) Head teacher seeks LEA approval for special allowances
(7) LEA informs head teacher of capitation allowance and any special allowances
(8) Head teacher produces final allocation list and informs heads of departments
(9) After 1st April, placing and receipt of orders for new financial year ensuring that 70 per cent of the allowance is spent by the end of July
(10) Staff review new textbooks and order specimen copies
(11) Departments spend remainder of allowance mainly on replacement stock, stationery and materials for practical work
(12) Near the end of financial year, heads of departments inform head teacher of any outstanding balance
(13) Head teacher confirms remaining balances with LEA
(14) LEA informs school current year's expenditure is to end
(15) Expedite or cancel outstanding orders, or exceptionally carry balance forward to next year
(16) Close current year's accounts

Allocations for the current year

	£		£
English	750	Careers	80
RE	100	Boys' & Girls' PE	400
Hist/current affairs	350	Commerce	200
Geography	255	Stationery	2,600
Modern languages	350	Visual aids	350
Maths	500	Library	636
Science	1,650	Remedial department	540
Project work		Petty cash	33
Boys' practical subjects	1,450	Periodicals	80
Girls' practical subjects	800		
Art	815		
Music	400	*Total*	£12,339

This leaves a balance of £137 for emergencies, extra demands, etc.

Other allowances

Sales of craft work produce an income which is used as a reimbursement of part of the capitation allowance. Occasionally a special allowance may be granted where a sound case can be made out, for example an increase in the size of the intake, for which £250 was allowed in the current year. A separate allowance, of the order of £370, is made for the library. Part of the capitation allowance can also be spent on library books.

Petty cash

For items to be bought locally, such as specimens for biology or art and electric sockets and for postages, the secretary borrows £10 at a time from the school fund. At the end of six months the petty cash expenditure is met by a cheque from the LEA and the borrowing from the school fund is returned. The LEA go through the petty cash account and debit to the capitation allowance those items which would otherwise have gone on requisition forms.

Annual financial estimates

Certain items of capital expenditure, listed separately under 'Equipment' and 'Building Work', which would otherwise make heavy inroads into the capitation allowance, have to appear in estimates for approval by the governors. These are listed on priority ratings graded A, B, C or D.

Estimates for visual aids and music department capital items are dealt with by the LEA's specialist advisers.

Reception of goods

These are received by the heads of departments concerned, delivery notes are checked and invoices certified correct and countersigned by the head teacher before being forwarded to the LEA for payment.

General school and office stationery, the largest single item of expenditure, covering such items as exercise books, file paper, files, duplicating paper and sundries, writing materials and examination paper, is ordered by the deputy head with the assistance of the head of the history department in upper school and a woodwork master in lower school, who arrange the issue of certain materials to pupils.

Special responsibilities

A teacher is in charge of visual aids and he decides the allocation of expenditure in this field.

One of the school secretaries includes among her duties looking after requisition books.

Textbooks are stamped and dated in the office before being handed over to heads of department. When books are issued, each carries a slip on which the pupil's name is entered and he/she signs it. This personal responsibility helps to ensure that the book is good for several years' use.

The school office reflects the work taking place on requisitions and the budget in the rest of the school. A considerable amount of time is expended upon correspondence to the various suppliers. Approximately 1 hour per week is spent sorting, filing and entering invoices, and a similar time on phone calls about orders and queries from the local education office accounts section.

There is also an additional workload falling upon ancillary and auxiliary staff and upon the school office. When it is not absolutely clear if responsibility for an order rests with an individual department, e.g. broadcast pamphlets issued by the BBC and ITA, then it is the school office which takes on the work.

What occurs at your school?

What procedure exists for receiving goods, books, etc., and signing for them as received in good order? Who signs the delivery note? Who informs heads of departments that their equipment, etc., has arrived? Whose responsibility is it for initiating consultations between departments, and what steps are taken when disagreements exist?

At the sampled school, some 286 hours were recorded by senior staff upon budgetary and requisition procedures during the year, although the real figure must be considerably higher than this. There was a constant workload throughout, with peaks at the end of the school year, and also, for this school, where major spending was to be complete by the end of December, at the end of the Autumn term. Examination of diaries shows little discernible difference in the content and pattern of work between, for example, a deputy head, a senior mistress, a head of department and a lab technician, all of whom spent the major part of their time on this task working alone on clerical activities. The head's activities seemed to be largely dominated by the allocation of extra monies to departments, discussing with departments their future requirements and signing requisitions.

Here is an entirely different budgetary procedure evolved by another school—school 2. At this point it can be formulated as follows:

(1) *Capitation allowance*

The local education authority allot a sum of money calculated upon a rate per pupil head. The exact amount to be made available is therefore known by the school in advance. The headings upon which the capitation allowance is spent is seen in the attached information sheet from the headmaster to heads of spending departments. In addition to capitation the school receives money under the following three headings: special purposes, major items and flexibility allowance.

(2) *Special Purposes* is used entirely for travel.

(3) *Major Items*: This is a supplement to capitation and is a fund to allow the purchase of items of equipment costing more than £100.

(4) *Flexibility Allowance*: The school is allowed total 'flexibility' in spending this sum. It can, for example, be used to buy additional members of the teaching, ancillary or auxiliary staff, or it can be spent on materials. In practice, the money has usually been spent on auxiliary staff. When the residual sum is approximately £500 or less, it is usually allocated either to part-time secretarial help or to materials. The flexibility allowance is credited to the academic year, not to the financial year.

Procedure

The system of allocation of monies at present adopted by the school is one that has evolved out of the practice of the last two or three years, a practice which initially related to the heading 'Major Items'.

Since 'Major Items' is supplementary to capitation the head teacher invites departments to make bids for the purchase of specific items of equipment. The problem lies in the allocation of the money. Rather than the head teacher taking the decision himself as to how to allocate the sum, a meeting is held for all those who are concerned, but anyone else who is interested can attend. The purpose of the meeting is for departments to substantiate and defend their claims to each other and to talk their way into agreement over the distribution of the money. This has worked extremely well in practice.

The claims, once agreed within the school, are formally submitted to the governors and ultimately to the local authority.

The success of this procedure led to a determination to revise the method by which the capitation allowance was allocated. However, one further precipitating factor existed, and this was that teaching was becoming increasingly resource based and the difference between practical and 'chalk and talk' subjects was no longer easy to sustain. A more equitable distribution was necessary, and this meant that the 'rich' must lose to the 'poor'. It was necessary to devise a mutually acceptable way out of this dilemma.

Heads of departments held a series of meetings over several weeks to try and provide a solution, and the periods between meetings provided an essential opportunity for further deliberation. The whole proved to be a lengthy and arduous process. They finally proposed a new measure of costing based upon the number of pupil hours taught by a subject department expressed in hundredths, which is subsequently modified by the different weightings given to raw material and resource material respectively.

Initially arbitrary figures were allocated to the costing in an attempt to approximate to a figure within a range of what the department would formerly have anticipated. The figures were stabilized for the current year for the upper school at £14 per 100 pupil hours for the basic allowance, but after that the different departments were supplemented in ways which are not exactly the same. Some departments are estimated at £8 per 100 pupil hours for raw materials and equipment, but others (who do not receive a 'raw materials' allowance) are given resource material at a rate of £4 per 100 pupil hours. There are just two cases, science and music, who receive supplements under both headings. It is because of this differential treatment that there is still recognition that science uses more expensive material than most other subjects and that even when the humanities are resource based they are still not using up as much raw material as for example the technical or needlecraft subjects.

The full table of allowances for the upper and lower schools is attached below. This sets out the figure the department would have claimed, the sum allocated to them via the new method of costing and the grand total. Last year's figures are presented as a guide.

The actual allocation for the year in this trial stage was in fact determined by the headteacher meeting with the cabinet. Certain modifications were in fact found necessary, e.g. a sum of money was held back to help those departments where pupil figures proved to be larger than anticipated after pupil option choices were completed. It was also necessary to ensure that no departmental allowance fell below last year's allocation.

The scheme has met with enough success within the school for there to be a desire to persist with the approach.

Head teacher's information sheet

To Heads of Spending Departments

CAPITATION

We have just received our allocation which amounts to £19,164 plus £1,009 for Special Purposes.

(1) *Capitation* The sum allotted, although less than our overall total, seems safe enough because it will be supplemented in the autumn. Accordingly, I give below the allotment to departments and the calculations on which they have been based. They do not differ greatly from expectations aroused at our most recent meeting.

(2) Offset litho and TV/film studio expenditure must be allowed for by departments using these facilities.

(3) *Summary of capitation:*

Departments		15,175
General Admin	} both sites	1,250
Maintenance		1,600
Libraries		900
Classroom furniture		400
Classroom stationery (rough books)		400
A/V aids		250
Arts Subsidy		100
Careers		100
6th Form General studies (pro student hrs)		80
Matron		75
		£20,340

This sum should be made up by the increase in the autumn. As 'Reserve' we have allocated the nearly £500 which comes from Progress Unit subsidy, sale of children's practical work, and FE classes.

(4) *Special purposes* (travelling) May I have bids again for this sum in the light of your capitation allowance?

It can be settled easily in first week of May, if you will let me have bids during the holiday.

(5) *Major Items* agreed by us last autumn have all been approved. Application for order should be made to bursar.

(6) *Safety Measures* Since it is absolutely *imperative* that no-one overspends and presents us with a *fait accompli*, I propose as follows:

(a) Not more than 60 per cent of any department's allocation may be spent before July 20th without specific reference to myself.

(b) When 60 per cent has been spent, the bursar will inform the department.

(c) Those departments like science and technical, which sub-allot to subjects, remain responsible that these subject departments do not overspend. They should therefore inform the bursar of the sub-allotment so that it too may be subject to the '60 per cent by July' reservation.

12th April.   Head Teacher

11 Tyne Road,
Bishopston.
September 29th

Dear Headteacher,

I have from the beginning of this term, got three children attending your school. I have just received your usual letter asking for contributions to the 'School Fund'. This will now amount to 70p.

I feel I must express my resentment at being asked for this contribution without ever knowing the use to which past amounts have been put. I am fully prepared to help the school in matters which are of direct benefit to the children but would like to be sure that the 'Fund' is not used for items such as office typewriters, etc., which I feel are the responsibility of the Education Authority.

I would like to suggest that a 'Balance Sheet' be sent to each parent at the end of the school year stating the purpose for which the funds had been used and feel sure that most parents would appreciate this and possibly even feel inclined to increase their contribution knowing that the children benefit directly. This is my own personal feeling but I certainly do not like the idea of sending money without knowing exactly, the use made of it.

Yours faithfully,

E. M. Nash

Would you advise the head to send out a balance sheet?

What in fact should a school's policy be towards raising funds from outside sources?

UPPER SCHOOL	Claim	Allowance £14 per 100 pupil hours	Raw Materials and Equipment £8 per 100 pupil hours	Resource Material £4 per 100 pupil hours	Total	Allocation	Last Year
Maths	840	917			917	840	700
English	800	914		261	1,175	950	650
Science	1,908	1,079	616	308	2,003	1,900	1,700
History and Econ	750	535		152	687	680	535
Geography and geology	800	486		139	625	625	450
Languages	695	637		182	819	695	*800
Social studies	710	419		120	539	650	617
RE	140	117			117	115	100
PE/games	482	624			624	525	*440
Art	370	219	125		344	340	300
Technical	1,300	583	276		859	1,150	950
Home econ	500	285	163		448	430	400
Needlecraft	650	192	140		332	400	400
Music	550	158	100	45	303	300	230
Typing	110	118	(piano tuning)		118	115	75
History/English	100				100	100	
Progress unit	500				500	350	400
Technology	200				200	200	200
Design	400	101	58		159	350	200
Remedial	120				120	120	100
Totals					£10,789	£10,835	

LOWER SCHOOL	Claim	£12 per 100 pupil hours	Raw Materials and Equipment £8 per 100 pupil hours	Resource Material £4 per 100 pupil hours	Total	Allocation	Last Year
Maths	300	602			602	350	455
Humanities	1,440	1,050		350	1,400	1,300	1,100
Science	750	615		205	820	800	700
Languages	850	655		219	874	500	*
Design	2,000	575	383		958	1,000	750
Music	385	205	100	68	373	250	200
PE/games	103	410	(piano tuning)		410	150	*
Totals					£5,437	£4,350	

| Total for Upper and Lower Schools: | | | | | £16,226 | £15,175 | |

*Last year Upper School and Lower School were taken as one.

POINTS TO CONSIDER_____

(1) Does the practice adopted by School 2 resolve the dilemmas that the strategy of School 1 reveals?

(2) 'Given that much educational expenditure is already fixed centrally, then one may gain credibility as an administrator by being efficient rather than effective in the disposal of resources, i.e. having adequate lines of communication, everyone knowing how much they have to spend, having running totals every month so that no-one overspends, controlling staff, controlling headings of expenditure so that the budget is balanced, etc. However, this is all part of the minutiae of control, the bursar function. *The key objective* for a manager ought to be to have as much flexibility as possible in moving money about the organization'.
—*Head of Resources Centre*

Can schools ever control their own development without having full financial control of their affairs? Should schools have control over the disposal of their income?

(3) With regard to the previous point—should schools have some control over disposal of their *income*?—Why do you think LEAs retain such tight financial control—aren't schools after all staffed by professionals?

(4) The school each year should undertake an educational audit as well as, and at the same time as, a financial audit. This would determine how well the school is meeting its aims and objectives. E.g. for slow learning children:

are the present arrangements satisfactory in the school?

what are the inputs necessary to determine an improvement in performance, and
how do you measure the inputs?—
an increase in the numbers of classes;
an increase in the numbers of periods classes taught;
a decrease in the size of classes;
an increase in the numbers of staff teaching these classes;
no remedial groups left in the school.

What body should do this?

One should of course be aware of the contentious nature of these measures; both teachers and the public might be tempted to strongly disagree with them.

Role play a meeting of a group of governors, parents, pupils, the LEA, teaching and non-teaching staff, to determine what represents effectiveness for the output of a school.

(5) What are the budgetary and requisition procedures that your LEA permits to a large comprehensive school?
What items are covered by capitation?
What items are excluded from capitation?
What restrictions are placed upon a school?
To what extent do differences in *per capita* allowances still exist between authorities?
What additional compensatory expenditure of a direct support nature is provided by your LEA? and so forth.
Perhaps you could get a finance officer from your LEA to provide you with this information.

(6) Since a school is (usually) financed annually, the inability of an authority to add to a school budget, but the authorities power to reduce the budget places the school in a dangerously exposed position. A school's budget should be clearly allocated into Capital, Continuation, Developmental and Manpower headings to ensure that the effects of reductions are more clearly identifiable. Do you agree?

Staff Development

in the Secondary

Comprehensive School

'For most teachers staff development means nothing more than looking at the back pages of the *Times Ed.* every week.'

—Male assistant teacher

CONTENTS————

Acknowledgements

This document makes extensive use of a number of sources.

The presentation of the various patterns of staff recruitment are taken from a research project, 'The Administrative Tasks of Head and Senior Teachers in Large Secondary Schools' LYONS, G. A report to the DES, University of Bristol, 1974.

Information about teacher careers from 'Teacher Careers and Career Perceptions' LYONS, G. A report to the DES, University of Bristol.

The structure of this document is based upon DAVIES, J. L. and NEWTON, J. discussion paper for EARAC conference: *Staff and Organization Development*, Anglian Regional Management Centre, 1973.

The documents concerned with the interview simulation and the more formal outlining of a scheme of staff development draw heavily from information published by a number of industrial training boards and from material published by the following:

ANDERSON, D. K. (1972) *Staffing*. Coombe Lodge Report, **5,** 4.

BELL, F. E. (1969) *Improving the efficiency of departments in Technical Colleges*. Coombe Lodge Occasional Paper.

GOVER, A. S. and RUSSEL, T. J. (1973) *Staff Development in Further Education*, 1973, *Staffing and Staff Development*, Coombe Lodge Report, **6,** 1.

Staff Development in Further Education. Report of a Joint working party. ACFPE/APTI. 1973.

Particularly from WEBB, P. C. (1973) 'Staff Development in large Secondary Schools,' *Educational Administration Bulletin*, **2,** 1.

Staff Development in Education. Proceedings of the first annual conference of the British Educational Administration Society. Councils and Education Press 1973. edit. Pratt S. particularly.

LIGHT, A. J. *Staff Development in Education*. Responses by HOYLE, E. and WEBB, P. C.

BRIAULT, E. W. H. *Staff Development in the Institutional Setting*, and GLATTER, R. *Off-the-Job Staff Development in Education*.

The particular problems of probationer teachers are excluded from the discussion here. For those who may have interests in this area see:

TAYLOR, J. K. and DALE, I. R. (1971) *A Survey of Teachers in their First Year of Service*. University of Bristol, and BOLAM, R. (1973) *Induction Programmes for Probationary Teachers*. University of Bristol.

For a more general orientation to the problems that underlie promotion in schools see:

HILSUM, S. and START, B. (1974) *Promotion and Careers in Teaching*. Slough: NFER.

Every effort has been made to give full reference to all sources used in this chapter although this has proved especially difficult where secondary sources are involved. Where difficulties were experienced then the reference given is to the secondary source.

INTRODUCTION

It might at first sight appear to be tendentious to suggest that schools 'generally' ignore the development of their staff. They assume, rightly or wrongly, that any development is either, wholly the responsibility of the individual concerned, or, means no more than attending in service training courses.

The aim of this particular document is to examine some of the constituent elements of staff development programmes developed for other organizations and, in doing so, to discuss the more significant problems that stand in the way of a programme being successfully applied to a school: also, to see the way in which these other organizations have attempted to find solutions to the problems. The major sections of this document thus become concerned with an examination of:

1. Why a systematic programme for the staff of a school is felt to be necessary; and
2. How such a programme may be brought about in a school.

Implicit in the above is a hidden value judgement and that is that a programme of staff development should be applied to a school in the first place: this assumption is, of course, open to question.

A staff development programme cannot be a universal panacea, it will not provide an instant cure for all problems although it might help in identifying their roots. The symptoms for which staff development appears to be a ready cure might be very different from the true nature of the organization's ills.

One of the more important aspects of any systematic staff development programme is that of staff recruitment: many intractable problems can have their roots in bad recruitment. Accordingly, it has been dealt with separately in two appendices. Appendix 1 contains:

An outline of staff recruitment programmes found to be existing in sampled schools;* and,

A more didactic recruitment exercise using simulated settings for the production of job specifications, undertaking short listing exercises, an interview simulation and so forth, can be found in Appendix 2.

This chapter is based upon a number of premises. Amongst the most important of these are that:

The term 'teacher' is not very explicit when one considers teachers' careers by implying a homogeneity which does not exist.** There are, in fact, many different types of teachers who had different motivations for entering the profession, look to different satisfactions within it, and whose experience over time is differentially mediated by factors both internal and external to the school.

A career is composed of stages, compartments, or whatsoever, sequentially arranged. Pertinent questions may therefore be asked about: the knowledge which those at any career stage may have of other stages, and of how they acquire this knowledge; what are seen as the necessary conditions for entry, or alternatively, to remaining in or leaving, any stage; who produces, controls, maintains, elaborates, and so forth, these conditions, and with what aims in view is this done; which stages are seen to have the greatest significance by the incumbents; how are timetables of career stages generated; what rituals are used to mark the transference from one stage to another—and so forth.

In practice it seems as though it is the task of the individual teacher to be solely responsible for his own career development, the man most likely to be successful therefore is he who has most knowledge of the career game. However, to set up in a school a scheme of staff development of necessity exposes a situation which is contentious, ambivalent and not ordinarily revealed to the scrutiny of a wider audience: staff development has about it an air of unfamiliarity when one thinks of schools and appears to carry disturbing overtones, for there seems to be lurking somewhere within it an implicit threat, for it is necessary to devise a scheme whereby individual and institutional development

* LYONS, G. (1974) *The Administrative Tasks of Head and Senior Teachers in Large Secondary Schools*. University of Bristol.
** LYONS, G. *Teacher Careers and Career Perceptions*. Report to the Department of Education & Science. University of Bristol.

can proceed hand in hand. It is necessary also for a rational assessment of teacher performance to take place, a feature which will in practice prove exceedingly difficult to bring about since such an aim runs counter to some of the most profoundly held beliefs in the profession. It is here, of course, that the major threat seen by teachers to themselves in the adoption of any programme of staff development will be found to exist.

Perhaps the most significant of all the steps for a school to take to bring about the successful adoption of a programme is that in order to plan rationally both for institutional and for individual development, it is necessary for the school to set for itself clearly determined goals or targets. By definition, the school cannot do this without involving all staff (or a representative selection of them) in the determining of these targets, since the targets must be meaningless unless there exists some consensus of opinion about their feasibility and desirability. Inevitably the role of the head teacher and others of the most senior members of staff will be profoundly influenced as staff are directly involved in participatory decision making at the highest policy level.

The school must set these 'fulfillable goals and targets' through a body which is charged with this task. What the relation of this body should be towards the existing decision making structure, and to the governors, is most imprecise. And further, there are some teachers whose sense of 'professionality' debars them from ever participating on such a body; it also assumes that it is possible to forge a consensus of opinion about goals or targets.

There is a clear need in schools to inform staff of career possibilities and in the immediate future it seems as though this must take place against a background of contraction and not of organizational expansion, a very serious problem to any organization but particularly to a school which might be attempting to incept a staff development programme.

It seems to be a fact that some of the roots of existing schemes of staff development can be found in industrial practice. Whether the theoretical model which would best describe the needs of industry can equally serve the needs of schools seems to be an open question, and begs the question of what other models might more pertinently fit schools. To apply to a school in an unassimilated fashion the sorts of thinking that can be applied to a factory may lead to an unprofitable discusson. Further, schemes of staff development contain implicit assumptions if they are based upon a 'Weberian' conception of bureaucratic authority, and these assumptions should at least be discussed. Though the 'Weberian' model might fit the needs and circumstances of many schools, the question of whether schools are bureaucracies, or being developed as such, still remains, and if they are, then should they continue to be?

It has already been remarked that a programme of staff development may appear to be threatening to those concerned. The usual view is to regard such behaviour as irrational and it follows therefore that those involved simply need to be reassured. However, the nature of the threat may lay in the theoretical perspective of the organization that was adopted in the first place. If this is an inevitable outcome of an existing view of an organization, then participation in staff development can never be more than optional. Does this then destroy the whole basis of staff development? Does a member of the teachers union need to be present at the assessment interview? Is self-appraisal capable of meaning any more than, ' "Oi" isn't it time that I was promoted?'

The point of this discussion document is to bring to the schools' attention, the essential constituents of any programme of staff development, *it is not put forward as a model scheme*. As far as the author is aware, a model has not been developed which successfully fits the needs of the large school. The aim in presenting this material is to allow the school an orientation and an opportunity of specifying needs with respect to their programme. The school must look, taste and judge; does it want to adopt all of it, just some of it, or none of it? From that point, they must go on.

The document proceeds upon the assumption that the school has responsibility for staff recruitment and that the governing body and/ or the LEA do not exclusively exercise this right. When appointments are made directly by governors or the LEA then clearly a considerable task of negotiation confronts the school before the proposals advocated here can begin to be entertained.

1. WHY STAFF DEVELOPMENT?

The line of argument most frequently advanced for the adoption of a staff development programme is as follows:

1.1 Objectives of staff development policy*

(a) *In individual terms*
To help academic staff to do their jobs more effectively;
To enable them to keep up to date;
To encourage a positive response to change;
To broaden experience;
To increase job satisfaction;
To prepare for different and/or increased responsibilities;
To identify and prepare those ready for advancement.

(b) *In organizational terms*
To increase the 'schools' capacity to predict and cope with changing circumstances in terms of pedagogic, organizational and subject development;
To provide a vehicle for planning effective management succession in the school

1.2 The bases upon which such views are advanced are as follows, that*

Staff training and development is a continuous process, with a relevant contribution to make at each stage of a teacher's career;

* DAVIES, J. L. and NEWTON, J. (1973) *Staff and Organization Development of Management Departments*. Discussion paper for EARAC conference. Anglian Regional Management Centre.

137

Policy for staff training and development must be sufficiently wide and flexible to meet the needs of all staff;

Individual consultation as an ongoing process should be the basis for the training or development proposals made for any member of staff;

Job satisfaction comes from doing any job well and is not to be associated with only those offering hope of advancement;

Each member of staff seeking assistance for his own development must show readiness to make his own contribution to it;

Whenever possible and appropriate the 'school' will draw upon its own resources for the implementation of this policy;

The 'school' intends to provide opportunities whereby members of staff can develop their interests, skills and abilities: it does not follow, however, that each member of staff can claim such development in a particular way or at a particular time.

1.3 The strategy of development*—The options open, and the assumptions

There is a fundamental decision to be made about the kind of approach to staff development that should be adopted.

Basically there are two kinds of approaches:

(i) The 'peripheral' approach which views staff development programmes as important but nevertheless only a fringe activity compared with the organization's main business.

(ii) The 'integral' approach which views staff development programmes as an essential component which enables the organization to pursue its business.

The 'peripheral' approach is characterized by *ad hoc* provision for individuals or to meet particular circumstances. Hand-to-mouth attendance at courses, conferences, and seminars (however good these may be) often passes under the guise of staff training and staff development.

On the other hand, the 'integral' approach is characterized by developing co-ordinated policies, practices and procedures that aim to recruit, train and maintain staff in a way that satisfies both the needs of the individual and the needs of the organization. The 'peripheral'

* Davies and Newton, *ibid.*

approach (which is much the easiest to administer) tends to be either individual-needs orientated or job-needs orientated, whereas the systematic 'integral' approach endeavours constantly to maintain a balance which is monitored and regulated through feedback.

It will be apparent from the above that the tenor of these proposals leans heavily towards the 'integral' approach. (Our) underlying assumptions are that an 'integral' approach is:

(a) necessary because it clearly establishes staff development as one personnel management function in relation to all the others: to consider it independently would be no service to (our) colleagues;

(b) advantageous because it starts with ends and only then identifies means;

(c) requires a dynamic view;

(d) is considerably less threatening to the individual in the manner by which training needs are identified, because it focuses attention on the 'institution' as well as the individual;

(e) necessitates a broader information base upon which to make decisions;

(f) enhances the prospect of transfer of learning.

Some discussion points:

1. Does it seem meaningful in your eyes for a school to set objectives for itself? How would you suggest it recognizes:

(i) when it has achieved a stated objective?

(ii) the stage it has reached at the moment?

2. Which of the following views most closely approximates to the practice you are acquainted with?

(i) It is necessary for a school to determine the structural framework necessary to achieve its objectives and to discover its manpower needs. It must simultaneously give staff fulfilment, utilize its resources to the utmost, assess staffs suitability for a particular post, and thereby respond to training needs (or decide to 'buy in' staff). It must also set up a means of allowing appeals from aggrieved staff.

(ii) The strength of the existing system is in the knowledge that the head teacher has of his staff.

(iii) The principal type of problem that a school faces is how to find a quiet backwater for someone on a scale 4 who is not up to his job.

3. Will teachers, since they are professional people, resent having their careers planned for them?

4. We take it for granted that major changes to mobility, function, promotion, and so on, will come from personal motivation and not from institutional need. Is this the case? Is your career something you do for yourself or something that is done for you?

2. SETTING OBJECTIVES AND SUCCESSION PLANNING___

Assuming that a school wishes to implement a staff development programme, one of its first tasks must be to set out the overall objectives which will act as a guide to its activities (and, of course, the body which will set these objectives) and to which the staff development programme will contribute.

A checklist may help in doing this.

2.1 A logical starting point is for the school to state its objectives (and for the faculties or other sectors of the school to state their objectives in the light of these broader school based objectives). The headings within such a development plan may be*:

(i) A statement of the aims of the school in terms of the client groups and sectors which it purports to serve; area of operations; behavioural objectives in relation to client organizations and individuals;

(ii) A statement of the activities which the school undertakes, or proposes to undertake, to fulfil these aims, and the precise

* Davies and Newton, *ibid.*

139

form of behavioural achievements pertinent to each of these activities;

(iii) A phased development programme over, say, five years, on the basis of a rolling plan, indicating precisely the timing and nature of developments, together with alternative options;

(iv) An analysis of the resource implications of the above developments, and spelling out the nature of staff and the numbers required;

(v) A series of evolving organizational charts indicating the development of new ideas and relationships deriving from the phased programme.

2.2 Succession planning:

The development plan must also relate to a systematic approach to future needs in terms of vacancies and numbers of staff. The steps to be taken in forecasting staff requirements are these:

(1) Produce an accurate organization chart as it now is showing functions, levels and incumbents.

(2) Produce an organization chart of the school (department) based on the development plan showing the projected functions and levels.

(3) Compare the two charts, noting positions or functions that may have become redundant and new positions or functions to be filled.

(4) Take account of known retirements, estimate wastage (as a percentage based on experience) and arrive at replacement figures.

2.3 Within this wider organizational framework, individual requirements can be stipulated. However, this is only one side of the coin. The marrying of individual and organizational requirements is a delicate and difficult task since many individuals will (quite rightly) see their needs from the standpoint of their own perception and not that of the organization. The problems of assessing and promoting will be dealt with below, but let us firstly look at what can be learned from more 'general issues' concerned with individual requirements and their consequences to organizational development.

3. INDIVIDUAL CAREER PERCEPTIONS___

Any organization is likely to achieve its purposes more successfully when its staff work in harmony with its avowed aims and are happy and enthusiastic about their work. To this end, it should become involved in an individual's career and development. Why people want to get on, what their motives are, and so forth, are essential ingredients to any programme of staff development. An organization should be prepared to modify its programme at any point of time to suit the needs of the individuals within it.

Is this really the case?

3.1 Individuals and their careers: a research perspective*

Teachers hold very different perceptions of their total career and of the methods by which they should achieve their career goal—let us call it a map of their career. The table below shows the proportions of teachers in a sample drawn from five comprehensive schools, who had never held a map of their career, who had acquired a map of their career, or, who had always held a map of their career.

* Lyons, G., *ibid.*

140

			Map always %	Map never %	Map acquired %
Males	...	...	31	43	26
Females	...	...	20	57	23
Total	...	...	26.4	48.8	24.8

This is not significantly different for males or females, for any age or for any status.

The most common method by which such maps are acquired seems to be a 'gradual cognizance' of the possibilities that lie ahead, and these possibilities seem to be structured in terms of a limited time span. 'You have to feel your way a step at a time.' One of the consequences of such a piecemeal view of a career is that the realization of an ultimate destination may be acquired at the same time as the knowledge that there is no longer the opportunity of satisfying the necessary conditions of entrance to the post.

The large comprehensive school has created totally new career patterns. Many teachers in those schools are simply unaware of this change and of the career requirements that they must now satisfy if they wish to be promoted.

3.2 (a) Success or failure in a teaching career. Two contrasting viewpoints*

The difference between illusion and reality is one of the most piquant aspects of any career, for the recognition of this contrast is in itself a coming to terms with hopes and yearnings that may never be fulfilled. It may be so traumatic that, for some, the recognition will be too painful to be admitted. It seems that one of the crucial differences between teachers lies in the setting of fulfillable goals by those whose careers seem to promise a likely achievement of their ambitions; as opposed to the unfulfillable, even unspecified, goals on the part of those who have been more concerned with the tasks in hand, and who only realized too late that they have been bypassed. Success and fulfilment go to those who map out their careers, and set out to achieve a particular

* Lyons, G., *ibid.*

objective. The strategy is of importance, the recognition of the need for a strategy is vital. For some teachers, there is an inevitable sense of tragedy in their dawning awareness of the career structures that do exist within education, because although their motivations, sources of satisfaction and ultimate goals may appear to be in harmony with the avowed aims of current educational practice, the nature of the educational organization may be such that the pursuit of these ideals does not result in the promotion which they apparently deserve. In the absence of any coherent source of information other than staffroom folklore, about the requirements for promotion and the types of career structures which actually obtain, it seems unavoidable that this sort of tragic situation will occur, and will lead to a degree of malaise within the teaching profession which might be thought unacceptable, offset as it may be by the other sources of satisfaction which may be found in the teaching profession.

3.2 (b) Male teachers who achieve top posts*

The eleven male teachers in the sample now holding top posts (head teacher, deputy head, head of upper/middle/lower school), were all graduates. The reasons they gave at interview for having chosen teaching as a profession were various, and not noticeably different from those given by other interviewed teachers; it is worth noting, however, that the two youngest top post teachers had not originally thought of teaching as their future career.

These teachers claim to have realized the possibilities ahead at an early stage of their careers:

'I picked up the career possibilities very quickly. My first grammar school post was the right thing for me to do at the time, it gave me 6th Form and examination experience, and then I talked my way onwards.'

'My grammar school head expected staff to be young, to stay for 2–3 years, and then be promoted away: it was the pattern of the school.'

Specifically, the aim of these teachers in the early stage is a headship

* Lyons, G., *ibid.*

141

of a department, within the first five years of teaching. All the top post males in the sample achieved this, and several emphasized its importance:

'When you enter the profession, you come in wanting to do a good job, and you don't look 10 years ahead. The ambitious want to be a head of department within five years. After four years I started applying for this post and got it after five.'

Having gained the post of head of department, the sampled top post teachers took different routes: some moved to take a larger department or to a larger school, or became a head of house in a comprehensive school. For all of them, however, there appears to be a consensus of opinion that it is unwise to stay in a median post for more than another five years:

'Don't stay here for more than four years,' warned one, and a general comment from another was:

'Length of teaching service is irrelevant; length of service in a particular school is irrelevant: those who get promoted are those who jump from job to job.'

This last point is borne out within this sample—the top post teachers had made significantly more promotion moves between schools (as opposed to promotions within a school) than had other sampled teachers and show a higher rate of promotion between schools than within schools when compared with the remainder of the promoted sample.

An implication of this finding is that those teachers in mid or graded posts are more likely than top post teachers to have been promoted within schools. This suggests that a characteristic of top post teachers is their willingness to move schools for the furtherance of their career; not all the top post teachers, however, have manifested this willingness by actually having moved schools for promotion—what seems more important is that state of mind which makes such movement possible.

Seven of the top post males undertook degree or diploma awarding courses of further professional study. The courses taken were normally Masters degrees in their own subject, and were undertaken partly from an interest in the subject, and partly from the point of view of improving their career prospects:

'I took a part-time MA mainly for career reasons. I saw in my probationary year that I needed this type of qualification: others were doing courses and I realized that it was the thing to have done—but I did get interested in it!'

'Last year I took a diploma in curricular studies, both for things that are immediately valuable and for things that will be valuable in the future. I used to think that one of the reasons for not getting interviews was because I had a funny (non-honours) degree, and having no professional qualification was a disadvantage. Things are better now.'

The pressure of ambition is perhaps strongest at this point in the top post man's career. The eleven such teachers in the sample achieved their first top posts after, on average, ten years of teaching (range from 6 to 14 years), and they are generally aware of a sense of urgency:

'You have to be a deputy head by the time you're 35, otherwise you're too late.'
'I realize that I need to be a head teacher by the time I am 38–40 otherwise I will have failed.'

Up till their appointments to top posts these teachers had been heavily involved in extracurricular and extramural activities, often specifically with an eye to improving their career prospects:

'Extracurricular activities have a very favourable effect on promotion—they show a readiness to give of yourself to the school outside prescribed limits.'

Once having achieved a top post, however, these activities seem for a variety of reasons to go by the board:

'I used to organize a lot of clubs and societies for the kids, but I don't any longer—there's just so much other pressure on my time.'
'Of course, these things help a lot up to the stage of deputy head. After that, you shouldn't be too involved in any one thing.'

Having reached the goal of a top post at the age of, say, 35, most of the sampled teachers found their possible futures problematic, and seemed unsure as to what they might do for the rest of their working lives. Two of the older teachers, just pre-retirement, had been headmasters of more than one school and this is a line which appeals to some of the younger ones:

> 'I certainly want to be a head, but may then want to go on and I don't know to what. Will later have to decide to go for a second headship until I retire or to branch off in my career (i.e. into LEA administration or a training college.)'

The options of administrative work or tertiary education are ones that these young teachers wish to keep open; attendance at in-service training courses is one way of doing this:

> 'Courses are important to meet the right people: advisers, lecturers, LEA administration officers and education officers. I attend a course once each year to which both the CEO and his deputy go.'

Early in their careers these teachers, who are capable, have been able to perceive the possibilities ahead of them, and perform in a highly efficient way in the competitive world of the teaching profession. It seems, however, that there is a real likelihood of their undoubted abilities being wasted in the latter part of their lives, since they are in a situation where any move would probably involve a cut in salary (e.g. from head of a large comprehensive to college lecturer) and where most factors encourage inanition. One young teacher puts this well:

> 'I am very conscious of the fact that I face thirty years of headship.
>
> For the first ten years the school will benefit, but after that it becomes very serious as to what happens to head teachers.'

It seems as though 'success', by achieving a top post in a school, presents the school, and the wider educational system, with a basic paradox:

> Although society at large encourages and rewards ambition, the necessary steps for achieving promotion in schools indicate that an attitude of mind concerned with achieving promotion and a willingness to move fairly rapidly between schools (if necessary), are prerequisites. But—so the ideology would say—schools are about the quality of relationships between pupil and teachers and such relationships can only be developed and fostered over time.

Are we, in fact, placing in positions of power in schools those whose values are antithetical to the ones we believe 'should' exist in the school?

Are we placing such key staff in an impossible position by asking them to encourage in other members of staff values that they themselves do not share?

Alternatively, are such staff more likely to be representing society's values? It is those of the school that are out of step.

On the other hand, is there any reason to believe that such an able and capable collection of men and women at the top of the profession can do anything other than good for the schools?

3.3 Women and a teaching career

The table below shows the distribution of staff to posts in a secondary comprehensive school according to Male/Female, Graduate/Non-Graduate status, where the staff pupil ratio was 1 to 18.1.

	Graduate (or grad. equiv.)		Non-graduate		Total
	Male	*Female*	*Male*	*Female*	
Senior post	2	1	—	—	3
Head of Dept.	8	1	3	2	14
Welfare post	—	—	6	1	7
Other allowance	2	2	9	10	23
Assistant Scale 1	1	6	6	7	20
Totals	13	10	24	20	67

Part-time and temporary assistants excluded.

Does the above table show the distribution of posts that you would anticipate finding in the large secondary comprehensive school?

1. Do you think that the careers advice that female teachers need is totally different from that needed by males?

2. How would you advise a female teacher to plan her strategy for re-entry into the teaching profession, after a break for child rearing? e.g. will she want the same job, will she need retraining, will she have to take a more junior post . . .?

3. Do you believe that employing mature women teachers presents a school with an opportunity of stabilising what might otherwise be a high staff turnover?

4. It is often said that women do not apply for any position involving responsibility. But with the image in front of them of a typical Senior Mistress' job—i.e. to handle that which the senior male executives in the school do not want to touch, plus an assorted collection of bits and pieces left over from anywhere to justify the salary, can you really blame women teachers for not wanting to be involved?

Look at the advertisement below, which appeared in the *Times Educational Supplement* of 9 September 1973. Does this resolve the dilemmas you have noted? This particular advertisement resulted in more than twenty applications from very good candidates.

> Required for January, a DEPUTY HEADMISTRESS for this Group XI school which is housed in excellent postwar buildings which are about to undergo a further major programme of modernization and extension. This appointment will complete a team of three career staff of Deputy Head status. Significant educational experience is necessary but it is also very important that applicants are of proved academic and administrative ability since ideally the school would like to make an appointment to ensure the oversight of all academic work in the Upper School, the development and oversight of courses, the conduct of examinations, the guidance of senior children in cooperation with the Heads of Houses and liaison with Further Education establishments in cooperation with the Careers Adviser.
>
> Although having a special influence as Deputy Headmistress the successful candidate will not be expected to adopt the traditional role of complete oversight of women members of staff and of girls' welfare although a deep concern for the pastoral care of children is essential especially within a school which has devoted a great deal of its time and its resources to the development of its system of care.
>
> Further details and application forms may be obtained from the Headmaster of the school.
>
> Generous scheme of grants for removal, lodging and disturbance expenses.

3.4 The end point of a career within teaching*

Apart from those who leave the profession early, it is anticipated that those holding self-perceived terminal goals will fall into three main categories: those who feel themselves frustrated in their ambitions; those who have redefined their ambitions to suit their circumstances; and those who have succeeded in achieving the goals of their ambitions. Not all of those in the latter category particularly will aspire to the most senior positions in a school.

Although the possibility exists for a teacher to reach what they consider to be their terminal goal in a comparatively short time, and this may in fact prove to be in a relatively junior post, it seems more likely that those who claim to be in a terminal position will fall into the older range of the teachers interviewed, and are more likely to be occupying mid-posts or top posts in a school.

Those who state that their present posts are terminal

Present post	Male	Female	Age	Male	Female
Assistant teacher	3	2	21+	0	0
Graded post	1	1	26+	0	5
Mid post	10	7	36+	2	1
Top post	5	3	46+	17	7
Total	19	13	*Total*	19	13

How would you advise a late entrant to the teaching profession to plan his or her career?

The consequences to a school of an aging staff is likely to be profound when it sets out to design and implement a scheme of staff development. Do you agree?

* Lyons, G., *ibid.*

4. APPRAISAL___

4.1 Appraisal is a damning word.

It does not seem in the least surprising that wide ranging schemes of appraisal are seen to be threatening by the teaching profession, as damaging to their individual as to their professional integrity. It would be much neater to remove the word and replace it by 'review' which is much closer to the spirit of the intention. However, the crucial point is that staff development must be based upon the right sort of information, and this information has to be collected—and in a large organization this means in a 'bureaucratic' manner.

One of the fundamental planks of any programme of staff development is that it must rest upon an appraisal. Accordingly, it is vital that staff, at all levels, agree to being appraised, that they see it as developmental and not restrictive, and above anything that they do not feel *it is staff inspection*. The only way to create this attitude is for all staff to demonstrate their willingness to participate and this should include the head teacher's participation.

The problems then raised are of course: who assesses the most senior members of staff and arranges their development programme; and the need for developing LEA wide programmes because of the limit to what any one school can accomplish.

What is it, do you think, that the school should attempt to assess? Clearly, the answer lies in the use to which they intend to put the information they have collected.

Should a school collect information about a teacher's personality traits; about the professional performance of his duties? . . .

What do you think?

What are the views of the teachers' organizations on this point?

4.2 How should a school collect 'information' about its staff?

Schools successfully manage to perpetuate themselves, to recruit and promote staff and so forth, in fact virtually all senior staff in schools at this time are products of the existing system. What clearer indication can you need that the existing system is viable and does not need changing? Or does it?

Ask the head teacher how he learns about the performance of a junior member of the English faculty.

Ask the head of English the same question.

Ask the junior member of staff concerned.

What do you think you will learn by a comparison of their answers?

As the school becomes larger it is clearly impractical to expect one man, the head teacher, to have a detailed knowledge of the performance of individual teachers. He cannot get round the school any more, he cannot see or hear the noisy classes. Listening over coffee cups, listening over lunch, is no longer a reliable source of information. It is not immediately apparent that middle management staff in the school understand or, in fact, want to take on responsibility in this area. Nevertheless, decisions have to be made, references written, staff recommended for secondment, promotion, and so forth. It seems to make sense therefore to do rationally and systematically that which is being done unsystematically.

4.3 The history of assessing individual needs is fraught with peril in many different types of organization, and a considerable amount of resistance has developed, as a result of the methods which may have been adopted. The school might attempt to use:

(i) *A personnel audit:*

A record to be kept for each member of staff containing at least the following information:

> age, qualifications, experience before joining the department, experience since joining the department (including publications), courses attended, extracurricular activities, curriculum development projects participated in, and so forth.*

This audit needs updating regularly.

What does the staff record card in use in your school look like? Perhaps members of your group or syndicate would like to provide illustrations of the record sheet in use in their schools, or of those in use in local firms, colleges, the local authority, and so forth.

(ii) *Performance appraisal*:

The following guidelines are suggested:

(a) Each staff member to write a description of his present post using an objective-orientated standard format;

(b) Agree the job description with head, section head, or departmental head;

(c) Agree standards of performance and specific short-term job-related achievement targets related to department plans;

(d) Review performance standards and achievement targets at regular intervals;

(e) Training needs are identified in phases (c) and (d) when appropriate action is agreed and initiated. They may be related to individual needs (the desire for the individual to extend and develop himself); or job-related needs (the need to develop or acquire new knowledge, skills, expertise in order to progress some part of the 'departmental' development plan); thirdly, and probably more commonly, training needs will be a mix of individual and job-related needs.

* Davies and Newton, *ibid.*

(iii) *Potential appraisal*:

The purpose of potential appraisal is to assist each individual member of staff to realize fully his potentialities as an educationalist quite independently of allegiances to particular institutions.

You might adopt the following strategy:

(a) ** Each staff member is invited to draw a career line on a graph. One axis represents time and the other, level or function (for example, head of department, and so forth). This line should be both historical to date and projected to the future. In those many cases where members of staff have been employed in industry before entering teaching, 'level' could be related to salary on termination of each employment. The line when drawn represents an explicit statement of career to date and to the individual's future career expectations. As such, it forms a basis for:

(b) a discussion with nominated senior staff or others at appropriate levels who may help or guide the individuals concerned. The point here is that potential appraisal needs to be carried out by people with knowledge and experience of the level to which the individual aspires.

The graph becomes a revealing way to discusss the individual's future, e.g.:

— did you have difficulty projecting your career line to the next post?

— what do you see as your terminal post?

— what alternatives are open to someone at your career point with the experience and qualifications that you have?

— what are necessary pre-conditions to achieve your next 'desired' post?

— what is to happen where organizational and individual aspirations for any one individual are not in harmony?

** Markwell and Roberts, *Management Career Planning*. Quoted by Davies and Newton.

What is the best career stage to adopt this approach, do you think?

Discussion points

The nub of the whole system will lie in assessment. Because of the burden of effort this will place on a school, the major part of assessment must, after the initial targets are agreed for each individual, rest upon self reporting. Is this ever likely to work in a school, do you think?

Having made an initial appointment most subsequent appointments are made from within 'a school'. What implications does this have for staff appraisal?

On the formal appraisal interview rests one of the fundamental planks of any programme of staff development. No one should have the responsibility of undertaking an assessment interview until they themselves have been interviewed by a superordinate. Do you agree with this view?

How long do you think it will take for a staff development programme to work through the school on this basis? The time lag could, of course, be shortened by including all new teachers into the programme from the start.

How would you recommend a school to cope with the following—all of which are likely to be associated with the appraisal interviews?

Ensuring that everybody does not jump on to the boss's favourite subject area;

Ensuring that the head's least favourite areas are undertaken;

· A junior with far more competence than the senior interviewing him;

Two members of staff who have so little respect for each other that the interview is conducted in only the vaguest of generalities.

The formal appraisal interview is a danger to the system and should never be tolerated. Do you agree with this opinion?

5. HOW DO YOU HELP INDIVIDUALS?___

Matching organizational and individual needs is a tricky business if one is to ensure that an individual is not subordinated to the overwhelming pressures of an organization. It is necessary to build a bridge between the two.

But what constitutes a good bridge?

It almost certainly will lie in the quality of interpersonal relations that exist in the school—counselling is possibly one way of formalizing this, and the head's style of leadership is clearly another important element.

Does the head need to adopt a role of 'counsellor' before this knitting together of organizational and individual needs can take place? In fact, is this the most important role for the head of a school to undertake? Can anyone else in the school offer this type of help?

5.1 The career needs of any individual teacher will be compounded from an amalgam of:

the motives that brought him into the profession;
those elements of his job from which he derives satisfaction;
his terminal (or next) goal;
plus those direct pressures upon him which are part of his environment but which are external to the school, e.g. family and financial requirements, the location of the job, and so forth.

Motives for entering the teaching profession (ranked)*

Q. What made the teaching profession attractive to you?

Academic/subject interest	45 mentions
Enjoys contact with children	43 „
Enjoys actual teaching process	29 „
Family history of teaching	23 „
Generally liked job, disliked alternatives	21 „
Altruistic reasons—a worthwhile job	19 „
Suggested by others	18 „
Always wanted to be a teacher	16 „
Working conditions (hours, holidays, pay) ...	14 „
Job security	11 „
Best career for a married woman	8 „
Drifted into teaching, no particular reason ...	8 „
Secured a safe job in the 1930s	7 „
Was aware of career possibilities for teachers ...	6 „
Status of profession	6 „
Admired own teachers at school	4 „
Wanted intellectual stimulation, contact with colleagues	2 „

These motives show no significant variation between graduates and non-graduates, for both of which the rankings of the first ten categories are nearly identical.

5.2 Should a school attempt to reconcile the unfulfillable career ambitions of its staff? If not, then whose responsibility is it?

Teachers' ultimate goals*

	%
Top posts (in school)	21.3
Multi-goal	18.9
Other educational	17.2
Terminal	15.6
Don't know	10.7
Mid posts (in school)	9.0
Non-educational	5.7
Asst graded posts (in school)	1.6

* Lyons, G. *op. cit.*

This table reveals that just over a fifth of the sampled teachers were aiming for top posts in comprehensive schools. It is apparent that the number of teachers who hold such posts in the country does not amount to anything like this proportion of teachers in general. Indeed in the schools which contributed to the sample the ratio of more junior to top posts approximated to 17:1, and it is against this background of fierce competition that the preceding and following discussions of factors affecting promotion must be set.

Just under a fifth of teachers interviewed were categorized from the point of view of their ambitions as being multigoal. These were teachers who were unable at the point of time when the interviews took place to decide between two or more clearly visualized goal positions:

'I could become a headmaster or I might go into a college of education as a lecturer.'

Generally the picture which emerges shows the young teacher at the beginning of his career as being uncertain as to the goals to which he may reasonably aspire. He may perhaps have some ideas as to the type of post he wishes ultimately to hold, but be unable to choose between various possible goals, and if he does choose, he will apparently set his sights low on the educational ladder. As he gains experience and his first promotion, however, the path ahead becomes clearer; his situation is, perhaps, analogous to that of a man climbing a mountain: at first he can see the distant summit, and he can see the path immediately in front of him—what he cannot see is the course of the path all the way up the mountainside, its branchings, twists and turns, and the disused paths which once led to the top, but which have been carried away by the landslide of educational change. When he reaches the top, too, he may find that there are other, higher peaks beyond, to which he may aspire; he may rest there; or even start down again preparatory to climbing another mountain nearby. The latter point is one of crucial relevance to those who achieve a headship in their thirties and ask of themselves what they may expect of the post for another thirty years.

5.3 The degree of satisfaction or dissatisfaction the items mentioned below give to the teacher in his/her present post.*

	PERCENTAGE				
	Very satis- factory	Quite satis- factory	No reaction	Unsatis- factory	Very unsatis- factory
Contact with pupils					
Security in job					
The actual teaching process					
Degree of personal responsibility and independence					
Relationships with colleagues in a similar position					
Working conditions, hours and holidays					
The sense of personal achievement					
The administrative content of the job					
Salary prospects					
Time to pursue personal interests					
Opportunities for professional advancement					
Recognition by the community					
Time to pursue academic interests					
Recognition for work well done					
Total					

The shaded sections show the proportions of teachers who find the statements given in the vertical column 'very satisfactory', 'quite satisfactory' . . . etc.

*Lyons, G., *op cit*

Although the number of items singled out by the interviewed teaching staff as being a source of dissatisfaction is not disproportionately large, any source of dissatisfaction must be of concern to a school.

It is worth considering a hypothesis that these sources of satisfaction or dissatisfaction will vary according to a number of predictable variables, e.g.:

— the older the teacher, then the more likely he is to find the administrative content of the job a source of satisfaction, and vice versa.

Would you agree?

Could one source of dissatisfaction have been that poor or incomplete information was given to candidates at the recruitment stage, and that this could have been avoided? See, for example, Appendix 1 and 2, recruitment of teaching staff.

6. OPPORTUNITIES AND TRAINING

6.1 A wide variety of training opportunities must be available if an appropriate choice is to be made for every member of staff, at each stage of his career. Although each opportunity will undoubtedly have a specific aim they must be seen collectively as a spectrum from which careful and appropriate selection can be made: moreover, although one approach may be right for one member of staff, the same purpose may be achieved for another by using quite a different method. It is stressed that the nature and timing of training should be related to the outcomes of performance appraisals (which are themselves linked with departmental development plans) and potential appraisals. The training needs thus identified, within the context of the organization, will be concerned with acquisition, development, and maintenance of knowledge and skills. Training provision can be on-job or off-job.

6.2 Methods of staff development will include:

Induction training:

The need for induction training is becoming more widely recognized although this has largely centred on the needs of probationary teachers. In this lies the beginnings of a coherent programme of staff development.

In-service training:

Possibly the main source of staff training and development that presently exists. It usually implies attendance on courses mounted by agents external to the school, thus the 'off the job'

training situation automatically entails all the problems of transferring the knowledge or skills gained into the 'on the job' situation.

Secondments:

(To work in other institutions;) rarely occurs in schools (apart from secondment to attend full time courses), although occasionally those involved in, for example, giving careers advice may have experience of working in industry. Much greater use of this type of secondment could be profitably used by schools. As a means of training it is still in its infancy.

Consultancy:

In many schools skills and experience are built up which could most profitably be deployed in the wider educational system. Generally, the nearest that the educational system ever reaches to harnessing this expertise is to invite a member of staff to give the occasional lecture on an in-service training course.

Job rotation:

As part of the planned training programme of any individual teacher, and also to avoid staleness.

Interchange between establishments:

It appears to be unthinkable in the educational world. Clearly underpinning any coherent programme of staff development is the involvement and the participation of the LEA itself. However, recognition of the need for this type of training need not wait for LEA initiation and the basis of a lively correspondence with the CEO is readily to hand.

There are many other forms of training, providing they are used in a planned way to develop a member of staff:
research, project work, participation in working parties, and so forth, are amongst them.

It is the constructive use that the institution makes of these potential means of training that is the crux of the matter.

6.3 Training needs questionnaire*

The following list of information forms the basis of a questionnaire to be used in a review of a manager's training needs as a short term solution to the problem where no formal appraisal scheme is in operation. If an authority prefers to interview all or some of its officers who have a considerable management function, the list could also provide the framework of the interview.

PART 1: This information will only be required where there is no adequate system of training records:

1. *Personal details*

Name

Age

Post and grade

Posts held while employed in local government—when, with which council and at what salary grade

Posts held while employed outside local government

Are there any health or other factors which affect the officer's mobility? (e.g. is there anything that would prevent his attendance at a course which involved being resident away from home or being sent on a temporary secondment?)

2. *Education*

Qualification(s) taken before completion of full-time education

3. *Qualifications*

Qualification(s) of an administrative or managerial nature taken since completing full-time education

Qualification of the above type being taken now

Qualification(s) of a professional nature taken since completing full-time education

Qualification(s) of the above type being taken now

4. *Courses attended*

Courses associated with a qualification where no qualification was obtained, give reasons (e.g. 'qualification failed', course taken for interest only', etc.)

* The above is taken from the initial document 'Management Development, Local Government Training Board, Training Recommendation 2, 1969, Appendix 2' produced by the Board. An area which the Board has subsequently developed.

Courses dealing with an appreciation of specialized techniques (e.g. network analysis, work study, etc.) used in management, but not associated with a qualification

Courses dealing with the development of managerial skills, but not associated with a qualification

5. *Application of skills*

What projects involving development or appreciation of managerial skills has the officer been engaged on? Give all projects whether or not they were associated with a course or a qualification previously mentioned.

PART 2: This section seeks an evaluation by the officer of his past training and his proposals for future training. Both opinions are expressed from two viewpoints: the officer's personal ambitions regarding his development as a manager; the managerial demands made by his present job considered in isolation from his personal career.

6. *Evaluation of courses*

Which of the techniques you have learned about on courses do you use in your job?

How often do you make use of the techniques?

Have any of the courses greatly increased your own management expertise without concentrating on particular techniques?

Which course would you like to repeat?

Which courses were too short?

Which courses were too long?

7. *Specialist professional work*

Which aspects of the specialist side of your work do you find most demanding?

Do you feel that you need any further training to assist you in meeting these demands? If so, do you already know of any course, conference or special experience which would meet this training need?

8. *Managerial work*

Which aspects of the managerial side of your job do you find most demanding?

Are you, as far as you know, employing all the management techniques which might help to ensure that the work within your area of responsibility is being carried out as efficiently as possible? If not, would you be in a position to employ more techniques if you were trained to use them, or to supervise their use?

Do you feel you need any further training in management skills and techniques to enable you to do your present job better? If so, in which particular field should this training be? Do you require merely an *appreciation* of the skills or techniques concerned or an ability to *use* them?

Do you feel you need any additional training to enable you to take up a more senior post than your present one? If so, what sort of training do you need?

Do you feel you need any further training to meet anticipated changes in the organization of your authority or the methods in use (e.g. a Maud type re-organization or the introduction of, say, a computer)?

Some discussion points

The relationship between the school's and the LEA's responsibility for staff development is likely to be tenuous, since the basic provision of resources must come from the LEA. Although the LEA can delegate substantial responsibility to an individual school the sanctioning of, e.g. in-service training, is likely to be retained as their responsibility, unless it can be in school based. But it is self-evident that the school cannot cope with all needs: it lacks flexibility in terms of the opportunities of job rotation; a school cannot develop its own head teacher; it lacks the resources to cope with a 50-year-old on a scale 5 who is tired of teaching and so on; so if the school cannot legitimately satisfy the aspirations of all its staff; then in fact who is to do what?

What would you imagine to be the principal reasons why teachers would seek in-service training? Are the reasons you have advanced likely to be mediated by: the age and length of teaching experience of the teacher concerned?

It is an extremely important question to determine the proportion of the organizational resources and endeavour that should be devoted to the staff development task. With the resources that are available it is difficult to free staff—to go on training courses, or be employed in other developmental tasks and so forth, and to deploy the resources to back up the outcome of such activities.

In your view, what is the approach most likely to minimize problems of resource allocation and the logistics of staff release?

7. PROMOTION___

7.1 To the staff of a school the whole of the training or development programme is likely to be condensed into the issue of selection and training for promotion. It is contentious, competitive and therefore needs to be objective.

The following table is a reformulation of a list of questions used by Hilsum and Start. Look at the items in the list.

1. Qual in teacher-shortage subject
2. Being a graduate
3. Familiar with new educ ideas
4. Ability to control pupils
5. Expertise in partic subject/method
6. Administrative ability
7. Good relationship with head
8. Concern for individ pupil welfare
9. Experience in variety of schools
10. Flexibility in teaching methods
11. Participation in extra-curr activities
12. Willing to move to other areas
13. Attending in-service courses
14. Having strong personality
15. Being younger than 40
16. Length of teaching experience
17. Participation in innovative practices
18. Good relations with other staff
19. Contacts with influential people
20. Success with exam candidates
21. Publications (textbooks, etc.)
22. Conformity with inspectors' views

23. Participation in civic activities
24. Being native to area of post
25. Experience outside education
26. Being a parent
27. Having taught in area of post
28. Being married
29. Being a man
30. Experience in HE/FE etc.
31. Long service in partic school
32. Being a woman

The above table is a reformulation of a list of questions used by HILSUM, S. and START, B. (1974) in *Promotion and Careers in Teaching*. Slough: NFER.

Should a school be influenced by such views in devising its staff development programme?

Do you judge people for promotion, or give them information on promotion prospects?

7.2 From the original sample of 122 teachers,* 31 teachers were separated as top communicators** (i.e. the top quartile). Of these, 12 occupied top posts (head teacher, senior mistress, head of section, etc.) and 19 teachers who appeared in this group had communication scores that showed a departure from the scores of their peers. The groups thus formed were subjected to statistical and qualitative analysis of their responses.

When the career ambitions of these sub-groups of the total sample were examined in greater detail it was apparent that those with 'high' communication scores were more likely than any other group of teachers to have a clear idea of that senior position in school for which they were ultimately aiming.

* Lyons, G., *ibid*.
** For a further discussion of 'communications' in school—see the chapter in this book on 'Communications'.

	High Communicators	All Others
Professed ambition for a top post	13	14
Professed other ambition	18	77

This matrix yields a chi square value of 9.458, significant at the 1 per cent level. It should be noted that 'Ambition for a top post' means a *named* senior post in a secondary school, and that 'Other ambitions' may include those who were unable to decide between alternative senior posts in schools. The interpretation of this table is therefore as follows:

Those whose communication scores are notably higher than expected are more likely than other teachers to have a clear idea of that senior position in school for which they are ultimately aiming.

What other career and personality attributes might you ascribe to this sub-set of high communicators?

7.3 The examination of the promotion rates of the different experience groups suggests that teachers are promoted faster at the beginning of their careers than they are later, although there are several complicating factors which may mitigate the significance of this finding:

1. Although all teachers start at the same level, the attainment of a post such as, say, head of science, may be reached by several different routes involving different numbers of promotion jumps, where the jumps themselves are of different magnitudes.

2. Promotions early in a career are commonly small ones, e.g. from assistant teacher to a Scale 2 allowance; whereas promotions later in a career may involve a much greater leap, e.g. from head of science to deputy head.

When the rates of promotion of teachers are considered from the point of view of their present status, there is no significant difference between the groups, again because of the wide variance in each group. It is apparent, however, that although years' experience and status are closely related, top post teachers appear to have arrived at their posts more rapidly than their mid-post experience peers.

It seems then that the career of the average teacher is characterized by rapid, small promotions at the beginning of a career, and longer intervals later. For the teachers now holding top posts, however, it appears that the early, rapid promotion rate is maintained for a longer period.

If such progress is not achieved, then there appears to be a strong chance of the teacher being passed by and this is one reason why teachers who become aware of their career possibilities relatively late in their teaching lives may, in fact, have become aware of an unattainable goal.

7.4 How do you determine fitness or readiness for promotion?
The outline attached below is taken from the recommendations of the Engineering Industry Training Board.

A METHOD OF REVIEWING MANAGEMENT RESOURCES
The process of determining future management needs will have assembled much information about individual managers and about their place in the organization. It will help in succession planning and in reorganizing if the information is displayed in a form which shows up the areas of strength and of weakness. A simple way of doing this is illustrated on the next page.

KEY to illustration on following page.

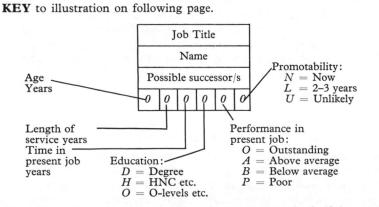

Note: Strengths and weaknesses will be illustrated more clearly if the panels are coloured according to a simple code, e.g. Red = Now, Green = 2–3 years, Yellow = Unlikely.

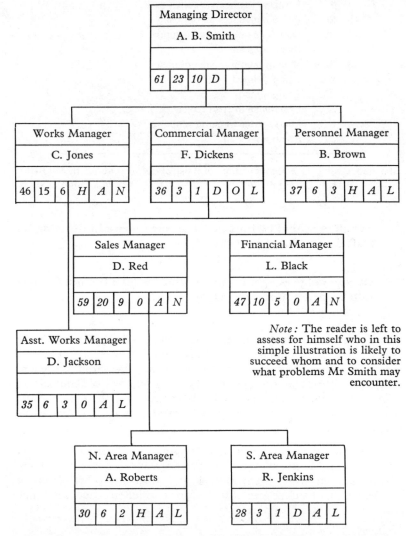

Note: The reader is left to assess for himself who in this simple illustration is likely to succeed whom and to consider what problems Mr Smith may encounter.

From: *Training Managers on First Appointment*, Booklet 19. Engineering Industry Training Board, 1973.

154

7.5 How do you determine 'fitness' or 'readiness' for promotion?

A number of sources have suggested that probably the most effective (and least disruptive) method of selection for promotion is rating by one's 'peers'. Clearly, if 'peer rating' were to be adopted and effective in a school then it must rest upon other than an ad hoc basis. The guidelines for procedures should be known to all and should be laid down by the staff themselves.

Attached below is the recommendation of a staff working party of a large secondary comprehensive school that was concerned with this issue.

Would their proposals fit the needs of your school, do you think?

STAFF APPOINTMENTS ABOVE SCALE 1

FINAL REPORT OF A STAFF COUNCIL SUB-COMMITTEE

On 1st December the Headmaster posted a list of 'Staff Appointments above Scale 1'. Subsequently, the sub-committee of Staff Council was set up to consider what criteria should be used in making such appointments. An interim report was discussed by Staff Council on 18th June of the following year, and the head master was interviewed a week later. This final report takes account of these discussions. It is suggested that this final report be the basis of a Staff Association discussion in the autumn term.

Points that were considered

1. In this context democracy should be interpreted as *responsible government* rather than rule by plebiscite.
2. The system that operates shoul be *clear to all, fair to all*, and seen to be both.
3. As far as possible staff should be rewarded according to their present value to the school, rather than on the basis of past performance. We recognized, and defined, the criteria of *responsibility* and *excellence*.
4. *Market forces* (e.g. national shortages of teachers in certain subjects) may necessitate the spending of extra points so as to attract suitable candidates.
5. Some colleagues feel that their talents are not well-recognized or fully appreciated. They should have ample *opportunity to present their cases* and, if rejected, hear why. Only if they are aware of their shortcomings are they able to act upon them.
6. Some colleagues feel that there are obvious injustices in the present distribution of points. The injustice may be real or imaginery—the feeling is certainly real and might be alleviated by *better communication*.
7. Our ideals could only slowly be effected.

Recommendations

1. The 'points cake' should be broken down into three parts. A large part should be distributed for *responsibility* in the traditional way; a second part should be awarded for *excellence;* and a small third part should be retained for *parochial flexibility*.
2. We recognize, and would reward, three different kinds of responsibility: academic, administrative and pastoral.

   Academic responsibility—We define the unique role of a head of department as 'ensuring the effective working of all members of the department'. (This might be the basis of a very worthwhile discussion). A rough measure of this responsibility is the number of persons in the department and we suggest an initial allocation of 1 point per person. The distribution of these points within the department should be discussed by the Headmaster, his immediate advisers, and the particular head of department. The results of these discussions should be publicized and should state specifically what responsibilities have been rewarded at each level.

   Administrative responsibility—We include here responsibilities such as audiovisual aids, examination entries, library, minibus. The headmaster, his immediate advisers and the particular member of staff should discuss the merit of each case and set down specifically the responsibilities and their rewards.

   Pastoral responsibility—We recognize the continuing state of flux in this field. We suggest for the present situation 6 points per year group. The distribution of these points should be discussed by the headmaster, his immediate advisers and, if there is one, the senior group leader. Responsibilities rewarded should be specified clearly.

F

3. *Excellence*—We would reward all those contributions which make a school more than a simple well-functioning machine, including commitments to teaching duties, to pastoral duties and to the general service of the school.

Particular commitment to teaching duties—This might involve the following: time spent on developing new courses and resource material, appraisal of published schemes and their suitability for the school, attendance at in-service training courses (particularly those outside teaching hours) and the like.

Particular concern for pastoral duties—Some colleagues do very much more as group leaders or form teachers than might ordinarily be expected.

General service to the school—We would include here such contributions as considerable help out of school hours with sport, music, drama, visits, etc., service as teacher-governor, work with PTA, etc.

Award of points for excellence—The two possible routes should be:
  (i) commendation to headmaster by his immediate advisers, heads of departments or senior group leaders;
  (ii) personal application to headmaster by those who think their particular merits are overlooked.

It could often be beneficial to those who are rejected to discuss the reasons.

4. A few points should be held in reserve so that the headmaster may 'buy on the market' in times of scarcity.

5. A list of 'Staff Appointments above Scale 1' should be published annually with comments on the responsibilities or excellence rewarded. To allay rumour and gossip, and to enhance general staff morale, all internal promotions should be quickly publicized and justified.

6. A copy of each newspaper advertisement relating to posts at the school should be displayed in the Staff Room.

Vaguely statistical appendix

There are about 115 points spent on the upper school and middle school site, and about 45 points on the lower school site. (The lower school is from the next academic year to become an entirely separate school).

For the upper and middle school situation at present we would allocate:

(a)	Responsibility points:	Academic (c. 60 staff)	60 points
		Administrative	7 ,,
		Pastoral (4 year groups)	24 ,,
(b)	Excellence points:		20 ,,
(c)	Parochial flexibility		4 ,,
		Total:	115 points

Presented to Staff Council on 16th July

7.6 What are the organizational implications of this report of the Staff Council?

If a programme of staff development was seen as a mechanism by which the headteacher sought to impose his will upon the school then such a programme would be doomed to failure. If there is a tacit acceptance of the aims of such a programme amongst the staff, then this would be the time to proceed slowly. It is necessary that they accept it upon their own terms.

It is likely that this is far more of a collective exercise than is normally current practice in schools in this country; perhaps the involvement of a body such as a staff council is a prerequisite for any steps in this direction. A report like the one presented above provides the basis to build upon. Do you agree?

The discussion should go on from here.

Some discussion points:

Should there be in a school an expected promotion ladder?

Should criteria for promotion be spelt out publicly in terms of qualifications, ability and experience?

  (a) How far should the school and the staff spell out their mutual obligations and expectations of each other, particularly about expected performance, training and development?

  (b) Is the interview the best place to do this?

  (c) Should these obligations and expectations be published in a document such as the staff handbook?

  (d) What, in fact, is the function of the staff handbook in a staff development programme?

(e) Do you think graduates are likely to be promoted earlier and further than non-graduates?

(f) In your view, does taking a further professional qualification correct any imbalance in the respective careers of graduates and non-graduates that you may have noted?

(g) What type of post would you realistically recommend a non-graduate teacher to make his career peak?

(h) Should a school recruit for long or short-term goals? If recruitment is for short-term goals, how should a school deal with the possibility of staff becoming redundant to the needs of the organization; and

(i) Would a career structure allowing the free movement of staff between school types, LEAs and tertiary education resolve this dilemma?

(j) Could two or more schools share in the appointment of a member of staff?

(k) What system of liaison would be needed in order to accomplish such a joint appointment?

8. RESPONSIBILITY FOR THE STAFF DEVELOPMENT PROGRAMME_____

8.1 'There can be little doubt that the head teacher is not only the proper person, but is the person that staff will naturally turn to for help, and for advice, about their careers. It is simply a non-sense to believe that another member of staff, however designated, can go to a colleague and say "Now, isn't it time you were looking for promotion?", "doing something about your career?"

'In my school I make it clear that I am the one responsible for careers advice, or equally I am responsible for recommending and selecting staff for promotion, and for staff recruitment.

'I use one of the junior members of staff, a young man on a scale 2 post to publicize the availability of in-service courses. He is keen, he does a good job, and he can draw the attention of his colleagues, senior or otherwise, to relevant courses without in the least appearing threatening to them.'

—Head teacher of a large comprehensive school.

8.2 A case history

Male, single, age early fifties.

Qualifications

1. Ministry of Education Certificate in Art & Crafts.
2. National Diploma in Design.
3. University Institute of Education Certificate in Education.
4. University Certificate in Counselling.
5. University Diploma in Education.

Experience

1. Assistant master, sec. modern school, art and general subjects —5 years.
2. i/c Arts and crafts, sec. modern school—3 years.
3. i/c Art and acting housemaster comprehensive school—7 years.
4. Unemployed.
5. Temporary posts, private schools—2 terms.
6. Assistant teacher secondary modern school—2 years.
7. Housemaster, comprehensive school—to date.

It is suggested that, in the initial stages, apart from some original difficulty in gaining entry to a certificate course (because of a lack of A-levels) the above represents a fairly normal career profile. However, towards the end of the third post mentioned above, a mixture of unfortunate family bereavements compounded by apparently intransigent attitudes on a head teacher's part, caused intense personal difficulties. The LEA did not prove able to offer help, suggesting a thick skin as the most powerful ameliorative. The teacher concerned offered his resignation, which was accepted. The head teacher refused to provide either a reference or a testimonial. Unemployment and a succession of temporary jobs followed. Very severe difficulties were experienced in re-obtaining any employment and, as time went by, interview panels became more and more suspicious of him as a candidate.

A proffered loan from one of the teachers' associations enabled him to enter university as a self-supporting student to study for a diploma. A hall of residence tutorship allowed him (almost) to make ends meet.

The year at university fortunately enabled him to obtain references and he was subsequently offered a permanent post in a comprehensive school. An appeal had to be made to the Department of Health and Social Security to enable him to live between the finish of the university course and the beginning of the new school year.

Do you agree with the following?

The power concentrated in the hands of head teachers is too great when this allows the power to damn a member of staff completely and to ruin a career.

That there may exist an ambivalent attitude on the part of head teachers and LEAs to awarding secondment.

Teachers should be able to take up an offered post when it is mutually convenient, and the insistence on starting a job only at the beginning of a term is too inflexible.

There is need for a staff welfare officer in all large schools.

There should be a panel that standardizes, within any education authority conditions of service, and this panel should be able to consider appeals from teachers.

Since there is a demonstrable need for teaching staff to have provided for them a counselling/pastoral service, who, in your view, should provide this help?

Would it be the LEA adviser? Should surgeries be held in the school, or in the local teachers' centre?

9. IMPLEMENTATION of a DEVELOPMENT PROGRAMME

At the beginning of this chapter in section 1, we looked at the opportunities which a staff development programme appeared to offer to a school. It should by now have become apparent that the implementation of a staff development programme is not necessarily easy.

CHECKLIST FOR A STAFF DEVELOPMENT PROGRAMME

1. Has the organization a 'manpower plan'? In detail is the following information readily available:
   (a) An organization chart?
   (b) Precise job descriptions for all posts shown on the organization chart?
   (c) An estimate of future staff requirements for five years ahead?
   (d) A training and development programme, designed to meet the estimated staff requirements?
   (e) A genuine assessment of the impact on these detailed plans of such imponderables as technological advance, sociological changes, and other local, national, or 'industry-wide' factors?
   (f) A procedure for keeping the manpower plan under constant review, so that it is flexible above all else?

2. (a) Has the organization 'personnel policies' which are written, published, and fully understood by all?
   (b) Does a clearly defined policy and procedure for 'promotion' exist within the organization?

3. Have the following been resolved?
   (a) Seniority or merit as the basis for promotion?
   (b) The extent to which senior appointments shall be filled internally or by recruitment from outside?
   (c) Providing members of 'promotion boards' with full job descriptions, and their training in selection and assessment techniques?

4. Is 'training' reviewed positively throughout the organization as the best means of increasing the productivity of all grades of staff?
   (a) Are training needs assessed effectively in the first place, priorities settled, and the standards defined?
   (b) Is a development programme then established for each individual likely to benefit from further training?
   (c) Does the organization provide its own training officers by withdrawing staff from line management for short periods?
   (d) Are those responsible for training and job instruction properly qualified in the relevant techniques?
   (e) Are those who return from outside courses positively encouraged to apply the techniques learned and to develop new ideas?
   (f) Are results of all training efforts followed up and evaluated?

5. Are individuals provided with precise job descriptions?

6. Are they properly inducted into the organization when they start? Especially staff coming from industry?

7. Are standards of job performance clearly laid down with measures of control?

8. Is there a regular formal assessment of how well these performance standards are being realized?

9. Are staff kept aware of research findings about the behaviour of individuals at work and the ways they function in groups?
   (a) Is the organization willing to participate directly in research work in this field?
   (b) Do staff know how to promote 'job satisfaction' and remove the 'frustrations' which individuals experience at work?
   (c) Are senior members of staff readily accessible to their subordinates?

10. Are the principles of 'participative management' encouraged within the organization?
    In particular:
    (a) Do staff agree 'targets' with their superiors for improved performance?

(b) Is special attention given to 'enlarging the jobs' of individuals, and is the application of this concept discussed with them by superiors?

(c) During performance reviews do staff help to identify 'organizational shortcomings' which hinder progress?

(d) Does the organization run a 'suggestions scheme' to encourage individuals' ideas?

11. Have senior members of staff been trained in an effective procedure for dealing with 'individual staff problems'?

Derived from *The Theory and Practice of Personnel Management* by M. W. Cumming. Quoted by Anderson, D. K., Coombe Lodge, 1972.

SOME COMMON ERRORS AND PROBLEMS MET IN THE STAFF DEVELOPMENT PROGRAMME

Perhaps the most fundamental and natural error is to see a staff development programme as too streamlined and mechanical. Quite the reverse, however; it is a sign of disorganization to overload staff who are in responsible positions, to appoint them prematurely and to fail to brief them adequately for a complex job, to select them without due regard for a job's requirements and challenges, to delegate duties and responsibilities without providing authority to make decisions, to send responsible people on courses before they can use the resulting information or expertise, or to set up a new structure of organization (and promote people into it) with inadequately specified tasks and functions. Creativity, freedom of professional expression, and opportunities to develop school relationships favourable to worthwhile learning are not inhibited by explicit and specific organization and planning, but given a stable, predictable context to operate in—and in education above all, this is surely vital.

Typical operational problems and errors include:

(a) Parochialism, over-administration, and other constraints on schools' autonomy. Parochialism tends to relate appointment to a job to other than the job specification's criteria: over-administration to over-standardize criteria for selecting, staffing structures, promotion and selection procedures—and admittedly this is often produced by pressure from teachers' organizations themselves, seeking 'fair' practice. It takes additional skills, in the head and top management of the school, to get the appointments, staffing structures, the personnel and training programmes they need, when parochialism and over-administration are powerful: too often the pseudo-political needs of such situations make them distort their own preferences, and styles of leadership and decision, and there is a danger that this may end by damaging their own credibility to the people who work inside the school for them.

(b) Lack of capacity at top management level. In cases where the top management is overloaded, or of inadequate capacity to cope with its load, thorough staff development and MBO formulation will almost certainly not occur; and even partial plans will not be consistently followed through. Staff will not receive the support and the confidence they need, often at (for them) crucial moments. The situation which occurs between an overloaded top and an inadequately briefed and supported middle management is in the nature of a vicious circle. This may be where external Advisers, consultants LEA support (including office/clerical support) and HMI advice can perhaps help.

(c) Settling for wrong or inadequate MBO structure of objectives and organization, particularly where this contains no assessment capacity for feedback and adjustment of programming. Staff may be wrongly briefed and trained, and aware of it. A faculty structure which does not meet the major challenges of curriculum development, or of the organizational design requirements for the school, particularly at its intake and tertiary sectors, or a guidance set up which is not effectively aligned with RoSLA needs, or delinquency problems, or assessment and progression schemes; these will put great stress on a school's executives if they are too rigidly set up for adjustment, especially in their early stages. This may be an argument for not appointing middle management executives or even for using temporary 'rotating' responsibility posts or team systems in situations containing too much innovation challenge.

(d) Incomplete analysis and communication of the MBO, which may produce the tendency typically in large organizations for different elements to see themselves as working to opposed or inconsistent briefs. Some organizational designs, especially those which sharply separate academic from guidance sectors, may lend themselves to this. But even within the guidance sector, inconsistencies between objectives relating to discipline, authority, teacher-pupil relationships and counsellor-pupil relationships often occur; and staff development in such a context is likely at best to be somewhat vague, at worst quite frustrating.

(e) Getting the timing wrong. This can take a variety of forms, for example starting in the middle by sending heads of departments and heads of faculty off on training courses while long and medium term objectives are still vague and without consensus; making key appointments before starting the staff development process; or before an effective personal or professional evaluation is available; or appointing the key staff to new organizational positions before considering the nature of the contraints they impose, and the accommodation and resources they may have to accept.

(f) There are difficulties for schools, in situations involving a great deal of change (for example in going comprehensive), in planning and structuring the work so as to create effective learning situations. Setting these up for the wide array of executives and other teachers to have adequate opportunities for personal and professional development at times when the school is changing rapidly may induce insuperable problems of planning, control and timing. This is an argument for organizing the rate of change, and phasing it over longer periods involving less intensive problems of timing.

(g) One of the greatest challenges in implementing this kind of planning and operational control is to the capacities of the top management itself. The chief problems appear to be difficulties in communication, for example in gaining consensus on detailed breakdowns of overall or global objectives, and in getting staff to accept and be involved constructively in techniques for appraising performance against objectives. Again at various executive levels, lack of experience in the processes of staff development and the over-riding problems of transfer of training and the learning of executive skills may make for difficulties of both communication and operation. Experience in the field of industrial training has shown, for example, that lack of skill and confidence in and of willingness to embark on, the kind of counselling and coaching work necessary between an executive and his immediate subordinate are often the crucial difficulties. This kind of problem too is an argument for gradual change in large organizations, rather than the adoption of the 'cataclysmic' approach to innovation in school organization.

From: PETER C. WEBB, HMI, 'Staff Development in Large Secondary Schools', *Educational Administration Bulletin*, **2**, 1, 1973.

10. OVERVIEW_____

Each school must make up its own mind whether or not it is to set up a programme of staff development. Once it has taken this step it must accept responsibility for its implementation and for the allocation of enough resources to the programme to ensure its continuing viability. The fundamental nature of the decision cannot be stressed too strongly for there is a serious need to re-examine at the highest level some of the issues which are raised. It might well be the case that programmes may not prove to be viable until they can be constructed upon an LEA wide base—to ensure the richness of experience and inter-changeability of posts that may be required, or, at a national level even, since the existing pattern of payment of teachers' salaries may prove a considerable hindrance, and there is equally a clear need to involve teachers' unions.

The unilineal nature of a teacher's career and its ever increasing specialization, the naivety of the employing situation which rests upon the view that classroom contact, giving satisfaction at the age of 22 will still be doing so 40 years later, the lack of inter-changeability between different sectors of the educational world, and those ever present old chestnuts—that promotion is out of the classroom, and, that the reward for teaching excellence is apparently promotion into administrative posts for which the teacher concerned has neither proven predisposition nor training are all factors in urgent need of examination and resolution.

Although there is clear evidence that the whole area of development of staff is generally neglected in the educational world, and that the situation is thus wide open to exploitation by those who are intent upon their own promotion it is not self evident that teachers will want schemes of staff development applied to their schools. 'Staff development described in programmatic terms could appear to be threatening and working against firmly held and traditional attitudes within the profession, particularly against the professional autonomy of the teacher to do his own thing in his own way in his own classroom. In this context isolation can be seen as security.'* The models for programmes of staff development that are available are not tailor-made to the needs of schools. It may well be that schools are unique institutions but it seems shortsighted to reject out of hand the experience that is provided; by industrial firms, professional organisations, from commerce, hospitals, and so forth, until models designed specifically for schools emerge.

This document is designed for no other purpose than to provide the basis of a discussion about programmes of staff development in a school. It does not present a model programme which schools can implement; such a programme does not exist. It is the hope that schools will begin to develop them.

It would appear to be a long and uphill task for staff to be persuaded that the adoption of a scheme of development will not only prove of benefit to themselves, but will best serve the interest of their school and the children they teach. The need is urgent enough. Perhaps anywhere is a good enough place to start.

Points for general discussion:

Is it within any sort of commonsense boundary to expect schools to develop forward looking programmes of staff development when they are financed annually by a task master who reserves the right to review the monies available and the headings under which they are allocated?

Staffing in the large secondary school is a function of Burnham scales and not of organizational or individual needs that may exist in a school. Do you agree?

The present system of staff recruitment and development relies very much upon a small group of staff who do not necessarily have any formal training in: interviewing, techniques of counselling, recruitment, and so forth. Does the large school, in fact, need a personnel department?

Staff development appears to prize the teacher out of the professional isolation and security of his classroom into the full professional view of his colleagues. Do you agree?

* A. J. Light, *ibid.*

Increasing militancy amongst teachers, and a potential move to have salaries paid by central government, could well see nationally determined duties for a given rate of payment. Would this be the death knell to a school's programme of staff development?

Can a school afford to concentrate solely on programmes for its teaching staff? To give coherence to its programme is it not vital to take into account the needs of ancillary and auxiliary staff in the school?

Is the school concerned with teacher development or with executive development?

What feedback is likely to come from the programme of staff development and is this likely to be what schools are looking for?

What do you think is the minimum size for an institution to have any hope of success with a programme of staff development and training?

Should a school feel disappointed about its staff development programme if a teacher decided to leave the field of education entirely?

How should you counsel and advise a member of staff to turn his back upon classroom teaching and go into administration?

It seems as though one of the most commonly held opinions expressed by teachers in the large school relates to their willingness to accept the existing pattern of hierarchical organization and the decision making structure that accompanies it:

The school must have a boss, they say, someone must be there to carry the can should things go wrong. Certainly teachers like to be consulted, but they do not want to make the important decisions and certainly not those concerned with staffing. Under these circumstances, is it, in fact, feasible to develop an effective programme where such a programme must rest upon the decisions of the committee the school itself sets up to determine its overall policy? Teachers do not want to be involved at this level; they want to be told what to do. Does your experience accord with this viewpoint?

The school is a unique institution and staff development models derived from other sectors are unlikely to be applicable. What we are looking for are ways of executive learning in the teaching situation. Do you agree?

Of what use is a programme of staff development to the children?

APPENDIX 1: PATTERNS OF STAFF RECRUITMENT___

One of the single most important items of any programme of professional development is that of staff recruitment.

'Teaching staff are not fixed assets (although in budgetary terms they might be so regarded), it is easier to change buildings than it is to change the attitudes and functions of members of staff.'

—Director of a Polytechnic

This document portrays several different aspects of staff recruitment that were in operation in the sampled schools.* It does this in order to draw attention to the wide variety of practice that exists and to stimulate discussion. The document does not purport to advance model schemes whereby the large school may recruit staff.

* LYONS, G. (1974) *The Administrative Duties of Head and Senior Teachers in Large Secondary Comprehensive Schools.* University of Bristol.

VARIATIONS IN RECRUITMENT PATTERNS

(1) Staff Recruitment: Procedure adopted in a particular School

There are a number of distinct phases in this operation so far as this School is conerned.

Phase 1 At the beginning of each autumn term the Headmaster and deputy head talk over possible staffing needs for the following September. Discussions are then held with senior staff (heads of departments) and tentative conclusions are reached. The deputy head explained that it has been necessary to start in this way, because since 1969 the numbers on the school roll have risen by approximately 100 per annum. The county education authority has reorganized this steady increase in numbers and has always been prepared to receive applications for an increase in staffing.

Phase 2 Following on the staffing discussions and the decisions made, negotiations with the county authority are then commenced, the headmaster working through the chairman of his governing body. The county authority is always somewhat argumentative about the proposed staffing increases for they are fearful of appearing to be too generous and then having the school quoted as an awkward precedent. A final decision is generally reached about the numbers of extra staff required by the middle of March, and this quite obviously is based on a realistic assessment of incoming numbers from the contributory primary schools and any evidence that may exist about increases in pupils because of new housing.

Phase 3 Once the overall staffing increase has been decided upon the school is left to decide its priorities so that appropriate advertisements can be inserted in the *Times Educational Supplement*. The school itself submits an appropriate draft for the *TES* advertisement but this must be sent through the county education authority office.

Phase 4 Completed application forms for individual posts are sent to the headmaster who arranges with the chairman of his governing body for an appointments panel. As these are permanent appointments to the staff a county official must always be present. Inevitably this is always a county local inspector or adviser in the appropriate area for which the appointment is being made. The headmaster makes his short list after taking advice from the chairman of the governing body, the deputy head, and the head of department concerned.

Phase 5 The interviews are so planned that the candidates have an opportunity to see the school and to talk to the staff. Once the interviews are over the governing body recommends the appointment of the selected candidate and it is left to the county authority to confirm this, subject to certain requirements such as medical examination, satisfactory records of previous service etc.

When posts above Scale 1 are involved and an internal promotion is going to take place the headmaster makes a recommendation to the governing body, after consultation with his deputy head and the senior master. This recommendation is submitted to the county authority and sometimes they have proved to be a little awkward about the recommendations made. However, since the headmaster is now so well established instances such as these are becoming less and less frequent. Generally speaking, he has a considerable amount of freedom to manoeuvre in this field. Internal promotions such as these are a delicate matter and if wrongly handled can cause unpleasant rifts in the staff common room.

When short term appointments are being made because of illness or some other absence, the headmaster and the deputy head are given a completely free hand. A suitable candidate can be appointed immediately with the approval of the chairman of the governing body and the appropriate forms are filled in then and sent to the authority office. This, however, only applies to short term supply appointments which may be either on a daily basis, weekly, or for a term.

(2) Staff recruitment: Procedure adopted in another school

(a) The head teacher works closely with a small sub-committee of the governing body and quite obviously is given considerable freedom.

(b) The first notification of an impending resignation or the need for a new post is made to the LEA staffing officer at county hall who initiates the insertion of an advertisement drafted by the head teacher.

(c) Applications are received by the head teacher's secretary, who lists and summarizes details of each candidate.

(d) The head teacher prepares a short list after close consultation with the senior staff concerned and candidates are interviewed by the head teacher and governing body staffing sub-committee. The interview is so arranged that all the candidates have time to see the school and meet the Head and relevant heads of departments concerned with the particular appointment. When senior appointments are being made the candidates are invited for the morning so that they can see the school, talk to staff and pupils before the formal interview in the afternoon. A representative (LEA official) only attends when their presence is deemed necessary by the head teacher who may wish for specialist advice over some particular post.

THE PROCEDURE FOR THE RECRUITMENT OF A HEAD TEACHER TO A SECONDARY COMPREHENSIVE SCHOOL

(1) LEA Area 1

Preliminaries A head due to retire realizes that it helps the LEA to know of his intention well in advance, and he intimates this informally. No action can be taken until his letter of resignation is received. The governors are then consulted, and the advertisement is then put into the educational press.

Procedure on receipt of applications Three or four people on the administrative staff attempt to put the applications into 'some sort of logical order'. The Articles of Government require that a committee, consisting of an equal number of governors and representatives of the LEA, draw up a 'long short list' but in practice this is done by the administrative officers and one governor. At this stage confidential reports are obtained on those whose names are on the list and their own referees are written to. The LEA do not read open testimonials as they regard them as valueless. In the past the people whose names are on the long list have been interviewed and a short list drawn up subsequently but this is not invariably done. Alternatively, the governors, including the chairman of governors, may reduce the long short list to a short list of six.

Short list interviews The Joint Committee as defined above carries out the interviews and recommends an applicant for appointment by the LEA. The committee does not meet before the interviews to discuss policy but the county education officer speaks to the candidates before the interviews. He enlarges on detail already supplied and deals with purely factual information. No official arrangements are made for candidates to see the school before interviews although this may well be done in the future. In practice most candidates arrange personally to see it by contacting the school themselves.

The *criteria* which the authority apply are only vaguely defined but in brief they are as follows: good experience including comprehensive school experience is looked for, limited range of experience would be regarded as a disqualification, promising deputy heads of comprehensive schools would be highly regarded, only an exceptional person who had had no experience of working with less able pupils would be appointed, graduate qualifications would be looked for implicitly rather than explicitly, and normally a person over 50 years of age would be excluded from the long short list. Considerable note is taken of the general educational principles of each candidate. Specific factors related to specific situations are important; for example, for a school which needed new and vigorous leadership, a young man would be sought. Local factors, such as the marked musical tradition of the area, its welfare needs, and public use of the school premises, would be very much in the minds of the LEA officers and of the governors.

At the interview, the chairman would say a few words 'to put each candidate at ease', the county education officer would then lead off with questions, anyone else could follow, and finally the LEA Inspector would question the candidate. The committee would then meet in private, the final three would be decided upon, confidential reports would be read, discussion would follow, a formal proposition would be made, and a vote taken. Usually a unanimous vote is necessary before an appointment can be made.

Handing over It is left entirely to the outgoing headmaster as to what he does about handing the reins over. The head teacher elect is expected to spend about a week in the school before taking up his appointment, and the LEA makes a request to his employers to release him for the necessary period.

When the new head teacher assumes office, the LEA inspector is a key person to him/her. The head teacher would meet the inspector in his office for a preliminary informal talk and would go direct to him with any problems. The LEA do not issue a handbook of guidance but a new head teacher would be expected to discuss proposals for change with the LEA inspector before embarking upon them. Once he has built up good relations with the governors, he would discuss changes with them also. The LEA officers keep out of head teacher/governors' relationships.

General points Only in one area of the county does the authority offer any help in the matter of *housing*.

The Governors of the school have various sub-committees which include members of considerable ability. There are normally able people on governing bodies of secondary schools including the chairman and vice-chairman of the education committee.

There are strong political currents in the town.

Applications for the headship of a large secondary school are made on the common application forms, without amendment, such as any teacher would complete for any teaching post.

(2) LEA Area 2

Stage 1 The chief inspector, after consultation with his inspector colleagues in the office and particularly the local district inspector for the school, compiles a concise summary about the appointment. It states clearly why the vacancy has arisen, gives factual details about the school, the salary attached to the post, so that all intending candidates have a preliminary picture before making their decision to submit an application. This summary of factual information is sent out to every candidate who requests an application form.

Stage 2 As applications are received they are quickly reviewed by the chief inspector, and a secretary has the task of listing and summarizing the details about each candidate. These give information as to age, qualifications, the present employment of the candidate, and a concise summary of teaching experience.

Stage 3 From these applications a long list of 12 candidates is prepared, and the chief inspector quite obviously spends a time over this in close consultation with his colleagues. He frankly admitted that he never reads open testimonials, but every effort is made to follow up references about each candidate that are known to be reliable, the educational world being such that in a large authority the chief inspector and his colleagues cover a very wide network of good contacts so hardly any difficulty is experienced in getting first-hand frank information about the candidates to be included in the first long list of twelve.

Stage 4 This long list is then submitted to a small schools executive committee and they have the task of reducing this to a short list of six candidates. In this they are guided by the chief inspector who obviously plays a very positive role indeed at this critical stage. The schools executive committee is quite high-powered, comprising the chairman of the education committee, the chairman of the school building committee and one or two deputy chairmen. All are people of standing on this committee, with a considerable knowledge of the educational world. It is clear that all these stages described are gone through without any reference to the governing body of the school at all; not even the chairman of the governors apparently figures in this preliminary screening.

Stage 5 The short list of six candidates completed, the governing body is then asked to interview and a date is fixed. Two days are devoted to the actual appointment. On the first day the six candidates on the short list spend the day in the school, looked after by the present Headmaster. At the end of the day the chief inspector makes it his business to seek the views of the headmaster to see how he had reacted to the candidates. The following day is devoted to the actual interview which is timed to start at 10.30 a.m. It is interesting to note that the chief education officer does not come into these appointments at all, other than receiving a formal summary about the six candidates on the final short list. Full responsibility rests with the chief inspector who guided by his colleagues and his knowledge of the particular school carry through the stages described above.

These further pieces of information were confirmed by the chief inspector:

(i) Nothing can be done about advertising a post until resignation is received in writing. When it is a case of retirement the education authority quite obviously knows from its own records that retirement cannot be long delayed, and very often the district inspector for the school will make polite inquiries. However, when a headmaster is moving to another post he is free to resign as and when he is appointed by his new authority, and this may well result in an interregnum when the deputy head has to take over.

(ii) There are no formal arrangements for the handing over of a school to a new headmaster, this is left very much as a professional matter between the outgoing head and the incoming candidate. It is assumed that the new man will spend some days at the school before taking up office.

(iii) The governing body interview quite obviously varies from school to school according to the quality of the individual governors, though one must never rule out the valuable 'horse-sense' of the governor who may not apparently know much about education but can recognize a good man when he sees one; this is probably one of the fundamentals of British democracy. Quite often most of the relevant professional questions at an interview are asked by the chief inspector or the district inspector for the school. Many of the governors never ask anything at all but do their best to assess the qualities of the answers given.

(3) LEA Area 3

'I applied for the headship of a Group II comprehensive school in South Wales catering for the 11–16 age group. I was shortlisted and invited for interview at the education office. I was not given an opportunity to see the school and was provided with sketchy details about its accommodation, curriculum and staffing.

'When I arrived at 9.30 a.m. I discovered that there were 12 candidates for two schools, the other being an 11–18 comprehensive. By 12.30 all 12 candidates had been interviewed and two new headmasters had been appointed. In addition there had been a coffee break.

'Each candidate was greeted by the chairman on behalf of the committee and was asked to answer two questions typed on a small piece of paper:

'What difficulties would you expect to meet in a large comprehensive school and how would you deal with the main ones?

'What kind of non-academic courses would you establish in the sixth form of a comprehensive school?

The chairman remarked that several more candidates were to be seen and that short answers would be appreciated.

'I write this letter with no feelings of bitterness because I became the headmaster of an excellent school within three months of this experience.'

—Aristides, *Times Educational Supplement*, 10.3.72

* (Published by kind permission of Times Newspapers Ltd.)

How would you appoint a headteacher

The most important appointment to make to a school is that to the post of headteacher. On the strength of the evidence that you have seen above, and together with the additional experience of those in your group or syndicate, what procedure can you propose that will result in the appointment of the most suitable candidate?

You might wish to offer your advice on the following points.

What personal qualities are absolutely essential for successful headship?

how would you determine that the candidate had these qualities?

would you recruit for an existing job or for a future job, in fact how would you determine what the school's needs are?

what groups or bodies would you consider it essential to approach for their views?

how would you seek the advice of the staff of the school?

who would you invite to participate in short listing?

to sit on the interviewing panel?

who in your view should make the appointment?

how long should you spend with the candidates . . . and so forth?

Does the procedure you have outlined vary in any striking way from the procedure which to the best of your knowledge is the one adopted in your LEA?

What is your reaction as a teacher to the information that your prospective headteacher has, to date, chosen to have his children educated outside of the comprehensive sector in direct grant, public or independent schools?

METHODS OF RECRUITING A NEW MEMBER OF STAFF

Two contrasting approaches

An education authority with no policy of appointing counsellors to its schools seconded one of its teachers to a Diploma in Education counselling course and when she returned considered where she could be best employed within the school service. They decided to offer her services to the school in their area which had the greatest interest in pastoral care and since the head was offered this addition to his staff, above quota, he readily accepted. The appointment was made in the last week of the Summer term and there was no opportunity to introduce the idea to the staff before the end of the term so that at the staff meeting at the beginning of the new academic year the head presented her to the staff as a full time counsellor appointed to deal with the personal problems of the children who would be invited to consult her. Now the staff of the school were very concerned with the personal problems of the children and prided themselves upon the caring reputation of the school and the housemasters and mistresses who were given a generous allowance of time and money for their work interpreted the appointment as a vote of no confidence in their abilities. The insecure counsellor did nothing to clarify her role or reassure the staff, indeed she seemed unaware of the resentment against her and since her motives were purely to help staff and pupils one can understand her naivety. She had a miserable time in the school, was under-employed, had several unpleasant interviews with house staff who resented 'their' children consulting her and were infuriated by her refusal to disclose details of her interviews with individual children. I talked to several of the house staff about the appointment and these quotations are typical.

'The counsellor will usurp the power of the house staff.'

'The pupils will play one against the other manipulating the counsellor to support them against the legitimate authority in the school.'

'House staff do not wish to be relegated to a punishing job while the counsellor appears as the kind person who is always sympathetic.'

None of these opinions was warranted, but what was important was that they were believed and acted upon until the counsellor, reduced to a distressed state of mental health, resigned her position and returned to class teaching in another town. It is sad that staff pride in pastoral care was not extended to a colleague and that the local authority have not repeated the experiment of appointing a counsellor to one of its schools.

Contrast this with the action of another head who, informed by his education authority that he could appoint a counsellor, called a full staff meeting and invited his teachers to discuss whether such an appointment was desirable and if it was, how such a person could best be used within the school. Having accepted the principle of a counselling appointment, further meetings were held to define a function and it was agreed that the school could best be served by a director of studies who would concentrate upon educational guidance. An appropriate advertisement brought in over 200 applications from which the head and senior staff made a shortlist of six. The head explained to the staff that since the appointment was for their benefit they should make the final choice and the shortlisted candidates spent a day in the school meeting the staff, accompanying them to class lessons, talking over coffee and lunch and free periods. After school that evening there was a full staff meeting, chaired by the head at which the decision was made to appoint one of the candidates.

At first this counsellor taught half time in the school so that he could understand the staff problems and be accepted by them as a competent colleague but as his work has grown and extended beyond the initial educational guidance function so his teaching time has been reduced. This counsellor is so valued and happy in his school that he is reluctant to move away although his qualifications and experience would fit him for a headship and the staff of the school have nothing but praise for the success of 'their' appointment.

Quoted from WILLIAMS, K. (1973) *The School Counsellor*. London: Methuen & Co. Ltd.

You might like to consider the following:

(1) Ascertain how your own school organizes its staff recruitment programme. In undertaking this programme, does your school take any major factors into account additional to those already noted?

(2) Compare the strategy of your school for this task with that adopted by other schools known to you or represented in the discussion group. If there are any differences in procedures, are these attributable to factors such as school size, or are they differences of principle?

(3) Can you, with the other members of your group, devise the outline of a more effective programme of staff recruitment that would more pertinently suit the needs of your school.

APPENDIX 2: A STAFF RECRUITMENT EXERCISE

INSTRUCTIONS FOR THE USE OF THIS SECTION

The recruitment exercise

This section is designed to form the basis of a recruitment exercise.

Against the background of either a real or a simulated school and for a post determined in advance, the group (or syndicate) should do some or all of the following: assess the job; produce a job and man specification; devise an advert; devise an application form; conduct shortlisting and so forth. If the group intends conducting simulated interviews then it should be arranged for them to have 'real' candidates. (Many teachers and students are glad to volunteer since it gives very realistic practice in being interviewed). If this is what the group intends then it is necessary for application forms to be devised and completed in advance of the exercise. To make the exercise as realistic as possible the candidates should be themselves and not attempt to represent fictitious characters, and, the application forms should be treated as strictly confidential and be destroyed as soon as the exercise is completed.

The group (or syndicate) should determine for themselves, the method(s) by which they wish to conduct the interview, and, the membership of the interviewing panel. In practice it proves rewarding to divide the panel into two halves allowing one half to function as observers. They can thus make a more accurate (and objective?) assessment of the candidates, and also comment upon the panel's interview performance should this be desired. The panel should be given total responsibility for conducting *all* aspects of the interview and this would include greeting and entertaining the candidates, setting out the interview rooms, and so on.

The course tutors' role should be that of observers.

Once the panels have made their selection for the post, comments in plenary session from course tutors on their rating of the conduct of the interviews invariably provides a very rewarding basis for discussion. It is equally rewarding towards the end of the plenary to re-introduce the candidates, this time to give their version of the interviews.

The interview simulation allows considerable scope to use closed circuit television should this be available.

'Bishopston School' provides a convenient background for the recruitment exercise.

Introduction

The appointment to your school of a member of the teaching staff, aged 25, at a salary of £2,500 per year, involves a potential minimum investment of £2,500 per annum for the next 40 years. You may well have committed a sum in excess of £100,500.

Does one 20 minute interview provide a sufficient basis to form a judgment and make a successful appointment?

How carefully have you determined the spending of this money?

Is it plausible that you could spend £100,000 on a building programme, for example, quite so easily?

We are concerned with what *we* can do *now* to improve the recruitment and selection procedure.

The recruitment and selection procedure inevitably implies a training procedure, possibly as its most important constituent. Staff recruitment and staff development are essentially constituent parts of the same process.

Considerable variations will be found between schools in the organization of their recruitment procedures, and in the practices adopted by different LEA's. Many schools do not have full control over their own staff recruitment procedures. In these cases, responsibility for recruitment may lie with the governors, or the LEA itself, and further variations exist according to the grade of staff to be appointed—the recruitment of a head teacher to a school usually calling for an entirely separate set of procedures.

Further information to illustrate these points and the range of practice in existence can be found in Appendix 1 of this chapter.

Assuming however that the school has been given a considerable measure of freedom in the recruitment of its staff—it has been suggested that the following are the steps that it will need to take:

1. Assess the job.
2. Attract a field of candidates.
3. Assess the candidates.
4. Make an appointment and induct the new staff member into the ongoing programme of staff development.

Staff recruitment is a complex process that involves time and teamwork.

1. Assessing the job

Is it an existing post that has fallen vacant? or

Is it a new post that has been created by the institution identifying future needs?

If it is the former:
Does it need to be filled?
Can the resources it releases be better diverted to other areas?
Can it be combined with any other job?
Can it provide useful training for an internal promotion?
Is it likely that a candidate will be easily found for the post?

In your opinion, what body in the school should make decisions of this sort and, should the decision vary with the seniority of the post involved?

Should teachers be involved in decisions of this type in the first place do you think?

What is the policy of your own school on this issue and what variation can you find amongst the experience of those in your group or syndicate?

In the light of decisions made, the organization should:

(i) Produce an updated job specification.

(ii) Produce a man specification, that is, a specification of the qualities and qualifications of a person who can perform efficiently the requirements of the job as shown in the job description.

Presented below is a job specification taken from the staff handbook of a large secondary comprehensive school for a Head of Department's post.

Does this in your view represent an adequate job specification?

If you feel it is inadequate, what amendments would you propose?

THE SUBJECT DEPARTMENT

From a School's Handbook

1. The subject department is the key instrument in the school in its vital academic role. It consists of all members of staff teaching a particular subject. Where a member of staff teaches more than one subject he may attend all the department meetings concerned. The purpose of the department is to strengthen and improve the

teaching of its subject for all academic levels by all the means it can devise.

2. It will be led by a *head of department*; members of a department may be given specific responsibilities by the head of department, and where a subject has many separate branches e.g. science or technical, members of staff may be responsible for a particular subject within the department. Every subject teacher is responsible to the head of department for the content, method and effectiveness of his or her teaching.

3. *Responsibilities of heads of department*

   (a) Responsible to the headmaster for the organization and teaching of the subject throughout the School.

   (b) Responsible to the headmaster for the teaching standards of the members of the department—for ensuring that teaching is effective, preparation sound and marking thorough.

   (c) Responsible for ensuring that new members of staff are settled in the school and are informed about school matters, general as well as departmental.

   (d) Responsible for ordering equipment, requesting estimates and keeping a list of stock. Orders should be sent to the bursar as set out on the back of the order form.

   (e) Responsible for advising the headmaster of the timetable needs of the subject—numbers of periods, use of rooms, disposition of staff.

   (f) Responsible for the preparation of a scheme of work for the subject throughout the school and keeping it up-to-date. Ensuring that this scheme is followed, and that members of the department work towards common standards of presentation and marking.

   (g) Responsible for planning any courses, visits, special activities in connection with the teaching of the subject.

   (h) Advising on and organizing 'out of school' activities connected with a subject e.g. English—libraries, magazine, literary competition; Geography—Geography Society; field study courses; Music—music at assemblies, choir, orchestra, etc.

   (i) Responsible for encouraging a team spirit within the department, passing on to the Headmaster the views and suggestions of colleagues, passing on to them decisions taken and matters discussed at heads of departments meetings.

   (j) Advising the headmaster on examination policy (external and internal) in connection with the subject.

   (k) Responsible for allocating pupils to groups and sets, and providing the headmaster with lists of these.

   (l) He will be responsible for advising and assisting students attached to his department.

   (m) He will work closely with careers staff where he may have specialized advice to offer, and with year tutors where the academic progress of a pupil needs to be considered.

   (n) He will chair the departmental meetings held once every 3 weeks.

So often job descriptions are little more than a list of tasks. Look at the job description for a head of faculty presented on the next page. Some of the fundamental differences between this job description and the one above for the head of department is that it gives evidence of 'performance indicators'—'I know how well I am doing in the job'. It allows a school to gauge much more accurately the sort of person they are looking for to do the job, and the likely training needs of the successful candidates.

2. Attracting a field of candidates

ATTRACT

INFORM

IMPRESS

IMPEL

Your Advert

Do you as a matter of course place all adverts on the staffroom notice board?

Does the LEA circulate to all its schools notification of all its posts that are becoming vacant?

Do you advertise locally or nationally, and which newspaper or journal gives the best return?

How best do you sell your school?

What should you include in your advert, how should it be laid out?

How can you best describe your school, its curriculum methods, and provide a job description to potential candidates?

Sample Job Specification—Head of Faculty

Arising, or derivation	Description and Analysis of Job	Training specifications
(1) Organizational structure	*Title:* Head of Faculty of . . . *Reporting to:* Headmaster, Academic Board *Direct involvement with:* Heads of other Faculties, Heads of Departments, Academic Board, innovatory groups *Scope:* Primarily curricular, records system, staff planning	
(2) MBO	*Functions:* (i) Define policy for faculty: values, objectives, aims teacher development, curriculum development, resources (ii) Plan development, phasing, access to resources (iii) Consult with heads of faculties, guidance heads, co-ordination of policies, plans, assessment, records (iv) Consultation and policy making with heads of subject departments within faculty (v) Responsibility for staff/teacher development within faculty, appointments, probationers (vi) Estimates co-ordination (vii) Control of standards; exams/assessments records (viii) Organization of functions overall within faculty: implementation of plans	
(3) from (1) & (2) above	*Qualifications, Skills, Attitudes, etc.:* (i) Education: graduate? Dip Ed? proved professional competence and experience (ii) Administrative capacity, thoroughness, executive skills, persistence, communication and PR skills (iii) Planning, co-ordinating skills, constructive and creative skills, attitudes (iv) Insight and scope of professional knowledge, flexibility of ideas, breadth of information, up-to-date knowledge (v) Skills in discussion, presentation of ideas, analytical capacities, committee competence, capacity as communicator (vi) Negotiation skills (vii) Personal qualities, leadership, diplomacy, sympathy, understanding. High personal standards, objectivity, persistence	(i) Professional upgrading qualification (ii) Admin/managerial training programmes and on the job rotation etc. (iii) Training programmes in planning techniques (iv) On the job training programme (v) Training in communication skills (vi) As for (v) above but with emphasis placed upon skills needed for negotiation and conciliation (vii) Management training, executive development
(4) Main effectiveness areas	*Performance indicators and assessment basis to be accepted and measures agreed:* 1. Organizational effectiveness of faculty as a whole: e.g. degree of acceptance of faculty its aims and goals by staff, clear plans agreed, resources adequate for task in hand, etc. 2. Scheme for staff training, guidance, and development agreed and in operation. 3. Effectiveness of co-ordination with other faculties determined. 4. Clear lines of communication established for contact wth other sections of school, particularly pupil welfare, and to parents, pupils and the wider community. 5. Adequacy of the modes chosen to review and assess curriculum agreed, etc.	

Adapted from WEBB, Peter C. (1973) 'Staff Development in Large Secondary Schools', *Educational Administration Bulletin*, 2, 1.

Bring examples of current adverts appearing in the press for jobs in industry, education, local government, etc., to your group or syndicate. Which of these most succinctly gives:

Key characteristics of the job and man specifications?

Information on the school and salary?

Which is the most successful advert?

What are the reasons for this, do you think?

Which is the best advert?

3. Assess the candidates

The selection process involves a study of the background and history of the applicant through:

(a) the application form
(b) shortlisting
(c) references
(d) interview(s)

and may also involve a measurement of attitudes, traits, etc.

(a) *The application form*

The application form should help to measure the applicant against pre-determined standards, and should be constructed to serve this purpose, not to collect a host of details.

The application form should be designed to help you short list.

It might also serve a secondary purpose, that is, to act as a framework for interview.

The following have been suggested as a checklist of possible headings for an application form:* .

Surname
Christian name
Marital status
Sex
Address
Telephone number
Age, date of birth
Health
Superannuation

* Anderson, D. K., *ibid.*

Education—secondary, further and higher with dates, examinations, certificates, diplomas, degrees (chronological order)
Teacher training details including DES number
Membership of professional institutes/learned societies with dates, grades, associated activities
Publications
Courses attended

Teaching experience. Complete chronological record with subjects taught
Administrative experience
Examinerships

Non-teaching experience. Complete chronological record with names of employer, title of post, duties and responsibilities

Service with HM forces

Particular details of present post: date commenced, salary, required notice, duties and responsibilities

Leisure interests

Referees

Letter of application

Would you add to, or remove any items from this list?

(b) *Shortlisting*

You may have determined the relative importance that certain criteria may have to the future development of your organization and wish to weight them at shortlisting.

The following* is presented as an example of the sorts of weighting that you may wish to be influenced by. *There are of course many other criteria that could be relevant to a post.* If desired, a score could be made upon an 'Interpretation Table'. Such a weighting can provide a helpful balance and be a useful counterweight to hunches.

Some suggested items to include in a weighted application blank:

The school should determine those items it regards as important to the successful performance of the post and personal qualities it desires amongst its staff and weight accordingly.

* BELL, F. E. (1969) 'Improving the efficiency of departments in technical colleges', *Coombe Lodge Occasional Paper.*

Age			Score		Education	Score
21–26	...	...	2 pts		Secondary comprehensive	2 pts
26–37	...	...	4 ”		Grammar school ...	3 ”
37–45	...	...	2 ”		College or university	
Over 45	...	...	0 ”		Graduate:	
					Pass degree ...	3 ”
					Hons degree ...	4 ”
Experience			**Score**		Master's degree ...	5 ”
Totally unrelated	...		0 pts			
Related	...	...	2 ”			
					Marital status	*Score*
					Married	4 pts
No. of jobs in					Single	3 ”
last 5 years			*Score*		Widowed ...	3 ”
1 ...	...	...	4 pts		Divorced/separated ...	1 ”
2 or 3 ...	...	...	3 ”			
4 or more	...	...	0 ”			

One suggested interpretation table for above.

Score			Interpretation
28–32	...	...	Favourable
21–27	...	···	Questionable
14–20	...	···	
7–13	...	···	Unfavourable
1– 6	...	···	

At what stage of the recruitment process should the criteria for shortlisting have been fully determined?

If you have determined to exclude; non-graduates, those younger than 29 or older than 38, married women with children of primary school age—why didn't you put this in the advertisement in the first place?

How would you justify to an applicant that he is being excluded at shortlisting by sets of criteria which are not being revealed to him?

STAFF SELECTION

The NAS have recently expressed disquiet at the great significance in the processes of selection for posts in schools of the confidential report of a candidate's headmaster. We can understand that a teacher whose relationship to his headmaster has not been wholly amicable may well feel uneasy about the degree of support which he may receive when seeking another post but we cannot suggest any method of avoiding this difficulty. Schools are justified in seeking the most reliable information they can obtain about candidates for appointment, especially in view of the great security of tenure which teachers enjoy. Headmasters go to great lengths to ensure that their confidential reports are fair and that the virtues of teachers are fully described. In large schools, particularly, they are likely to consult senior colleagues rather than rely entirely upon their own judgement.

—Extract from 'The government of schools,' a report from a working party of the Headmasters Association, 1972.

(c) *References*

It seems to be a general opinion that open testimonials are quite worthless. A personal reference can act as a check against an applicant's statements and can give information not otherwise discernible. But you can assume that the applicant will only give the names of those who have a good opinion of him. Will the referee give a reference good enough to get rid of the candidate or poor enough to keep him?

It is possible that you could be sued for misprepresentation

Is the telephone, therefore, the most effective way of providing information on candidates?

For the purposes of internal promotion, or for the production of a reference:

Who makes a report on you, (what do you think they look for) and, who would actually write the 'reference'? Is the above likely to be varied according to the level of staff concerned? Conduct a straw poll amongst your colleagues in the staff room for their views.

In your opinion:

1. Should the potential employer take up a reference from the existing employer whether or not the candidate has used him as referee?

2. If you are acting as a confidential referee to a colleague, should you always be willing to discuss with him the reference you have produced?

3. Apart from the head teacher, which other member of staff of a school might act as your referee?

4. At what stage of the process would you call for references?

5. If you have produced a 'good' job specification, have done your shortlisting properly and used the interview to select the man you want, bearing in mind all the above problems, what is the point of the reference?

The interview

The successful conducting of an interview is a complex task that calls for a considerable measure of expertise and experience, and, since it is a topic of such importance, it is also one of much contention.

It is highly desirable to base any decision taken in an interview situation upon as much objective evidence as is available and to be aware of the subjective nature of many judgments which are likely to be made.

The objectives of the interview should be clearly determined. It should be ensured that the candidate is suitable for the post, that he has been given an accurate picture of the job for which he is to be interviewed, and that all candidates are given a fair hearing.

It is suggested that the following are amongst the most common hazards to be met in interviewing:*

(a) brief, ill-prepared, unsympathetic interviewing;
(b) inadequate application forms—interview time spent on 're-covery questions';
(c) interviewer talking too much—less than one-third of time desirable;
(d) interviewer failing to establish rapport;
(e) interviewer asking leading questions—problem of the ultra-sympathetic interviewer;
(f) interviewers 'points scoring' off each other;
(g) excessive prompting of interviewee;

* Anderson, D. K., *ibid.*

(h) making too many generalizations about the interviewee too soon;
(i) the interviewer attempting to assess too much in the inter-view;
(j) time wastage by undirected interaction;
(k) out of context interpretation of given statements;
(l) failure of interviewer to *listen*;
(m) expressing disapproval of any statement/response by the interviewee;
(n) 'rushing' the 'flow of conversation';
(o) ambiguous/lengthy/multiple questions;
(p) comparison with stereotype;
(q) interviewer unaware of his own limitations as to his ability to assess certain traits/qualities, e.g. honesty, integrity;
(r) answers to interviewer's pet questions assuming dispropor-tionate weighting;
(s) not using language which is appropriate for the candidate;
(t) interviewer unaware of his own bias, etc. . . . and 'halo effect'. For example, there exists a common bias towards certain physical characteristics;
(u) the way the interview room is set out may prove critical.

RELIABILITY OF INTERVIEWING (2)*

1. Sixteen university graduates were interviewed by two boards of 4 or 5 eminent persons, including two professors, a chief inspector and a headmaster of a public school.

2. Each interview lasted 15–30 minutes.

3. The board had to assess: alertness; intelligence; intellectual outlook re 'value of personality for a Civil Service job'.

4. Members of each board gave a mark to each candidate. He was then discussed and an average mark agreed on.

5. The marks of the two boards for each candidate were then compared.

Extract from table to show the two Boards' ratings of candidates

Candidate	Board A Rating	Board B Rating
A	1	13
B	11	1

* Bell, F. E., *ibid.*

If there had been 6 vacancies to fill, 5 of the six recommended by Board A would have been different from those chosen by Board B.

As a way out of the dilemma of subjective bias (and recording), an interview rating chart might prove useful. The following is presented as an example. Other headings more appropriate to specific interviews could be added to replace headings presented here.

INTERVIEW RATING CHART*

	Excellent	Good	Average	Mediocre
1. *Physical*				
Health				
Appearance				
Manner				
Energy				
2. *Intelligence*				
Mentality				
Education				
Thoroughness				
Judgment				
3. *Personal*				
Initiative				
Self-reliance				
Persistency				
Tact				
Ability to gain respect				
4. *Value of services*				
Previous experience				
Accomplishments				
Willingness to assume responsibility				
Helpful to others, etc.				
Overall rating				

* Bell, F. E., *ibid.*

There are many different ways in which an interview can be conducted, but fundamental to any interview is that both interviewer and interviewee are wishing to communicate information about each other and to assess each other for suitability. In one sense, therefore, the best way to establish rapport is for the interview to be protracted and carried out on a one to one basis.

This plainly makes economic nonsense.

Construction of the panel

How should the panel (interview board) be constructed by a school?

Who would most profitably appear on a panel to appoint a second deputy head?

Would the same panel be most suitable to appoint a head of department? In fact, would the appointment of the various heads of departments require a differently constructed panel for each appointment?

Who would most profitably appear on a panel to appoint a Scale 1 teacher?

Would you ever involve parents, pupils, the secretarial staff, the caretaker, and so on, in decisions on appointing teaching staff?

Methods of conducting interviews*

1. *Regulated or patterned interview* (see details on page 176).
    (i) Contains no question relating to job skill.
    (ii) Attempts to measure aspects of personality, e.g. industry; motivation; stability; self-reliance.

    Basis

    'An applicant's future behaviour can best be judged by his past performance.'

2. *Non-directive interview*

    Avoids questions which easily produce YES/NO answers. 'Broad' questions substituted.
    e.g. What did you like about your last job?

* Bell, F. E., *ibid.*

Basis

The more freedom applicant allowed to talk about himself, the more he will reveal his personality.

3. *Stress interview*

    (i) Pressure purposely put on applicant in order to test responses. *e.g.* Rapid firing of questions by 'hostile' interviewer.

    (ii) Not yet any statistical proof as to validity of this method. It is also likely to place as much stress on the panel as upon the candidate.

4. *Group interview*

Applicants placed in a leaderless discussion situation, and observers note emergence of leader—how it is done, how others accept.

5. *Peer ratings*

The opinion of one's fellows is perhaps the best measure of personality.

A US Marine Corps study shows such a method to be the best predictor of effectiveness in combat—better than ratings of superiors, school, personality or intelligence tests.

Perhaps it should be left to the teaching staff to choose amongst themselves those to be selected for a post.

REGULATED INTERVIEW FORM (Extracts)*
(Manufacturing Company)

1. *Work history*

Begin with first job and work up to present.
How many jobs? How long in each?
Reasons for leaving each job.
Which job liked best? Reasons.
Strong loyalty to employer(s)?
Approximate earnings.
Ambitions? Initiative?
Is he past his peak?

* Bell, F. E., *ibid.*

2. *Family background*

Are parents living?
Father's occupation?
What sort of person is/was father?
Does applicant depend on him, or on mother?
Brothers and/or sisters. How successful is each?
Competitive stimulus in family?
Was he taught work habits and attitudes?
When did he start savings account?
Family background. Asset or liability?

3. *Educational history*

Subjects liked most.
Subjects disliked most.
Practical, theoretical or artistic interest?
Extracurricular activities? Offices held.
Any special courses he would like to take?
Does he persevere or give up easily?

4. *Present domestic situation*

Married? Or when expects to be?
Children? Age, sex and schooling of children?
Wife working? Or does she want to work?
Any enthusiasm in talking about family?
Is he loyal and considerate?
What is wife's attitude towards changing jobs?
Are wife's ideas important?
Will living standard need to be adjusted?
Is he self-reliant? Or dependent on others (e.g. wife).
Principal hobbies/interests?

5. *Attitudes*

Attitude towards superiors, colleagues, work?
Is thinking: wishful, emotional, hard headed, confused, etc.?

6. *Reaction to post under consideration*

Does applicant have any questions about post?
What is general reaction to post?
What particularly appeals?
What is likely to be his chief difficulty with us, etc.?

Making the appointments

On offering the post to the successful candidate do you consider that this forms the opportune time to negotiate 'performance indicators?'

Once an appointment has been made, there then begins the task of inducting the new member of staff into your ongoing programme of staff development.

The most important and difficult part of your task has now started.

Epilogue

Up to this point the orientation of the exercise has been to ensure that the school chooses the right man for the job. It is worth asking whether you have taken sufficient steps to ensure that the candidates have been provided with sufficient information for them to decide whether or not they want to come to you. It is essential that they have been provided with sufficient information, and the opportunity to make such a choice, for both parties to the interview can be seriously misled by the impression created on the day.

Arrangements for Student Teaching Practice

CONTENTS

INTRODUCTION___

The arrangements that schools make for student teaching practice exhibit some of those features which clearly distinguish major administrative tasks from the more routine and everyday aspects of schools' administration. Since this task principally serves the goal of an agency external to the school, the grounds for a potential conflict are present, both because of the additionally imposed workload on school staff and particularly because the inception and termination of the task are likely to be to the convenience of the training institution rather than to that of the school. The task itself displays a cyclical pattern, in that it

Figure 1: Arrangements for student teachers

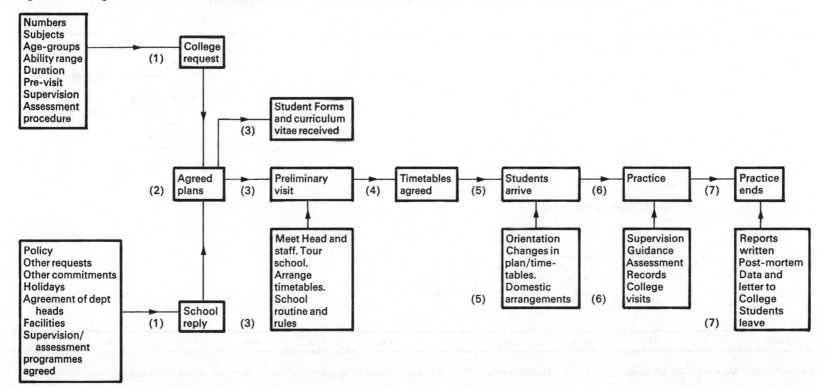

regularly re-occurs, although this periodicity does not conveniently fit the format of a school year. One other distinguishing feature is the way in which the task falls into distinct sections which makes it relatively easy to delegate responsibility for these different sections. So often it seems that the senior mistress is responsible for arranging the teaching practice. Assessment of student performance, however, is likely to be in other hands, and the senior mistress is not necessarily involved in this aspect of the task at all, overall responsibility for which invariably passes to the head teacher.

Presented in the form of a flow diagram is the scheme adopted by one large secondary school for arranging student teaching practice.

It is not presented here as a model programme—the intention is to indicate the complexity of the task and to stimulate discussion.

Figure 2: Bar Chart: Arrangements for student teaching practice (Practice to take place in the Autumn Term)

(The numbers relate to the numbers on the overall strategy diagram on Page 179)

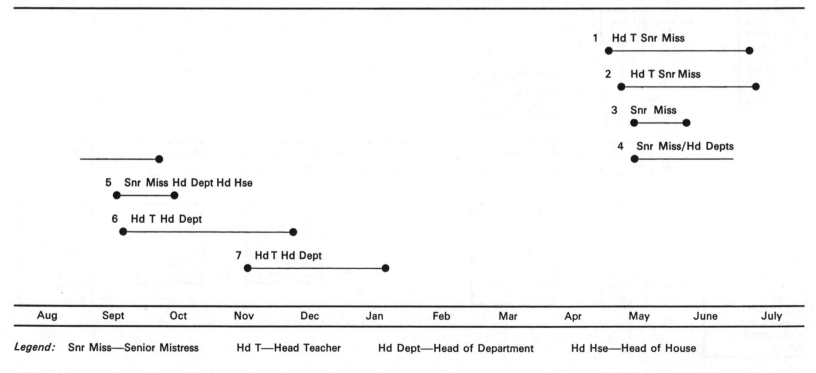

Legend: Snr Miss—Senior Mistress   Hd T—Head Teacher   Hd Dept—Head of Department   Hd Hse—Head of House

The bar chart shows, for each step in a single cycle of the operation:

  (a) the times of year at which the programme started, how long it continued, and when it ended, and

  (b) the member of staff responsible for its initiation, and the member of staff responsible for controlling the programme's progress.

The arrangements for each cycle of the operation are finalized in the term prior to that in which students are actually in school. Thus arrangements for students undertaking teaching practice in the Spring Term are made during the Autumn Term.

Attached below are two further items taken from the school's programme of arrangements for student teaching practice.

Figure 3 shows the amount of time expended in one year by the senior mistress in making arrangements for student teaching practice and the parts of the year in which this work occurred. In itself it does not represent a particularly heavy workload, although it is only one of her many duties.

It must be stressed that if the amounts of time expended by heads of departments, heads of houses (or years) and the head teacher on the supervision and assessment of students were taken into account, then the workload would appear to be far more substantial.

Figure 3: The amount of time spent by the senior mistress in a year on the arrangements for student teaching practice

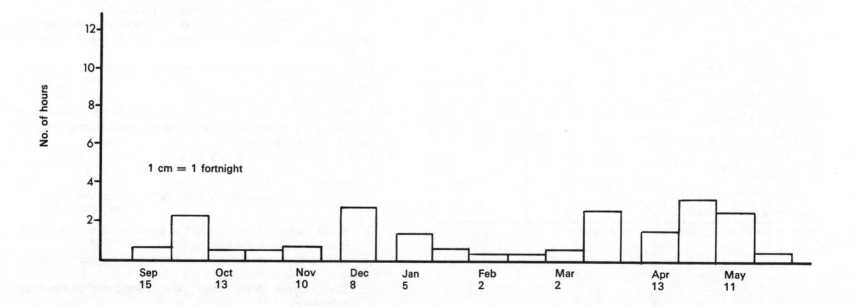

The form below is a pro-forma issued to the school by a training institution for the school's assessment of the student's performance.

Name of Student ....

Date of Teaching Practice ....

HEAD TEACHER'S ASSESSMENT

(It is not essential that all sections of the assessment be completed; some may be left blank if desired.)

Please place an X in the appropriate column indicating comparison with the standard of the average teacher	Out-standing	Good	Satis-factory	Below average	Failure
Aptitude for teaching					
Preparation of schemes and lessons					
Confidence in classroom					
Powers of expression: (a) Fluency & verbal facility					
(b) Standard of English					
Skill in presentation, to include use of blackboard, questioning, etc.					
Relationship with pupils					
Powers of control					
Originality as shown by practice					
Co-operation with Head & Staff					
Energy in teaching and school activities					
Enthusiasm shown outside the classroom, e.g. in accepting help from staff, etc.					

General Comments (*e.g.* Personality and Aptitude):

QUESTIONS

(1) To what extent do you consider that a need exists for a member of the school staff to have full-time responsibility for developing and maintaining training programmes for student teachers within the school, and liaising with external agencies? Are there other groups of staff for whom such a person could produce training programmes?

(2) To what extent do you think the school should evolve its own consensus on the pattern of supervision to be given by school staff to students and on the assessment procedure?

In fact, should the school accept the major responsibility for the supervision of teaching practice, and the assessment of students?

(3) How would you advise staff to respond to requests from students who have successfully completed teaching practice for your school to provide them with testimonials?

(4) If the procedures used by the college or department of education appear to conflict with those of the school, what action might be taken to resolve the difficulty?

(5) *Extract from a Head Teacher's diary:*

Duration	Mode	With	Topic
10 mins.	Discussion	Art Student	Standard of dress and appearance

(a) Should schools have the right to be involved in disciplinary processes against student teachers?

(b) Have schools any right to lay down arbitrary codes for the dress of adults working in the school?

(c) Does anyone really know what constitutes professional behaviour?

Aspects of Organization

in the Large

Secondary School

CONTENTS

This chapter cannot purport to do more than scratch the surface of an enormously complex subject, and in doing so, no attempt is being made to do other than adopt a series of disparate viewpoints.

INTRODUCTION

A school, by virtue of the nature of its educational activities and its clientele, is subject to a range of contraints in the organization of its administrative processes. Some of these constraints are well known and documented in a number of sources. Amongst the more obvious of them are the expectations of pupils, parents and employers, and the expectations of its professional staff. A considerable proportion of the school's time is taken up with the requirements of physical maintenance and the monitoring of its own adminstrative processes, a feature which is of course common to all large organizations.

Schools suffer from a lack of fundamental resources with which to carry out their work, and further the provision of these resources varies from LEA to LEA. The level of supply that would constitute adequacy from the schools' point of view is difficult to determine since schools have for so long coped with inadequacy that it appears inappropriate to turn to them for objective assessment.

Large schools certainly exist where senior staff have inadequate office provision and many make-shift arrangments are in existence. The research project* provided examples of a senior member of staff undertaking confidential interviewing in his car parked in the playground, and an inability to appoint an extra senior member of staff because there was no office in which he could be located. There are schools with no internal telephone system, with one external telephone line also serving as an internal system; schools with improvised and sometimes widely distributed teaching accommodation; and schools with markedly differential provision of secretarial, clerical and other ancillary and auxiliary staff. In such circumstances it is suggested that the school's resources, its time, its equipment or its buildings, are invariably fully committed, and that it is thus equipped that a school must cope with periods of maximum pressure. The school, at certain of the busiest parts of the year, appears to complete its work by exploiting the vocational and professional commitment of its teaching and of its non-teaching staff.

At some stage, for the school's benefit, if for no other reason, it seems necessary for a decision to be taken as to whether certain types of services may best be provided by the school or by other agencies.

Organizational practice in the large school seems to entail increasing bureaucratic processes, a subdivision of responsibility, and a need to store in a written form the information required in order to carry out work. Pupils, parents, the wider community, staff, all who use the school in fact, need to show an inderstanding of this. Knowledge of this sort must inevitably grow slowly within a community and the very quality of the relationship between teacher and child does not necessarily conform to organizational convenience. A child will, at a time when help is needed, turn to the teacher with whom he gets on best or, if the circumstances are urgent enough, then to the nearest adult he can find.

That there should be differences between the practices in small schools and large schools might appear self-evident, but the small school has long been the representative institution in the educational system of England and Wales, and it was in such institutions that the patterns or organization were formed, which were later to be applied to the large secondary comprehensive school. It is likely therefore that there may be a small school legacy still mediating relationships and procedures both within aspects of large school organizations and between the large school and its LEA.

* LYONS, G., *op.cit.*

184

STAFF RESPONSIBILITIES

Can you establish the areas of defined responsibility for the staff at your school?

How do these areas of responsibility compare with those found by other members of your group in their schools?

'The work undertaken by the different members of the senior staff owes more to the traditional organization of schools than it does to the needs of a complex and large comprehensive school.'

Would you agree with this opinion?

From a school handbook

STAFF RESPONSIBILITIES

I Head teacher

He is responsible to the governors and the LEA for the organization and administration of the school in all its aspects.

II Deputy headmaster

With the senior mistress, the deputy head has a large part to play in maintaining the unity of the School. To this end he will:

1. Deputize for the headmaster whenever necessary.
2. Under the headmaster, have direct responsibility for the day to day administration of the school which is on two sites. He will generally be on one site and the headmaster on the other.
3. Assisted by the senior mistress, be responsible for the maintenance of discipline and of pastoral care of pupils through the heads of lower and of upper schools, the year tutors and the school counsellor.
4. Assist in curriculum development by discussions with the headmaster, the director of studies, heads of department and all curriculum development committees.
5. Assisted by the senior mistress be responsible for maintaining good staff relationships and ensuring that adequate channels of communications are maintained.
6. Ensure through the director of studies and year tutors that records and reports are well maintained.
7. Have general supervision with heads of department over staff in their probationary year and assist the headmaster to produce the required reports on such staff.
8. Coordinate arrangements for members of staff to attend short courses.
9. Consult school-based tutor and/or heads of department regarding the placing with classes of students in training.
10. Liaise with LEA advisers, teachers' centre and Parents' Association.
11. Have general responsibility for arrangements for the various school functions and meetings.
12. Have overall responsibility for the fabric of the school and for the stocktaking of furniture and equipment.
13. Answer with the headmaster queries from the school council and year committees.
14. Prepare a report on school activities for headmaster as part of the general report to the school governors.
15. Assist the director of studies to prepare the timetables.
16. Ensure that parents are kept informed on matters of importance.
17. Whenever possible be available for consultation with staff or parents.
18. Coordinate arrangements for school detention.

III Senior mistress

With the deputy head, the senior mistress has a large part to play in maintaining the unity of the school. To this end she will:

1. Assist the Deputy Head to maintain good staff relationships and ensure that adequate channels of communication are maintained.
2. With the year tutors and the mistress in charge of lower school

girls be responsible for the pastoral care of all girls in the school.

3. Aid the year tutors and mistress in charge of lower school girls with communications to and interviews with the parents of girls who have personal or behaviour problems.
4. Coordinate and record school activities, visits, club and society meetings; as Chairman of the Calendar Committee prepare the Calendar of major functions—exams, committee meetings, parents' evenings, etc.
5. Prepare school uniform lists revising the requirements when this is considered necessary.
6. Have overall supervision of the attendance records for lateness or absence liaising with the school counsellor and the school welfare officer where this is appropriate.
7. Make arrangements for routine health inspections (through the School Health Service); maintain the level of first aid supplies in the school.
8. Have general supervision of grants and allowances for pupils.
9. Prepare probationary reports on girls and reports on girls leaving school.
10. Have general supervision over school charitable efforts.
11. Make arrangements for relief teachers in the upper school during the absence of staff.
12. Prepare a report on school activities for the headmaster's General Report to the School Governors.
13. Assist with annual stocktaking of furniture and equipment in the upper school.
14. Coordinate arrangements for parents' evenings, house activities in the upper school and for Open Day.
15. Have particular responsibility for the girl prefects and all girls in the sixth form, working with the sixth form tutors in this respect.
16. Keep a watching brief over stationery bought through the non-departmental capitation allowance.
17. Keep past examination records; distribute examination certificates.
18. Give permission for absence to upper school girls when acceptable reasons are forthcoming.

IV Director of studies

The director of studies is directly responsible to the headmaster for the following duties:

1. School Timetables—preparation of timetable analysis and overseeing completion of all timetables.

2. Curriculum choices
   (a) Oversight of school curriculum as it affects individual pupils and teachers.
   (b) Presentation to pupils and parents of various courses and options available to pupils in each year group; supervision of pupils' choices; course guidance.
   (c) Detailed arrangements for assigning pupils to subject and group choices; preparation of lists of pupils in each subject grouping.
   (d) Assignment of sixth form pupils to various course and subject groupings; preparation of lists of pupils in each group; estimates of numbers for new lower sixth.
   (e) Liaison with heads of department for suggested allocation of teachers in next year's timetable.
3. Development of curriculum in the light of educational developments:
   (a) Cooperation with heads of department for coordinating curriculum development, particularly where inter-departmental and new disciplines and techniques are concerned.
   (b) Liaison with heads of department about syllabuses and scheme of work.
4. Assignment of Year 1 pupils in cooperation with head of lower school, school counsellor, heads of primary schools.
5. Assessment and transfer of pupils within year bands, in cooperation with deputy head, heads of lower and upper schools.
6. Documentation: assistance with development of school records and responsibility for seeing that these are up to date—record cards, reports to parents, reports to other LEAs when pupils change schools; assignment of new pupils to optional courses.
7. Interviews with pupils and parents: advice about progress and curriculum choices, maintenance of high standards in pupils' attitudes to their studies. Pupils may be referred to director of studies by year tutors, heads of upper and lower schools, heads of departments.
8. Liaison with careers master to link careers work with curriculum development, with the school counsellor, heads of school, with other comprehensive schools, with the curriculum development committee etc.
9. Coordinating the activities of the sixth form tutors and overseeing the sixth form block, sixth form committees and prefect arrangements.

10. Higher and further education applications from form six pupils and guidance on choices of colleges and universities.

V Head of upper school

The Head of Upper School will:

1. Have responsibility for the day-to-day administration of upper school site, including care of fabric and equipment.
2. Liaise with caretaker and external agencies of LEA for maintenance and improvements of fabric.
3. Be a source of reference for year tutors and sixth form tutors for major disciplinary problems, particularly those relating to boys.
4. Be the coordinator of the team arranging prefects' duties in upper school.
5. Have responsibility for coordinating pastoral guidance of year tutors, sixth form tutors and if necessary for seeing parents in connection with such matters.
6. Be the coordinator of the team dealing with all arrangements for external exams and with all arrangements for internal exams in the upper school.
7. Maintain direct liaison with the WJEC in matters concerned with external examinations, i.e. ensuring that changes in syllabus are obtained, that examination papers are delivered in good time etc.
8. Have responsibility for issuing staff duty rosters in the upper school.
9. Liaise with the careers department for arrangements for visits by careers advisory officers and other guest speakers.
10. Be a member of the calendar committee.

VI Head of lower school

The Head of Lower School will:

1. Have responsibility for the day-to-day administration of the lower school site, including care of fabric and equipment.
2. Liaise with caretaker and external agencies of LEA for maintenance and improvement of fabric.
3. Be responsible for maintaining stationery stocks, requisitioning classrooms equipment and requisitioning/distributing furniture in the lower school.
4. Be a source of reference for year tutors for major disciplinary problems, especially those relating to boys.
5. Have responsibility for coordinating pastoral guidance of lower school year tutors and if necessary for seeing parents in connection with such matters and/or involving school welfare officer.
6. Liaise with lower school year tutors on care of registers and in scrutinizing them for persistent absentees and latecomers.
7. Arrange all internal exams in the lower school.
8. Arrange detention in the lower school.
9. Assist in timetabling where it affects the lower school.
10. Be responsible for drawing up duty rosters in the lower school.
11. Arrange daily substitutions for absent staff.
12. Liaise with primary school heads, director of studies and school counsellor on admission of new pupils and on placing them in the correct band.
13. Allocate pupils and staff in lower school to houses.
14. Coordinate arrangements for parents' evenings, house meetings, Eisteddfodau in the lower school.
15. Assist the deputy head in discussing suggestions emanating from year committees.
16. Liaise with director of studies, year tutors, form tutors on records and reports.
17. Liaise with deputy head, director of studies, year tutors on movement between bands.
18. Coordinate fire drill arrangements on the lower school site.
19. Be a member of the calendar committee.

VII Mistress responsible for lower school girls

While her specific responsibility is towards girls in the first three years of their schooling, thus complementing the activities of the year tutors in these years she nevertheless will assist with much of the day-to-day administration of the lower school. Accordingly, she will:

1. Have general responsibility for the care of girls' deportment, dress, behaviour and cleanliness.
2. Be a source of reference for year tutors for major disciplinary problems, particularly those relating to girls.
3. Work with year tutors and school counsellor for motivation and guidance of girls.
4. Interview parents who come to school at their own request or because they have been asked to.
5. Have oversight of reports sought when girls move to other areas or are placed on probation or are referred to the child guidance clinic etc.
6. Be responsible for the organization of medical and dental inspections and for emergencies arising through accidents.

7. Give permission for absence to lower school girls when acceptable reasons are forthcoming.
8. Assist the deputy head to maintain good staff relationships and ensure that adequate channels of communication are maintained.
9. Assist in the preparation of room timetables for next session.
10. Assist in general welfare and guidance of new members of staff, probationary teachers and students in training.
11. Prepare a report on girls' activities for the headmaster's General Report to the School Governors.
12. Liaise with senior mistress in connection with school charitable efforts.

VIII Year tutors

Year tutors have as a prime consideration the creation of cohesive year units within the school. Therefore, they will:

1. Coordinate activities in which the year as a whole is involved.
2. Inform the year groups of general school policy, examination arrangements, arrangements for special functions etc.
3. Assist form tutors to maintain acceptable standards of behaviour and dress by dealing with pupils referred to them for persistent breaches of discipline. Serious cases will be referred to the head of upper/lower school, senior mistress or mistress in charge of lower school girls as appropriate.
4. Cooperate with heads of department in maintaining required standards of class work and homework, ensuring in the weekly inspections that homework diaries are up to date and that the general appearance of textbooks and exercise books is presentable.
5. Ensure that pupils' record cards are maintained and kept up to date.
6. Ensure that end of term reports are completed and assembled by the agreed date.
7. Liaise with the director of studies, head of upper/lower school to arrange movement across bands and to disseminate subject choice information.
8. Liaise with the director of studies, careers staff to ensure that pupils receive guidance in academic and vocational problems.
9. Liaise with school counsellor, school welfare officer and appropriate outside agencies in social welfare and medical matters.
10. When requested or when thought necessary establish direct contact with parents for discussion of pupils' problems.

11. Conduct year tutor assemblies and ensure orderly movement to and from other assemblies.
12. Liaise with the deputy head and head of lower school in conducting such detention classes agreed on by the staff.
13. Assist the head of upper/lower school in the day-to-day running of the school.

IX Responsibilities of heads of departments

Heads of departments have complete responsibility to the headmaster for all aspects of their subjects as they are taught in the school. Therefore, they will find it necessary to:

1. Draw up a syllabus or scheme of work constantly reviewing it so that it deals not only with content but with method and technique. The syllabus should be in enough detail to indicate the work to be covered by each class in the year and that part which deals with lower school work should ensure that there is enough common ground to enable transfer between bands to take place.
2. Set and maintain the quality and standards of work in the subject. This includes the supervising of the setting of adequate classwork and homework exercises and the efficient and proper marking of all exercise books.
3. Be responsible for the supervision of the teaching of all staff in the department, particularly that of probationary teachers.
4. Discuss with the director of studies/deputy headmaster/school-based tutor the placing of visiting student teachers with classes.
5. Liaise, where necessary, with other heads of departments to draw up joint courses and methods of assessing such courses.
6. Requisition books, stationery, apparatus etc. needed by the department and to keep stock lists up to date.
7. Liaise with the head of upper school in matters relating to entries for external exams.
8. Arrange such tests and examinations that have been agreed as being necessary for purposes of internal assessment.
9. Liaise with the director of studies regarding the allocation of teachers to classes within the department.
10. Be concerned with subject arrangements for year group parents' meetings.
11. Attend meetings with the headmaster and other heads of department to discuss factors affecting the organization of the school.
12. Arrange regular departmental meetings, considering on an ordered agenda particular problems, departmental adminis-

tration, general and specific aims.

13. Carry out as required from time to time, by the headmaster or his deputy, any other relevant duties.

X Form tutors

Form tutors have general responsibility for being aware of the overall academic progress of pupils, for their pastoral care, for the setting of standards in their appearance and behaviour and for the fabric of the form-room. Therefore they will find it necessary to:

1. Use the form tutorial period to acquaint themselves with the background and interest of the pupils.
2. Use this period to check on the progress, social and academic, of the pupils.
3. Ensure that homework diaries are kept up to date.
4. Keep full, agreed record cards in order to counteract staff changes and provide information for references.
5. Ensure that pupils are aware of and conform to the required standards of appearance and behaviour.
6. Liaise with year tutors, school counsellor, careers staff, heads of upper/lower schools, director of studies, senior mistress, deputy head in connection with pupil problems that need further discussion.
7. Furnish year tutors with reports on those pupils who are frequently late or are unable to explain absences in a satisfactory manner.
8. Arrange the completion of pupils' reports by the nominated times.
9. Keep the form register up to date.
10. Ensure that any information circulars issued are given to the pupils and that any returns required are obtained.
11. Delegate responsibility for special functions within the group to certain pupils.
12. Conduct pupils to assembly.
13. Be responsible for the collection of any monies required from the form.
14. Attend as required, meetings convened by year tutors, heads of upper/lower schools, deputy head, headmaster.
15. Carry out, as required from time to time by the headmaster or his deputy, any other relevant duties.

The senior staff of the school as a team

There is considerable similarity in the non-teaching work undertaken by the senior members of staff of a comprehensive school, although there are also areas of specialization characterizing the differing positions. Some of these characteristics are shown in the descriptions below. These descriptions are given to characterize the posts. It is not intended to imply the apportionment of duties between such posts in any given school, or that any one school would necessarily have these posts.

The head teacher's time is distributed over all activites that concern the school, but his work is particularly characterized by his involvement in activities concerned with external contacts.

The deputy head similarly undertakes most types of activities but, unlike the head teacher, seems to be conerned primarily with routine ongoing activities within the school boundaries and he does not meet with the same range of external contacts. It often seems that his work is summed up in 'the timetable'.

The work of *the Senior Mistress* again involves a wide range of activities but her area of specialization relates to pupil welfare. As might be anticipated, much of this work is done in direct contact with those concerned.

The activities undertaken by *heads of section* (i.e. *head of upper, middle or lower school*) display some specialization in pupil and curriculum centred work, but they, together with the other most senior members of staff, interact on a day to day basis to resolve short-term administrative problems as well as being involved in the more routine functions of system maintenance.

Up to this point one of the most pertinent characteristics of the work of the senior staff examined is that the greater part of their working week is given over to non-teaching activities. For all other members of the staff of a school, teaching is the dominant activity.

The deputy heads of section in this sample were, with one exception, all females. Their work is clearly pupil centred and face to face interaction with others dominates their way of working. A clear manifestation of this is that, unlike all the other senior staff sampled, they spend more time working with pupils than they spend working alone.

Heads of houses or years. Reference has been made in other sections of this work* to the differential performance of tasks according to whether those undertaking the work are male or female and this is particularly true of the work undertaken by male or female house or

* See particularly the chapter 'Pupil Welfare and Guidance Systems'.

year heads. Pupil welfare activities occupy a substantial proportion of their non-teaching duties, but their time in school is principally committed to teaching.

Heads of departments. Administrative duties do not form a substantial proportion of their work—rather it is felt that administrative duties intrude into their work as teachers. The differential performance of a task according to the sex of the teacher was not applicable to heads of departments. As might be anticipated curricular activities, examinations, and equipment occupy a substantial proportion of the administrative work undertaken.

For further information about the nature and patterns of work of members of the senior staff of a comprehensive school, see LYONS, G., *'The administrative duties of Head and Senior Staff in large secondary comprehensive school'*, University of Bristol, 1974.

SOME CONSTRAINTS UPON WORK_____

It seems that many of the non-teaching activities undertaken in schools are subject to a whole range of contraints which condition the content, the quality, the pace and pressure of the work being carried out.

What steps can you take to alleviate these factors to ensure a more evenly balanced flow of work?

Pace and pressure of work*

It is difficult to find a quantifiable index which reflects with any degree of accuracy the pace and the pressure of work at certain parts of the school day or the school term. Events impinge upon one another and interruptions are in turn interrupted. Though much administrative work, and its character, stems from the immediacy of face-to-face relationships of staff and children, it must not be assumed that work undertaken with this degree of pressure is of a trivial nature. One deputy head of a large secondary comprehensive school of some 1700 pupils, using a tape recorder as an aid to diary compilation, logged interruptions to scheduled events at the following rate:

* Lyons, G. *op. cit.*

Time of programmed event	Length of programmed event	Number of interruptions	Rate of interruptions
8.30– 9.00	30 minutes	20	1 every 1.5 mins
9.00– 9.15	15 minutes	20	1 every 45 secs
9.15–10.00	45 minutes	20	1 every 2.3 mins
10.00–11.00	60 minutes	20	1 every 3.0 mins
11.00–11.40	40 minutes	16	1 every 1.9 mins
11.50–12.30	40 minutes	nil	—

At this part of the day, already identified as one of the busiest, the deputy head was undertaking activities which dealt with external examinations, staff absences, timetabling problems, lost property, parental interviews, and so on.

Whilst it is no doubt necessary that some key members of staff make themselves accessible not only to colleagues but parents and children as well, this accessibility, whilst shielding those members of staff whose time is largely taken up by teaching, inevitably leads to a seriously fragmented day for the senior staff concerned. The conflict experienced by such staff is likely on the one hand to lead to a hazardous situation in regard to administrative coherence and long-term planning. On the other hand their programmed activities may be so badly interrupted that in fact they fail to occur at all. While some activities seem to be more expendable than others (planned marking and teaching preparation seem to be of this category) and can be postponed to other parts of the day, a loss of teaching time through interruptions is a net loss. Bites out of the beginning and ending of lessons, since senior staff are inevitably waylaid on corridors on the way to or from classes, help account for the fact that one senior mistress was losing up to eighty minutes planned teaching per week, a considerable proportion of her scheduled teaching load.

Although senior teachers are subjected to an intensive pressure of work only rarely do the most senior of them, the head, the deputy head, the senior mistress, the heads of upper, middle or lower schools, fail to undertake any teaching at all. Teachers of the status of deputies to heads of sections, heads of houses or of years and heads of departments are largely timetabled to teach. Since teachers usually spend their working time in isolation from each other, access is inevitably restricted.

The timetable thus begins to form the framework around which other activities occur—the times between lesson changes, before morning school begins, after the end of afternoon school, during the morning break and lunchtime, become crucial periods in which substantial proportions of school administration are undertaken. One of the most apparent consequences of this method of undertaking work is that most contacts are for relatively short periods of time, and are verbal. The diagram below (Figure 1) sets out the number of administrative activities undertaken by senior teaching staff according to the duration of the event undertaken. Implicit in the distribution shown is the fact that one of the principal ways by which teachers undertake their work is in face-to-face contact, although working alone and writing also feature quite substantially.

Figure 1: The distribution and duration of administrative events undertaken by senior teachers

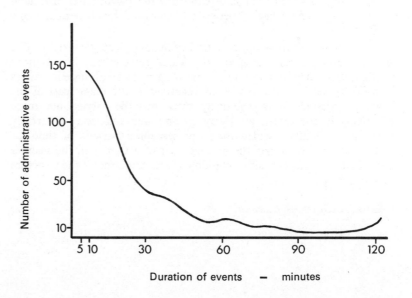

Pattern of the school day*

Table 2 sets out the mean times for administrative events according to the time of day they occur—sixteen schools were sampled. An interesting feature of the diagram is that (with one exception) the duration of administrative activities undertaken increases steadily throughout the day, the morning and particularly the time before morning school having activities of smallest duration. The diagram shows quite clearly that activities of a longer duration are associated with the period when school has closed for the afternoon, with evenings and with weekends. It is also of interest that a school lunchtime features heavily as a period when administrative work can be undertaken.

It is obvious that in the organization of a school day large tasks, unless they are to be undertaken piecemeal, must be postponed to non-timetabled hours. The beginning of a school day is clearly taken up with the host of problems that need a rapid solution in order to get the day under way, and also represents a period restricted in duration when staff and pupils have access to each other such that rapid, if not final, arrangements are made. Apart from the period after afternoon school has closed all breaks between lessons and lunch periods allow such access.

The school morning appears to be characterized by events of a shorter duration than the afternoon. Many reasons may be advanced for this: there may be a need in the morning to deal with urgent matters in order to settle down to what is regarded as the major part of the day's programme, or alternatively work may be carried out more effectively in the mornings. Evenings and weekends were invariably given to work that needed long uninterrupted periods of time for completion. Quite clearly the arrangement of activities in the manner described above is a result of working within and around the structure of a timetable.

* Extract from LYONS, G., *op.cit.*

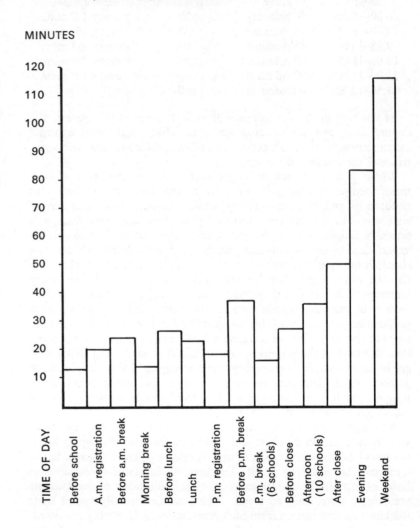

TABLE 2: Mean times for administrative events according to time of day in a sampled 16 schools.

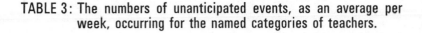

TABLE 3: The numbers of unanticipated events, as an average per week, occurring for the named categories of teachers.

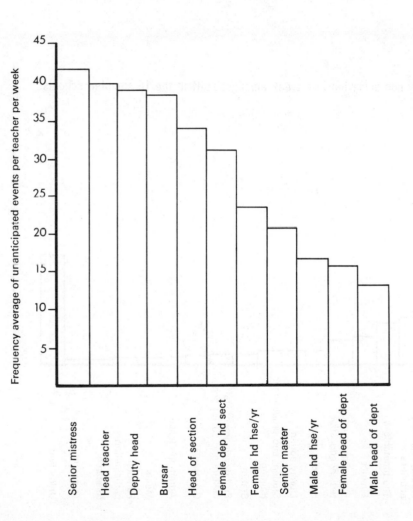

The dislocation of the anticipated day*

Table 3 shows the numbers of unanticipated events logged by the teachers who kept diaries in the sampled schools. This is expressed as a rate per week. It is obvious that those teachers who have the largest burden of administration within the school are those who must cope with the greatest number of unanticipated events. They are the ones who are most normally free of timetabled commitments and therefore more likely to be available when unexpected and unscheduled events occur. Since the most senior members of staff are normally free from timetabled commitments they are able to monitor ongoing activities and are accessible when importunate events occur; because of this availability they are able to build expertise and experience and to forge bonds of relationships which entails that they are automatically consulted as other events of similar character occur. In this way they are able to shield, to some extent at least, those others of their colleagues whose time is largely timetabled to the classroom.

That ongoing activities are subject to interruption is nevertheless still a source of frustration and irritation to senior staff. A head of department wrote:

'Today was particularly bad from the point of view of interruptions. My afternoon lessons were almost completely lost by an unexpected visitor. This often happens when a sales representative, visiting teacher, maintenance engineer, county adviser, and so on, come to see me in my official capacity.'

Many interruptions will be of a very fleeting nature—a request for information, confirmation of a point of view, and so on—requiring no more than a couple of sentences in reply, but cumulatively they help to account for the exhausting and wearing nature of the teaching situation. A deputy head wrote on a Friday's diary:

'A most frustrating day, with constant interruptions, ending as usual in taking home a good deal of administrative work to be completed by Monday.'

Those events causing most interruptions are, naturally enough,

* Extract from LYONS, G., *op.cit.*

193

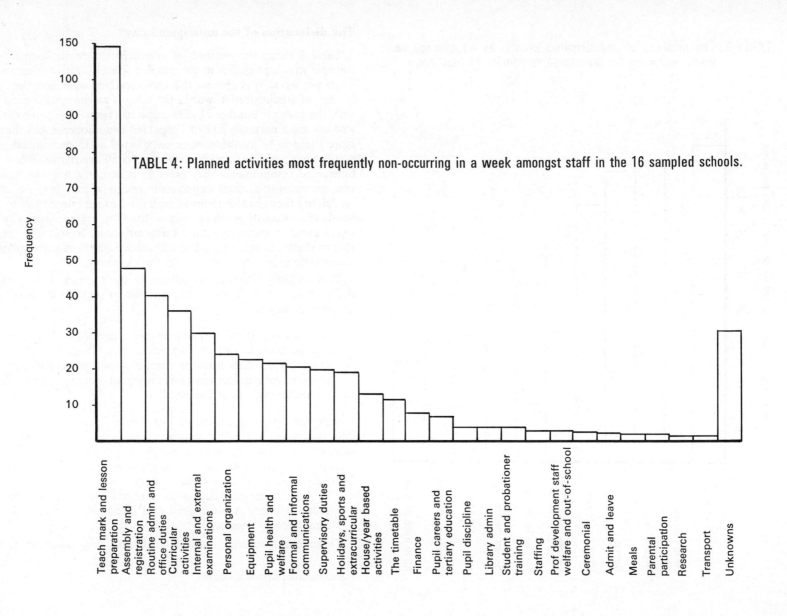

TABLE 4: Planned activities most frequently non-occurring in a week amongst staff in the 16 sampled schools.

closely related to those events occurring most frequently in schools. Typically they would include curricular activities, pupil health and welfare, equipment, internal and external examinations, pupil discipline, sports, holidays and extracurricular activities, the timetable, and so on.

Teachers constantly have to make decisions regarding the priority of events, but needless to say pupils in need of attention must come before any teaching or paperwork commitments, and telephones must be answered. It is not uncommon for teachers to experience interruptions to what was already an interruption and thus a large backlog of partially completed work may have accumulated at the end of the day.

Planned activities which fail to take place

In cases where an ongoing activity is interrupted two possible outcomes can be identified. In one case the ongoing activity may be resumed after the interruption and thereby completed, and in the other the interrupting activity may dominate the respondent's attention and prevent the completion of the former activity. The first of these two outcomes is most likely to occur when the interrupting activity is of short duration, particularly when less than five minutes, although because of the method of recording reported here it cannot be fully identified. It must also be mentioned that an interruption is not the only reason for leaving work incomplete—on many occasions an activity may be postponed for lack of further information or because individuals who should be party to an activity are unavailable.

In this context of considerable pressure of work, where the planned day is subject to both unanticipated activities and interruptions, it seems inevitable that activities planned for one part of a day should either be deferred to some other time or alternatively fail to occur at all. The latter gives indication of the real pressure of events, for most events that fail to occur during school hours are undertaken in the evenings or at weekends. Expressed as a rate per week per teacher, the number of 'non-occurring' activities is not excessively large, although any abandonment of scheduled activities must be viewed with some reservation.

Table 4 shows planned activities which most frequently fail to take place and, conforming to other profiles discussed earlier, shows those activities which take up the greater part of teachers' time to be those which also have the highest incidence of non-occurrence.

There is however a degree of subjective rating which faces a member of staff when he is confronted with a choice of conflicting events. In view of this, it is interesting that teaching, marking and lesson preparation are the activities which most frequently fail to occur. One might ask whether this is because their in-school frequency is amongst the highest or whether they prove easiest to drop.

Whereas administrative work which was interrupted may (theoretically at least) be resumed at some other time, interruptions to teaching incur a permanent loss and these were therefore investigated in some detail. Teaching lost, as defined here, refers to planned teaching time. It does not include teaching failing to occur because a staff member was away ill or out of school due to other 'planned' events e.g. professional development course, attendance at exam, LEA offices, and so on. (Table 5).

Work outside timetabled hours

The consequences of coping with inadequate resources and of a total commitment of these resources inevitably has long-term effects. In a situation where most members of staff are by their programmes principally committed to teaching, the emergence of extra or unanticipated activites, whether of an administrative or teaching category, must impinge upon the school's virtual total commitment of its resources. In coping with such demands staff need to sacrifice non-timetabled periods, to lose teaching time or to postpone activities.

For the school to get through its work, it must apparently rely heavily upon the sense of vocation of the staff and particularly that they are willing to sacrifice their free time.

A member of the senior staff of a large school is therefore subject to urgent demands from many directions. Because of this pressure he will need to undertake his administration in non-teaching periods (along with marking and lesson preparation), to defer the work to out of school time or to interrupt periods of the day already allocated to other activities. At certain parts of a school year members of staff with a full teaching commitment will therefore be carrying a very heavy burden indeed.

Table 6 shows the amount of administration, marking, lesson preparation, etc. that is undertaken before school begins, at lunch times, after afternoon school, in the evenings and at weekends. Not surprisingly

TABLE 5: Loss of planned teaching time per teacher per week.

TABLE 6: The average time spent per week on administrative activities in the teachers' own time.

TABLE 5: Loss of planned teaching time per teacher per week.

Hours per teacher per week

1·4, 1·3, 1·2, 1·1, 1·0, 0·9, 0·8, 0·7, 0·6, 0·5, 0·4, 0·3, 0·2, 0·1

Senior mistress
Female head of dept
Female dep hd of section
Male head of dept
Female house/yr head
Head of section
Male house/yr head
Senior master
Deputy head
Head teacher

TABLE 6: The average time spent per week on administrative activities in the teachers' own time.

Hours per week

15, 14, 13, 12, 11, 10, 9, 8, 7, 6, 5, 4, 3, 2, 1

Head teacher
Female hd hse/yr
Head of section
Deputy head
Senior mistress
Female dep hd sect
Female head of dept
Senior master
Male hd hse/yr
Male head of dept

the head teacher undertakes the largest proportion of the work done at these times, but the loads carried by heads and deputy heads of sections, heads of departments, senior mistresses and heads of years/houses are also quite heavy, particularly when the teaching load carried by these staff is taken into consideration.

Within each category of senior staff there proves to be a remarkable consistency in the work undertaken outside timetabled periods. If however the location of this work is examined, then an interesting difference in the strategies employed is revealed in a comparison of the sexes: whereas men tend to take their additional work home, women tend to undertake their additional work at school, before school begins, after the close of afternoon school, in lunch periods and coffee breaks, and during whatever other non-timetabled time might be available.

Patterns of administrative work in the school year

On examination, the school year appears to have a cyclical nature, to be characterized by clearly demarcated 'setting-up' and 'closing-down' operations, and has a content of tasks that varies according to the time of year, each term also showing a characteristic pattern. The distribution of this work entails that a number of cycles are ongoing simultaneously, but these cycles do not fit tidily into either a programmed year or into term times. In these circumstances vacations are necessary periods for undertaking work that has spilled over from a crowded term, each vacation in fact having a characteristic content of tasks. The distribution between administrative work and teaching activities shows a marked difference between terms and this is exemplified in Figure 2. (It must be emphasized that this diagram is a construct derived from returns made by separate schools and also only represents the sampled work of *senior* teaching staff in schools—not the work undertaken by all teaching staff in the sampled schools.)

It is mentioned above that the content of work does seem to vary according to the time of day, the week, the term, and the time of year. Although there is variation between schools in the weight allocated to any specific activity, the schools sampled appeared to spend between 72 per cent and 90 per cent of their administrative effort upon a relatively restricted number of topics: pupil health and welfare, holidays, sports and extracurricular activities, curricular activities, internal and external examinations, the timetable, pupil careers and

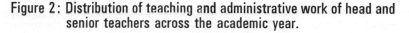

Figure 2: Distribution of teaching and administrative work of head and senior teachers across the academic year.

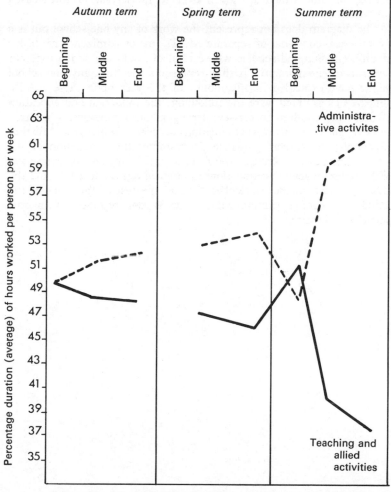

* assembly and registration activities are included as administration

197

tertiary education, equipment, buildings, grounds and upkeep, were amongst those topics taking up substantial periods of this time. The pupil welfare and guidance system also has allocated to it substantial periods of time which are given over to house/year or tutor-based activities.

The diagram does not represent the work of any one school but is a hypothetical construct of separate MATS (major administrative tasks) of different sampled schools whose total of hours are added together for each calendar month. It thus represents the work any one school might have expended in any month of the year upon these MATs. The MATs sampled were the following: the induction and allocation of first year children to classes; arrangements for mounting internal and external examinations; applications for places in higher and further education; the careers guidance programme; the production of the school timetable; recruitment of teachers; arrangements concerned with student teachers; requisitions; statistical returns to LEAs and the DES. It must not be overlooked that all the rest of the work of the school is ongoing simultaneously but is not represented in this particular diagram.

MATs AND HIGH-LEVEL DECISION-MAKING*

Any discussion of MATs involves some clarification of the definition of administration. It is used in education in a variety of contexts, usually associated with hierarchial levels. At class teacher level it tends to encompass everything from register marking up, which is not directly a part of the teaching task itself and which has a routine aspect: at Ho Dept level, it is used to cover organizing aspects plus clerical routines: ordering books, setting up exams, keeping mark schedules, budgeting and estimates and so on; while at top management level it implies anything at all to do with the organizing of ongoing functions concerned with the structure of school activities, and the deployment of resources. Many so called major administrative tasks are clerical, or very little more than clerical. At the other end of the spectrum, some have far reaching connotations for the quality of work and employment of expert professional effort in appropriate activities—in other words, management. The same range of implications also exist at LEA level.

For training or staff development purposes, and for clarity of thought in planning and decision making, it is important to distinguish as clearly as possible between the functions involved, since they require different

* I am indebted to Peter C. Webb HMI for his help with this section.

skills and different organizational contexts, or levels.

Ideally in large organizations a certain differentiation is needed in allocating the different tasks—purely clerical operations should be carried out by personnel trained for clerical work and paid accordingly, and similarly for the various levels of administrative and managerial tasks. Deputy heads should not be high level clerks or administrative assistants, teachers should not spend time typing and duplicating notes. But it would be a mistake to attempt to separate out administration totally from educational tasks—some administrative tasks have strong educational content and implication—construction of the timetable, allocation of pupils to teaching groups, reports on pupil performance and potential, and so on, are some of them. Hence the need for careful analysis and evaluation from an educational as well as an administrative (and managerial) point of view.

The use of the term major also needs attention—it can involve an emphasis upon impact as well as on load. It can also be taken to focus more upon the level of professional expertise needed in decision making terms as against an inherent content of routine, standardized procedures.

For these reasons MATs are best analysed by a number of classifications concerned with function, sector, level, impact and time span:

In sector terms it is useful for example to classify into (a) curricular, (b) academic, (c) welfare, (d) resource deployment, (e) managerial, (f) organizational, (g) financial—and so on.

In time span terms a different classification may be set up, possibly into the following, relating to the level of performance necessary to carry them out.

    (i) Top—long term, free of constraints from resources, finance; concerned with role and function for the organization as a whole, negotiation and planning and forecasting skills predominantly needed.

    (ii) Middle—medium term, constraints from (i) i.e. from defined role, resource availability, organizational function. Skills in budgeting, organizing, logistic planning, implementation, development: (curriculum, staff, resources, etc.) functional usually i.e. involving breakdown of overall plans from (i) into

divisions, departments, faculties, programmes, areas etc.

    (iii) Operational—short term, year by year, day by day implementation of (ii); control of standards, deployment of staff, organization of activities and operations and so on.

Some activities will be 'major' in terms of impact, professional level and administrative or managerial power within any of these time span or sector divisions. The time span division proves to be particularly useful since it admits of a distinctive hierarchical specification of responsibilities.

In terms of practice in schools the following was found to prevail:

A distinctive feature of a large school is that its size and complexity enforce formal organization of activities which in a small school would require no more than the assigning of a responsibility.

There is some tendency for schools to have a similarity of approach to a task and this may be attributed to a number of factors. Holidays, the beginning and ending of the school year, and of an individual term, impose a periodicity upon activities, e.g. interviews may be concentrated during term times and clerical work, which is less dependent upon other people, may be left over until school holidays. Tasks tend to have an underlying logic dictating their operation and are prone to be constrained by the demands of external agencies which, each year, occur at roughly the same time and in the same form. School systems tend to be inbred; there is a traditional hierarchy of authority which invariably in practice means the allocation of overall responsibility for the task to one person. Methods of paying teachers for special responsibilities reinforced this tendency. One consequence is that during the time that a task is operational only the 'responsible' member of staff is likely to be involved. There are MATs which by their nature involve a number of people working together, but the occasions when this occurs appear to be concentrated into relatively short time spans. Senior mistresses and deputy head teachers are frequently given the central responsibility for a task.

MATs seem to share with other facets of school administration a cyclical sequence of activities and the task may be initiated and terminated a number of times each year; particularly in that a series of 'organizing' sub-routines are continuously brought into play; or that an ongoing operation needs apparently to be suspended during a vacation.

The logic of an MAT seems further to dictate a rhythm of operation in that at inititiation a 'setting-up operation', particularly characterized by discussion between the head teacher, senior members of staff, and whoever may have overall responsibility for the MAT, is undertaken. Following this the more mundane, clerical aspects of the task begin to operate. This latter phase is specifically characterized by data collection and dissemination, the production of lists, interview arrangements, and notification of arrangements.

MATs display a periodicity dictated amongst other things by: traditional behaviour; the deadlines of new terms; a new academic year; the end of such periods; or by other fixed points on the calendar. For example, although arrangements for Christmas activities can take place at other times of the year, the occurence of the activities must be at Christmas.

MATs are also subject to the constraints of external agencies, e.g. local education authorities, the Department of Education and Science, External Examination Boards, who may require the school to enact administrative processes in order to meet deadlines that are set by the external agent and that are not necessarily convenient to the school.

The combination of such factors as those outlined above lead to a lack of flexibility in task devolution and planning. It also appears that they lead to periods of maximum pressure in a school year and cause resources to be stretched to their utmost.

The amount of time expended on any MAT seems to be related to the distribution of the task across a school year and those tasks ongoing for the greatest length of time seem to be those with the highest pupil or parent contact time.

The organization of careers advice in schools and the related task, applications for places in higher and further education, are examples of such work. They are further characterized by extensive interaction amongst members of staff and between them and outside agencies. Such interaction and continuous feedback of information and of decisions demands a sustained output of routine clerical activities; it needs an organizing and co-ordinating function to be applied to the work of other members of staff; and because the activities of this particular MAT cross school boundaries, it needs a senior member of staff with high executive status to implement and sustain the momentum of the task.

These two particular MATs also display the interrelationship that exists between MATs.

Logically, at least, it would appear that MATs display a sequential interrelation, and that this interrelationship particularly where these directly concern pupils together with the professional nature of the teacher role, imposes further difficulties for MAT rationalization.

(1) There might prove to be difficulty in establishing boundaries between tasks and in resolving boundary disputes.

(2) Any member of staff may feel he has the right to intercede on any aspect of school work or school life that concerns pupils. This would be acceptable as long as all members of staff understood the processes in operation, particularly how to extract and feed back into the system the relevant information.

(3) A problem in school has to be dealt with by whoever it comes to first.

(4) The quality of pupil/teacher relationships is such that e.g. a counsellor/housemaster/tutor might not be the person a pupil turns to for advice or help. The pupil will obviously turn to whoever he feels he can trust.

(5) The passing of information between the different sections of the school organization might not be centralized, thus careers and further education applications, option choices, external examination entries, etc., were observed to be collecting separately similar information from the pupils.

This latter difficulty is increased by the dilatory way that information is often returned such that expedition of pro formas and progress chasing can account for a sizeable proportion of the time of the person responsible for a task. Inevitably schools and the personnel involved learn more satisfactory ways of dealing with the problems, and experience gained often offsets difficulties that may at earlier stages have accounted for a considerable part of the operation.

Presented below is a list of those tasks that are here referred to as Major Administrative Tasks (MATs):

(1) (a) Induction of first year children to school

(b) Allocation of first year children to classes

(2) Allocation of other children to classes

(3) Subject choices of examination and non-examination forms

(4) Arrangements for mounting externally moderated examinations (including Mode 3 CSE)

(5) Arrangements for mounting internal school examinations

(6) Arrangements for pupils applying for places in further or higher education

(7) Careers guidance and the placement of pupils in employment (where separate from 6 above)

(8) Reports on pupils and subsequent meetings with parents where these tasks are separate from any mentioned above

(9) The production of a timetable for the next school year

(10) Staffing and recruitment of teachers

(11) Staff development and training, and
    (a) All arrangements concerned with probationary teachers
    (b) All arrangements concerned with student teachers

(12) Requisitions

(13) Stocktaking

(14) Budgeting, allocation and negotiation of capitation allowance, etc.

(15) Transference of pupils between schools where age range is 11–16 or any other permutation

(16) Statistical returns to LEAs or DES

(17) Arrangements of social activities, e.g. Christmas, school plays, sports days, etc.

You might care to review this list with an eye to: adding to the list; deleting items from it; or combining some of those that are presented here as MATs. You should do this from the standpoint your school adopts.

It has been pointed out that although the logic of a task stays roughly similar in all schools, the amount of time and staff a school devotes to a task varies considerably. Some of this difference is attributable to varying size of schools and the necessity of rationally recording and distributing information. (It could be argued that a small school is unable to devote the resources that a large school can bring to bear upon a task.) Certainly by virtue of the size of school, what may be no more than a temporary increase in work load for one or perhaps two people in a small school can in fact amount to work spread over a full year in a large school. The allocation of first year children to classes and staffing are examples. A small school particularly centralizes administrative effort, usually in a head teacher, whereas the large school must devolve the activities to other staff members and over as much of the year as is practicable, the head teacher of a large school perhaps never undertaking activities which the head of a small school would regard as his prerogative.

Some questions

1. Do you agree that there is a need to redistribute task effort over a (school) year?

2. What steps would you recommend a school to follow in order that they should significantly redistribute their workload?

    The following may be amongst the factors you would consider:

    (a) The combination of parts of MAT programmes in order to avoid duplication of effort.

    (b) The reallocation of MATs to parts of the year where task load is the lightest.

    (c) You might wish to produce a calendar that shows the timing of tasks to be undertaken.

    (d) An analysis of task to determine the relevant 'level' and 'function' necessary to ensure:
        effective delegation,
        staff training,
        forward planning,
        adequacy of monitoring procedures and effective review and feedback into the programmes.

3. The procedures that you have been examining are amongst those leading to a growth of bureaucratic processes within a school. Will you in discussing the rationalization of administrative procedures bear in mind those rationalizations most likely to lessen a potential

estrangement between the major administrators in school and the other members of the teaching staff. Perhaps you would like to discuss these measures in plenary session.

4. Should staff be inducted into the administrative procedures of their own school by a planned training programme? Would this resolve most of the problems you have noted?

PATTERNS OF DELEGATION

Closer examination seems to suggest that a member of staff holding two positions of responsibility is not necessarily undertaking twice as much work as a member of staff who only holds one position. From an inspection of the returns made upon diaries it is suggested that probably the pressures of a school situation on multi-office holders will almost inevitably entail an uneven distribution of time between posts. A woman jointly holding the positions of head of middle school and senior mistress is likely to spend more time as senior mistress, and a head teacher who is also head of geography will devote a minimum amount of time to the geography department. It would be interesting to pursue in greater detail the circumstances dictating which posts, of multi-status posts, held primacy at a particular time, and the consequences of conflicts entailed.

A further factor of some importance is that when multi-status positions cross-school organizational sub-divisions they can in fact negate such sub-divisions reducing, for example, a supposed three part school organizational sub-division into a *de facto* two part division, e.g. when the deputy head is also head of lower school.

It must be stressed that the actual designation of an office does not necessarily imply that the work functions are being undertaken exclusively by the office holder or holders—it seems self-evident that one should be prepared to deal with whosoever undertakes the work and not with whoever exercises titular responsibility.

Certain patterns of school organization determine the possibilities of administrative delegation and lend themselves to the ease by which delegation can occur and the recognition of areas of defined competence. Thus schools subdivided into upper middle and lower sections show a greater potentiality of the range of possible delegation than schools divided into upper and lower sections only, or schools not subdivided into separate organizational systems.

It is already known from work reported in other sections of this report that the majority of senior staff are largely timetabled and this is particularly true for staff of the level of seniority of heads of year or house and heads of department. Assuming for this purpose that three schools were of the same size, other variables held equal, but were organizationally differently subdivided, then excluding house/year masters and heads of departments (since they are primarily committed to teaching) the school divided into upper, middle and lower sections can delegate its work to ten organizational positions, the school divided into upper and lower sections to eight positions but a school without this internal subdivision must share this same work load between four positions. As was pointed out earlier the propensity for delegation does not necessarily match the actuality.

Although there are quite striking differences between schools, it is the similarity rather than dissimilarity that is initially most noticeable. The schools show a large number of categories of staff all reporting directly to the head teacher, plainly representing the academic, social/pastoral and routine administrative side of school life. Inevitably, it seems the Head must be deeply involved in running the school on a day-to-day basis.

The differences are most noticeable between schools without internal organizational subdivisions and those divided into either upper, middle and lower sections, or upper and lower sections, schools not organizationally subdivided show a much simpler chain of command. In the latter situation it seems inevitable that the head, deputy and senior mistress must cope with an enormous burden of day-to-day detailed problems without anyone being in a position to filter or mediate the flow of work coming to them.

ORGANIZATION AND THE FUTURE____

One of the characteristics of organization charts is that they represent a clear hierarchical ordering of command. There is a tacit assumption that all roles and all jobs are known and there is likely to be great security in these roles to the staff concerned. It is suggested that this type of organizational framework is most suitable to an organization where the rate of change is likely to be leisurely, for such a structure is likely to be slow in responding to change. A school that teaches steadily to a syllabus set by an external examining body ideally sums up this pattern.

Because of the stability brought to a school by an organizational framework of this type it is quite possible for it most nearly to fit the needs of a large secondary comprehensive school in its early stages of development. However, once the school is fully developed the inflexibility of such a structure may prove a serious handicap.

The information presented below shows how one large school and community college in the Midlands has attempted to cope with this problem. They set as their two prime objectives: people's needs and adaptability.

The pattern of organization which they adopted (see page 206) is in the form of a matrix structure. To simplify the philosophy represented: One side of the chart, the personnel side, represents the users; the other side (resources) represents the holders. A tension is assumed between the two. It is necessary for the holders to 'sell' to the users their resources. The users will however only 'buy' that which ideally suits the everchanging needs of their pupils or students. Thus a process of continual bargaining is brought into play between the two axes of the school.

The executive and supervisory teams, constituted from staff involved in this process, is nevertheless deliberately set aside from the normal day to day processes of the school in order that it may retain overall command, and direct and develop the future of the organization.

THE SCHOOL AND COMMUNITY COLLEGE
Management and Organization

1. Management is that which gets effective results out of resources and people. Implicit in this statement is the need for management to define what are effective results, and be able to measure progress towards them.
2. In a large and complex organization, many people are managing for some of the time. A person is managing if he or she is helping to formulate policy and plans, deciding what are effective results, and using resources and influencing the behaviour of people.
3. Management is team work. This organization permits teams of people to work co-operatively towards objectives, and credit is given to team work rather than individual supremacy.
4. Set out in this document is a model of the organization structure showing how teams of managing people relate with others. Job descriptions are brief so as to give people the maximum chance to show initiative and be flexible.
5. A situation full of change and of the unknown calls for a flexible and dynamic approach, and although it is necessary to design an organization structure to indicate in some measure the relationships between people, strict adherence to a mechanistic and authoritarian system would slow down the decision making and inhibit initiative. The structure is organic, and groups of people co-operate with each other to identify and solve problems which concern them; and commitment to the objectives of the school and community college override faculty interests and pride.
6. All staff are invited to participate in the formulation of policy and objectives, but within that framework individual staff members are expected to make and execute decisions—to get on with the job—and accept accountability for their actions.
7. All staff are urged to see their work as concerned with the whole community of which the school is a vital and definable part, and they are encouraged to manage or assist with 'out of school' and 'non-school' activities either voluntarily, or in exchange for time off during school hours or for remuneration for some formal activities.
8. Thus our community—those people who are serviced by it and who make use of its facilities—play a major role in developing future policy and plans, and managing their own activities, using the staff as advisers. People serviced by our school and community college are pupils of compulsory school age, students beyond school-leaving age, and community members of all ages.
9. The care and the development of all members of our community is the concern of all members of the staff. The house staff have particular concern for the care and development of the school pupils, and relations with parents. The community staff have similar concern for all the non-pupil members of the community, The work of these teams is the responsibility of the deputy who is the director of personal development (DP).
   Inevitably and rightly the work of these groups overlaps. Senior house heads co-ordinate the work of the houses and head of community activities co-ordinates the work of the community staff.
10. Curriculum development and the provision and control of activities is the concern of all members of the staff. The faculty staff have particular concern for the provision of suitable programmes and resources both for school and community, and work of these teams is the responsibility of the deputy who is the director of resources and services (DS).
11. Administrative services necessary to support the activities of the enterprise, and the personal management of the non-teaching staff is the responsibility of the administration officer (AO).
12. The day to day supervision of the activities of the school is the responsibility of the head of upper school (HU) and the head of lower school (HL); and the supervision of the community activities and the community use of the premises outside school hours is the responsibility of the head of community activities (HC).
13. Excellence is encouraged, but there are no departments which aim for departmental excellence for its own sake. Faculty heads exist for the provision and care of resources, curriculum development and the development and guidance of staff, but staff are not the exclusive property of any one faculty head and work in several different disciplines alongside staff from another faculty.
14. School pupils are grouped in years (360) and houses (120) within the years. The house behaves in many respects like a little school, so that pupils feel to belong to it, and regard the house head like

the head of a small school. Within a common curriculum, this small school is provided with resources and services to meet its needs. In this way, the advantages of size are retained along with the advantages of smallness. The house is the learning unit, and teams of staff visit the House to carry out education programmes.

15. Each year of 360 pupils provides three houses of 120 pupils. Each house has a house head. The pupils are encouraged to look firstly to the house heads as the person looking after their total development. Senior house heads are appointed from the house heads to co-ordinate the work of a number of houses.

HOW THE ORGANIZATION OPERATES

1. The executive team determines the overall aims and policy for the co-ordinated school and community operation within which the other teams develop objectives and plans. Members of the executive team are *ex-officio* members of all other teams and monitor their performance towards their objectives.

   The executive team often incorporates the supervisory team into its meetings where appropriate.

2. The supervisory team plans the co-ordinated supervision of the school and community activities.

3. The three operations teams (upper school, lower school and community) determine objectives and plans in detail to meet the specific needs of those parts of the school and community enterprise.

4. Resources and services teams determine objectives and plans which enable teams staff to provide a curriculum and programme of activities serving the requirements of the schools and the community.

5. House heads team determine objectives and plans which enable the house staff to provide an effective pastoral care and guidance service for pupils and to develop home-school links.

6. The administrative team determines objectives and plans to provide a range of back-up services to the school and community operations working particularly in the functions of secretarial and communications, security and maintenance, catering, accounts, and bookings.

7. Teams of teachers (4 to 6) who work with groups of pupils (120) do the detailed curriculum planning and execution. The team has a leader appointed from amongst its members. The team is guided by a faculty head to see that its work supports the overall curriculum objectives of the School.

8. The house staff associated with the house do the detailed planning of house activities.

TEAM ORGANIZATION

The following teams are constituted. They should meet as infrequently as possible to do essential business. Detail should be delegated to individuals or other teams. Groups other than those listed below may meet from time to time.

(a) Executive team—ET (HD, DP, DS, AO)

(b) Supervisory team—XT (DP, HU, HL, HC)
   Frequently, the ET and XT meet together to discuss policy and implementation.

(c) Upper school operations team—UT
   (HU, Upper School House Heads, Faculty Heads, representative of CT)

(d) Lower school operations team—LT
   (HL, Lower School House Heads, Faculty Heads, representative of CT)

(e) Community operations team—CT
   (HC, CA, CY, CW, CR, AE, (CG), representative of school teams)

(f) Resources team—RT (DS and Faculty Heads and HC (DP))

(g) Services team—ST (DS, RS, CL, TR, IS, AE, CG)

(h) House heads team—HT
   (DP and the House Heads (Lower School, or Upper, or combined))

(i) Administration team—AT (AO, SS, OS, CO)

(j) Teams of teachers (4 to 6) who work with groups of pupils (120) are responsible for both detailed curriculum planning and its implementation.

(k) House head and house staff

NOTES:
Members of the executive team are *ex-officio* members of all other teams. Service heads (RS, CL, TR, IS, CG) and may be co-opted on to UT and LT.

OBJECTIVES

1. An enterprise should always be achieving updated and stretching objectives within each of the following areas:

   (a) *Reputation*   — with the pupils
                             — with the parents

THE SCHOOL AND COMMUNITY COLLEGE ORGANIZATION

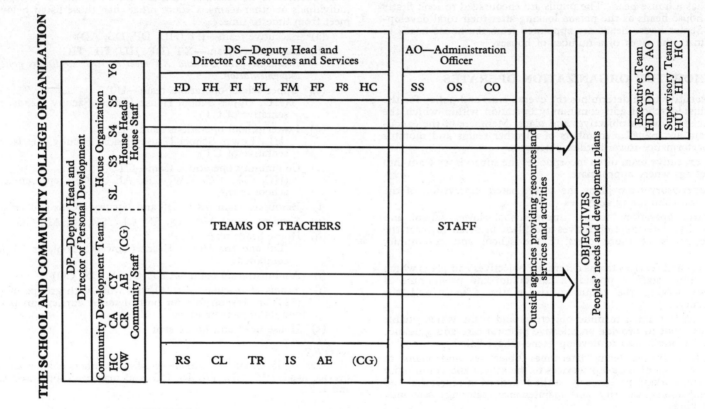

Executive Team	HD DP DS AO
Supervisory Team	HU HL HC

DP—Deputy Head and Director of Personal Development

House Organization
SL S3 S4 S5 Y6
House Heads
House Staff

Community Development Team
HC CA CY AE (CG)
CW CR
Community Staff

DS—Deputy Head and Director of Resources and Services

FD FH FI FL FM FP F8 HC

AO—Administration Officer

SS OS CO

TEAMS OF TEACHERS

STAFF

RS CL TR IS AE (CG)

Outside agencies providing resources and services and activities

OBJECTIVES
Peoples' needs and development plans

KEY TO THE ORGANIZATION CHART

HD—Head
HS—Head's Secretary
DP—Deputy Head, Director of Personal Development
DS—Deputy Head, Director of Resources and Services and Curriculum Development
AO—Administration Officer
HC—Head of Community Operations
HL—Head of Lower School
HU—Head of Upper School
Faculty Heads
    FD—Design
    FH—Humanities
    FI—Interdisciplinary Work
    FL—Languages and Communication
    FM—Maths and Science
    FP—Physical Education and Recreation
    F8—English as a Second Language
CM—Co-ordinator of Maths

CG—Head of Career Guidance and Employer Relations
RS—Head of Remedial Services
CL—Co-ordinator of Learning Resources
IS—Head of Information Services
TR—Resources Centre Technician
Y6—VIth Form Tutor
S3, S4, S5—Senior House Heads for 3, 4, 5 Year
SL—Senior House Head, Lower School
House Heads (Year and colour—e.g. H3R .. 3rd Year red)
CA—Community Worker (Adults)
CY—Community Worker (Young Persons)
AE—Adult Education Co-ordinator
CR—Community Recreation Warden
CW—Community Warden
SS—Services Superintendent
OS—Office Services Supervisor
CO—Catering Officer

(a)	*Reputation* (continued)	— with the staff
		— with other community members
		— with the teaching profession
		— with colleges of education and universities
		— with other colleges
		— with the LEA and all other LEA schools
		— with the city in general
		— with employers
		— nationally
(b)	*Innovation*	— curriculum development
		— learning processes
		— management of the organization
		— co-operation with other schools and colleges
(c)	*Productivity*	— use of staff
		— use of buildings and equipment
		— use of learning media
		— contribution of pupils and others
		— timetabling
(d)	*Purpose*	— aims and objectives and programmes relevant to the needs of those served by the enterprise
(e)	*Resource acquisition*	— generating income, money raising
		— voluntary help
		— finding resources from other agencies
		— economy and conservation
		— influencing the LEA
(f)	*Staff development*	— individual development programmes for staff
		— team work and sharing experience
		— motivation
		— communication
(g)	*Community relations* (pupils and others)	— counselling and helping people
		— participation in planning by people
		— care of people
		— recognition and reward of people
		— attitudes to people
(h)	*Public responsibility*	— care of public property
		— good neighbours

2. Every team and every member of staff should recognize for themselves key activities, and key targets within those activities, which are supportive of the objectives of the enterprise. (To be 'key' they will be few in number. It is better to succeed in a few key items than flounder in a piously large number.)

3. (a) A key activity is an activity performed by a team or individual which is crucial to the success of the enterprise.

   (b) A key target is an actual event within the activity which, when achieved, makes a significant contribution to the objectives of the enterprise.

4. *Examples*

   (a) A team recognizes a key activity as the development of continuous assessment processes in interdisciplinary studies. Its key target is the design and acceptance of a Mode 3, CSE examination in a particular interdisciplinary activity by a certain date.

(b) A group tutor recognizes a key activity is to gain parental co-operation. His key target is to have visited the homes of all his pupils by the end of term to explain to them the programme for their children.

5. Teams and individuals should identify for themselves, in conjunction with team managers and heads of functions, appropriate key activities and key targets. Teams and individuals should continually review their progress towards these targets, and seek help when in difficulty. Heads of functions should help their teams and individuals to

(a) set realistic targets,

(b) achieve them,

and should monitor progress and provide necessary resources and stimulus.

6. Key activities, targets and progress should be recorded in writing—briefly. This is helpful for individuals, teams and heads of functions, and a satisfactory way of collating the progress and change in the whole enterprise.

Would you consider the following:

1. In your opinion does the matrix provide a better basis for the design of a school's organization? The example presented is not necessarily the only model that could exist for a school.

2. Can you work out a matrix pattern of organization to resolve the problems of organization you have identified as existing in your own school?

3. How would you suggest interpreting such a system to parents and pupils?

4. How would you recommend inducting school staff into working a matrix pattern of organization? What would be the principal problems you would expect to meet in the first few months of operating the new system?

5. Is it possible for a school to design a matrix pattern of organization under existing Burnham patterns of payment?

6. Does the matrix structure aid or hinder instruction, and, is it likely that the matrix will ultimately convert itself into a more traditional hierarchical structure?

7. Does the matrix superimpose an unsupportable decision-making structure on the school, and is the consequence a generation of an indigestible volume of paper and committees?

Points for further discussion

1. To what extent is the kind of organization your school has suitable to planning the future of the school? Who has the time for it?

2. How much of the time of the senior staff at your school is likely to be taken up by their dealing with 'organizational things' as opposed to dealing with people?

3. If the four fundamental areas of school administration can be said to relate to 'curriculum leadership', 'resource allocation', and 'personnel' and 'public relations',

(i) which member of staff would you place in charge of each section?

(ii) Does this accord with the practice followed in your school, and, if not, which members of staff have responsibilities in these areas?

4. Do you agree that:

(i) non-teaching positions create their own workload?

(ii) specialization is counter productive, e.g. 'I cannot do it, it needs to be referred to Mr X, I should however send him a memo to report on progress.'

(iii) specialization is alienating to junior members of staff who have a ready response in 'it's so and so's job—he's paid for it.'

5. (i) One of the problems with schools nowadays is that they have rushed 'willy nilly' into doing work where really they should have hesitated and asked as a first question, should we be here to begin with. If this had been done it might have led to an easing of the burden of work, and a reduction in the complexity of some of the problems that they have to deal with. Do you agree?

(ii) If more resources were made available to a school, how should it determine how it is to allocate them. In fact, how do schools determine what they should be doing?

6. Forward planning of any real depth or consistency is virtually impossible for schools because of the way that they are financed, that is, on a year to year basis with little real knowledge or control as to how much money will be available to them in the following year. The LEA (and therefore the school) should be able to budget for a quinquennium in the way universities do. If this were the case, then a school could plan its future. Curriculum development, staff development and so on, would all become realistic possibilities. Do you agree?

7. The job descriptions provided by schools are usually no more than lists of tasks. They give little indication of the existing pattern of responsibility. More importantly, it is only rarely that performance indicators are incorporated into the job description to enable an objective measure as to how well the person is doing in the job to be made, and therefore allow the job to be seen as developmental. Do you agree?

8. As a task, your group might like to outline a typical hierarchy of responsibility for a traditional secondary school; or for a public school.

What is the shape of the outline like?
How many positions of real responsibility are there in it?

9. We have already seen how a lack of resources seriously constrains the flexibility of a school in organizing its output. It might be necessary for a school to spread its effort thinly over a large number of activities or, concentrating on those it thinks most valuable, expend no more than minimal effort on the others. Do you agree?

10. The procedures that you have been examining are amongst those leading to a growth of bureaucratic processes within a school. Will you in discussing the rationalization of administrative procedures bear in mind those rationalizations most likely to lessen a potential estrangement between the major administrators in a school and the other members of the teaching staff. Perhaps you would like to discuss these measures in plenary session?

11. Should staff be inducted into the administrative procedures of their own school by a planned training programme? Would this resolve most of the problems you have noted?

Communications

'*Too much paper, we haven't time to bother with it*'

'Consideration needs first to be given to the arrangements which the institution can make within its own resources for the people who work within it. Of these, good communication is of first importance. In a large institution and particularly in a large administrative department, this may be very difficult to organize. Many good managers, whether a head teacher, a principal or an education officer, will lay down a pattern of communication which provides for channels of information flow in both directions. The snag is that a failure of communication at a particular point along a particular channel cuts off the information flow beyond that point. So many practical exigencies arise which can cause this to happen. We fall back upon or try to supplement the channels with blanket means of communication: the circular notes, the file of school instructions, the departmental circular, the staff magazine with a copy to every teacher. Back comes the cry: "too much paper, we haven't time to bother with it".'

—Dr E. W. H. Briault, Education Officer, ILEA,
quoted from
*Staff Development in the Institutional Setting**

'Third, chaos, and lack of time. "That was the fourth fire drill this week. The kids are always setting it off. If it's not fire drill, it's the Tannoy blasting into the classroom, telling you to perform some irrelevant task like taking the register and sending all names of absentees to the office. You can't get on with anything, even if you succeed in getting the kids quiet". "I had a first-year boy who was meant to go to a special maths lesson the other day; he wandered round the school for 20 minutes and never found it". Genuine education either gets sunk in a surfeit of administration—or withers through a complete lack of it.

'Fourth, low morale among the teachers. "Fifteen teachers off today. I haven't . . ." '

—From the *Times Educational Supplement*,
2nd March 1973

* A paper prepared for the Annual Conference of the British Education Administration Society, November 1972.

CONTENTS

INTRODUCTION

'It is most important to stress at the outset that a study of communications requires an analysis of the school as a whole—as an organization, as a structure or system involving resources, locations and processes, as a social entity; and as an economic activity in which people come as it were to bargain with it as to how much of their time and energy they are prepared to give, and in return for what. A study of communications in a school is really a study of the school itself in 3 or 4 related facets or attributes, and not a study of something to be added on to it like a poultice, that is mysteriously, going to cure it of its problems.'*

* Mr Peter C. Webb, HMI.

THE NATURE OF THE PROBLEM___

The large comprehensive school poses communication problems which are of a different order from those encountered in smaller traditional schools. The numbers of staff and pupils, the likely size of the school campus, and frequently the geographical separation of the school's buildings are factors likely to have influence on the speed and efficiency of information flow within the school. The traditional methods of creating and maintaining a sense of corporate identity, by amongst other things, frequent full staff meetings, daily school assemblies, and the continual encounters of staff and pupils, are often no longer feasible. Other approaches must be found.

Many teachers are aware that all is not well with their schools in respect of communications, although they appear to have no very clear idea of what is wrong, and vague expressions of dissatisfaction are unlikely to provide much by way of answers. The first task is to attempt to isolate the various aspects of the general problem.

Schools have a need to:

collect items of information relating to children covering a wide range of topics, and to store this information in such a way as to maintain confidentiality and yet allow immediate access for those who require it;

pass information and instructions in a routine way through the school, so that it reaches the designated person within the required time;

transmit decisions concerning all aspects of school life to all those people whom they affect; and these people should to a greater or lesser extent be able to participate in the decision-making process.

There is also the social aspect of communications, the process whereby staff and pupils come to experience the school as a community, and where sudden or unexpected events, such as a child's illness, may be rapidly and efficiently dealt with.

The 'professional' aspect of communication is however a central matter. It is a question of the level of commitment to the corporate aims, and philosophy and of professional involvement in its processes and development. The opposite of commitment becomes alienation or rejection. Thus commitment or alienation are likely to be direct concomitants of the communication process. We should thus be prepared to look at communications in school in terms of the structure, personal relationships, authority and so forth.

In the most general terms a communication might be classified as 'internal', taking place entirely within school boundaries, or 'external', passing from the school to outside agencies or vice versa. Similarly communications may be considered as urgent/priority, or alternatively to be routine.

Important factors which may influence a communication and its modes of transmission are the identity of the originator and recipient of a communication, and the direction in which communication proceeds between them. Thus a head teacher is likely to employ modes of transmission according to whether he is in contact with junior teachers in a part of the school, or only with his closer and more senior colleagues; similarly, both content and style of communication will differ in these situations. It is also apparent that in communicating with even a single person he may select one or more of three major types, *viz.* he may request information (interrogative); he may give information (informative); or he may issue orders (instructive).

The methods of communication which he chooses will to a certain extent depend upon the type of communication, e.g. a brief note might well be appropriate for the issuing of a simple instruction, whereas a face-to-face interview might be necessary for an exchange of opinions, to gather information and to make decisions.

It was mentioned above that the recipient of a communication to some extent dictates the mode of transmission employed. Recipients might be broadly classified into three groups: general (anybody and everybody); limited (a particular group of people, e.g. science teachers or Form 3 pupils); and particular (a single individual). It is apparent that whereas a notice on the school notice board(s) or an announcement at assembly is appropriate to general communications, a meeting of the science faculty would be more appropriate to limited communications, and a chat in the staff room might be the best means of contact with a particular individual.

Thus the recipients' perception is one of the chief factors in determining the effectiveness of a communication, and this perception may be a school-wide feature in that it has a socially determined base. The problem then for the originator of a message, is to forecast the nature and the extent of distortion likely to be induced by the perception of others. It is equally likely to affect individuals, groups and committees and tends to have powerful historical and cultural continuity.

The selection of the most appropriate method however is not the end of the process—there are further constraints. Amongst these might be the layout of the school, the disposition of the internal telephone system, the characteristic working methods of communicator and communicatee, and so on. An example of how the 'most appropriate' method might be modified by force of circumstances is the situation where the head wishes to contact a teacher whose department is physically isolated from the staff room. In this case, although a staff room meeting would appear the best means of contact, in fact it is not possible as the teacher does not frequent the staff room. Another method must be found.

You might like to consider the following points:

1. Do LEAs recognize the problems that a large school may have in its communications? What would you expect them to do about it?

2. Is it possible to organize the monitoring of communications such that breakdowns can readily be:
   (a) detected
   (b) located
   (c) rectified?
   What in your view constitutes a breakdown in communications?

3. Is it inevitable that there will be a group of people who do not want to be involved, who 'don't want to know'?

4. What sorts of personality factors can hinder communications? How can such difficulties be best overcome?

5. Is there inevitably an informal network of communications in a school? Is this network centred around one or more particularly 'sympathetic' members of staff? In what relationship might such a figure stand to the senior staff in the school? What functions does this network have? Is it appropriate that this network should be used to the best advantage of the school community and, if so, how may this be done?

6. 'The problem is that the head stands aloof from the rest of the staff.'
   This viewpoint tacitly accepts that authority in a school is vested in the head teacher. How do you incorporate this point of view into a situation where everyone feels that they know what is going on, that they are involved?

7. We all know of the game where the players sit round in a circle and a message is whispered from ear to ear. When the message has gone full circle and reached the original sender, it is usual to find that it now bears little resemblance to the original. What safeguards may be built into a communication system so as to minimize the corruption of information?

8. If a parent comes to the school during the day with an urgent message, how do you find the child? Can you in fact find the child at other than registration periods?

9. The fire alarm will empty the school in three minutes, but what else is as urgent as this? A satisfactory minimum time for the retrieval of an item of information is 15 minutes—do you agree?

10. 'If you stand on the playing field of the lower school when there is a fire drill, 1300 kids come out onto that field, and I know 30 of them. That's the only class I teach down there,' Head of Department.
    Is this opinion something that should be of concern? Why should the head of department know children he doesn't teach?

11. Internal telephones at all key locations in the school and in all offices and teaching rooms is an absolute minimum necessity. These phones should be equally accessible to pupils and staff. Do you agree?

AN EXERCISE

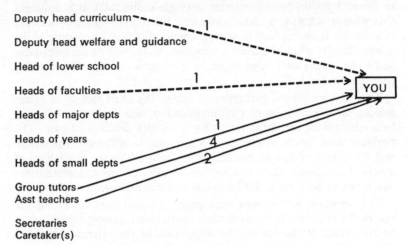

Head
Deputy head curriculum
Deputy head welfare and guidance
Head of lower school
Heads of faculties
Heads of major depts
Heads of years
Heads of small depts
Group tutors
Asst teachers

YOU

1
1
1
4
2

Secretaries
Caretaker(s)

Together with other members of your group you might like to keep a simple log of the communication processes you are involved in during *one school day*.

Bring to your group to aid the discussion some of the examples of the communications you sent or received. See pro-forma on page 216.

You might also, together with other members of your group, wish to produce the outline of a diagram like the one shown opposite, listing all the staff in your school in order of seniority.

The aim is to *estimate* the number of staff *who contact you* about *school work* in the course of a day, a week and a term.

What you need to do

Using coloured pencils draw a red line from the box marked YOU to all those staff in school who contact you about school work *each day*, whether on the phone, by memo, by seeking you out for a chat and so on. Use a green pencil for the number of such contacts *in a week*, and a blue pencil to mark those people contacting you over *a term*. Write the number of people involved on each of the lines you have drawn.

You might produce a diagram that looks like the one following:

Using another outline diagram repeat the process but this time indicating the number and levels of staff *that you contact*.

Using these two small pieces of work, which admittedly oversimplify the 'real' situation, what can you learn:

1. About the volume of communication in your school?

2. About the direction of most of the communication in your school?

3. About the flow of communicatin between those in senior, mid-post, and junior posts in your school?

4. Which appears to be the most common mode of communication in the school?

5. Which is the most common mode chosen for communication to you from:

   (a) the head

   (b) the deputy head(s)

   (c) Heads of section

   (d) Heads of faculties, and so on.

Communications sent by you

Who is it to?	Does it give information, ask for information or give instructions?	Topic e.g. Pupil Welfare, Options, Timetabling, etc.	Mode (circular, memo, phone, informal chat, in committee, etc.)	Comments about factors likely to have influence upon this particular communication

Communications received by you

Who is it from?	Who is it to (apart from you)?	Does it give information, ask for information or give instructions?	Topic e.g. Pupil Welfare, Options, Timetabling	Mode (circular, memo, phone, informal chat, committee)	Comments about factors likely to have influence upon this particular communication

And vice versa?

What can you deduce about the factors likely to be influencing their choice?

6. About which topic do you:

    (a) receive most communications?

    (b) send most communications?

7. (a) What proportion of the communication you receive informs you of events to take place?

    (b) What proportion asks you to do something or asks for information?

    (c) What proportion instructs you of a course of action you are to follow, and so on?

8. With what levels of staff do you have the largest number of contacts?

    Since there are more teachers of the grade of group tutor/ assistant teacher in the school, it would appear reasonable to assume that most contacts are with these staff. Is this true in your case?

9. What can you deduce about communications between the various levels of staff in your school?

    Is this experience similar to that shared by other members of your group?

WHAT TEACHERS THINK ABOUT COMMUNICA-TIONS

In the course of interviews with a sample of teachers from each of five schools, the interviewees were asked for any comments they might wish to make concerning the 'communications' within their schools. The wide range of topics about which teachers volunteered comments, suggestions and opinions reveals that the subject cannot be considered as a precise, well-defined entity, but rather as a 'bucket' category into which teachers conveniently insert all the various organizational ills from which they feel their school suffers. An analysis of the types of comments made is shown in Figure 1, in which the total numbers of comments in various categories are given in the form of a histogram, with broadly favourable comments in any category appearing above the zero line, and unfavourable comments below the zero line. The categories in which the comments were coded appear as follows:

1. *Inter-staff communication*

This category refers to the organizational characteristics of the school, particularly to the hierarchical structuring of staff relations, both inter- and intra-departmental, and between senior and junior staff either individually or considered as members of groups. Examples of comments in this category are:

'Some things take an awful long time to get down the grapevine.'

'They're improving. You can see a chain of people now, as there wasn't two years ago. The comprehensive school has settled down.'

'The head and his underlings have no contact with us—they have no idea what really goes on.'

'Within our department (communication) is good, because we are all in one collective area. It's difficult to communicate with anyone else, though.'

2. Staff-pupil communication

This category refers to staff-pupil relations within the organizational framework of the school, particularly to sections (i.e. upper, middle, lower schools), houses, forms and sets, as well as to pupils in their capacities as, for example, prefects. In this category fall such comments as:

'The house system militates against effective communication with any band of kids. There is no effective way of getting 400 children of one band together, to gain or give information or instruction, because they are all in separate house or tutor groups.'

'Communication with children extra difficult particularly if in sets.'

'We are divided into three schools, staff teach in all three but children don't mix. House system doesn't knit school together. Ideas don't get through. Perhaps upper school pupils could help in lower school not necessarily as prefects but as form helpers—give younger pupils someone to identify with.'

3. Physical

This category refers to the physical characteristics of the school. Included are its geographical size and the numbers of people it contains, its layout with regard to classrooms, office facilities, staffrooms, and specialist subject facilities, e.g. science laboratories, home economics and craft rooms. In this category fall such comments as:

'Big schools are going to burn off a lot of teachers; it is tension-producing as well . . .'

'I walk miles looking for people, and have to organize things so they can be taken in one journey.'

'You should have one room for your subject so that you don't have to carry equipment and books all over the place.'

'Men and women have separate staffrooms, and this is a real difficulty.'

'Two schools create problems. If it's raining and you haven't a car then you get wet. In four days each week travel 14 times between schools. Don't complain because don't bite the hand that feeds you . . .'

4. Resources

This category refers to the equipment whereby communication between members and parts of the school may be carried out. Included are internal and external telephones, Tannoy systems, notice boards and pigeon holes, duplicating facilities, and ancillary personnel in their communicative capacities as, for example, secretaries. This category includes the following comments:

'The internal phone is a blessing . . . Using the correct channels (e.g. pigeon holes) it is quite possible to contact everyone you need within a day . . . I find no difficulty . . . If I want to get in touch with someone, I can.'

'Pigeon holes have improved things, and internal phones.'

'We have a compromise microphone; at present it is broken which has meant enormous extra paper work. Announcements were daily or twice daily over the microphone, while the children were with their house tutor, who then reinforced what you've said, gets it all clearly understood. Now he has to get it all down on paper, which is a huge work load.'

'The secretaries do a grand job under the conditions. We need a photocopy and duplicating office. Now it wouldn't work if everyone began to use the available facilities.'

5. Location and access

This category refers to the ease of establishing personal contact for work purposes, including the problems of finding members of staff and pupils, the ease or lack of it, with which information may be obtained, and the role of the staffroom in inter-staff relationships. Comments in this category include:

'It takes so long to be able to make contact; to find out where people are, consulting timetables, sending runners . . .'

'Worse trouble is trying to reach a particular child at a particular time. You have a copy of everybody's timetable, and look up index of the form you want to find. (You need) a daily diary of room changes, absences, class visits. (You use) referral slips—write down the name of the pupil you want to see on each slip, and the tutor's name, and send it off . . .'

'One of the biggest problems is contacting the children; there is no one person you can go to. Any one class can have up to 32 tutors, you can have to write out 32 messages and put them into registers.'

6. *Information channels*

This category refers to the channels which are established for the passage of information, and includes 'bureaucracy' in general, circulars, weekly orders, timetabling changes, meetings and committees. Examples of comments in this category are:

'People say size militates against communication, but if we worked it out organizationally, communication would follow naturally. On the whole, information comes through.'

'Hand outs are very numerous. Staff moan about the amount of paper, but at least it proves beneficial.'

'Very good. There are weekly and monthly staff meetings and regular notices pinned up on the board.'

'Contact with other members of staff through weekly orders is in theory O.K.; but we don't have enough face-to-face contact.'

'There's so much on the notice boards that you can never find what refers to you. Most people don't bother—you find out in time, anyway.'

'My pigeonhole is in a staffroom in the lower school. I seldom get there in time for urgent messages, so people have to send a kid with a message.'

The following categories, 7 and 8, differ from those examined so far in that they relate to the individual's personal feelings about working in the large school.

7. *Personal*

This category refers to the position of the individual staff member, and includes expressions of isolation, frustration, apathy and exhaustion. Representative comments in this category include:

'I have the feeling that I don't know what's going on in the school.'

'Staff feel there is no way they can have an effective voice in the school—lack of interest or a lack of constructive outcomes.'

'There's a basic lack of communication as to the *general principles* on which we work. I'd like to be more aware of basic thinking behind the philosophy, so I'd know how I stood a little bit more.'

'I felt I was a member of a community, but now the community feeling is destroyed—and this destroys the basis of communication.'

8. *Professional*

This category refers to the individual staff member's perception of the system in general terms, and includes comments on informal communications. Examples are:

'If they could give more time to consultation, to assist teachers, than they do, would be an improvement. Things have been decided in advance, rather than to discuss the issues—this is a feeling about the way the school is run—want more open discussion.'

'The system here works reasonably well once you have mastered it.'

'I feel for the children, too great a flood of information, and they "turn off" defensively. Ditto the staff. Too much pouring in. No breakdown of info., only clogged pipelines.'

'On the whole good. Because school's philosophy is that *people matter*, hence communication is of prime importance here, not secondary as it is if you don't care about people.'

'People are very cagey about things which are everyone's concern. They don't pass on info from senior staff. No frankness in the school. An atmosphere of mystification. This is the only flaw in my relationship with colleagues.'

'There is a ghastly breakdown. But what else can you expect in a school like this.'

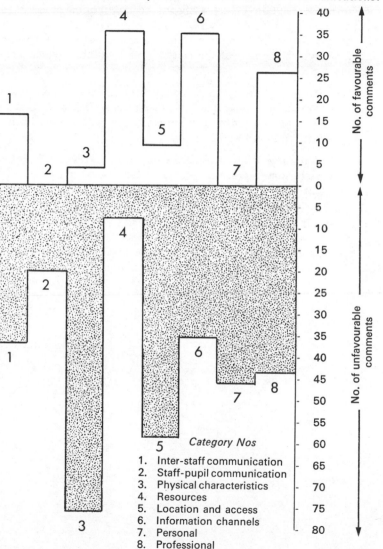

Figure 1: Comments made by interviewed teachers on communications.

No. of favourable comments

No. of unfavourable comments

Category Nos
1. Inter-staff communication
2. Staff-pupil communication
3. Physical characteristics
4. Resources
5. Location and access
6. Information channels
7. Personal
8. Professional

You might like to consider the following points:

The block diagram Figure 1 shows the distribution of comments in the following way: broadly favourable comments in each category or where an aspect was simply mentioned, appear above the zero line, and those which mentioned the category unfavourably appear below the zero line.

(1) The largest proportion of comments made were unfavourable. Do you think that this is because teachers asked to comment about any aspect of school organization are far more likely to criticize than to praise?

(2) **Category 3** 'Physical Characteristics', **Category 5** 'Ease of establishing personal contact for work purposes' and **Category 7,** relating to the position of the individual member of staff, were almost wholly mentioned in critical terms.

   If this related to your school and if you were the head teacher, what action would you take? Could you draw any comfort from the responses made to **Categories 4 and 6,** relating to 'Resources' and 'Information Channels'?

PARTICIPATION AND CONSULTATION

Staff consultation: two viewpoints

(a) 'The Interim Report of the national Working Party, which was accepted by the 1972 Annual Conference, said this about consultation: "There need be no delay, however, in the achievement of consultation and we recommend, as an interim measure, that the Union immediately declares it should be the right of all members of staff to be consulted on matters affecting the school in general and their own work in particular, and that it should be obligatory for head teachers to make satisfactory arrangements within their schools for such consultation".'

From: *The Right of Teachers to Consultation*, a Declaration by the Executive of the National Union of Teachers, April, 1972.

(b) 'Control could easily fall into the hands of an unrepresentative group. This might be a reactionary band who would oppose all change: it might equally well, in some schools, be an idealistic and enthusiastic group determined to make revolutionary changes but lacking the experience to see either the difficulties which would arise or the need for careful preparation. We can appreciate the enthusiasm and the promise of many young teachers without feeling that we could with confidence entrust the direction of our schools to them at this stage. We would add that those keenest to acquire power are not necessarily those whose judgement commands our greatest respect.'

From: *The Government of Schools*, a Report from a Working Party of the Headmasters' Association. August, 1972.

Staff meetings*

Regular meetings are one of the most commonly used methods of communication. The head regularly meets with senior staff on a weekly or fortnightly basis, thus seeing all his heads of departments, heads of houses or years and heads of schools. These meetings serve many purposes but one of their main functions is undoubtedly for staff to report to the head teacher. At one school regular briefing meetings took place each morning for any senior staff wishing to attend, these meetings usually beginning at 8.25 a.m. In a large comprehensive school it is not usually possible to hold regular staff meetings where all staff attend, and it is also an opinion that such meetings are far less useful than meetings where a genuine interchange of views can take place. The full staff meeting seems much more characteristic of smaller schools where, for example, 'Weekly staff meeting is held Friday p.m. during afternoon break with all staff over afternoon tea. Short, urgent matters only are dealt with.'

The department is a sub-unit of a school small enough to allow meetings where a real interchange of views can take place. At one large school eight of the fourteen heads of department kept diary records of their departmental meetings during the Spring Term. Thirty-six meetings were recorded of which half were attended by all departmental staff and half were sub-departmental meetings, e.g. head of science holding a meeting for the physics staff. A wide variety of approaches was found in this one school—at one extreme a formally organized process was in existence, meetings were arranged in advance, an agenda was circulated, discussion was through the chair, and minutes were kept, and at the other extreme, no meetings were arranged because members of a department were said to be in 'daily face-to-face contact'.

* Extract from LYONS, G., *op. cit.*

What is it do you think that determines attitudes, and relationships in committees and under whose control are the factors that are involved?

Is the point of a committee meeting to get the business done as quickly and effectively as possible, or, to achieve a full and frank exchange of views with as wide a representation as possible?

The timing of staff meetings*

Schools are staffed by professionals who expect and desire to be consulted in decisions which affect the running of the school. The traditional ways to effect such consultation are either informally, through a chat in the staffroom, or formally, through committees. The nature and pattern of the work in a large school creates difficulties to consultations of this type.

Schools inadequately supplied with the resources necessary to do the job are continually working at considerable pace and pressure with a total commitment of their resources; the importunate nature of events, governed particularly by pupils in a dependent relationship, leads to a discontinuous work pattern. The timetable, effectively ensuring that staff spend the larger part of the day in isolation from each other, provides a framework around which all other work has to take place. Thus the times between lessons, breaks and lunchtimes are of necessity taken up with ongoing or urgent events. On a large campus staff may be physically isolated from each other and the opportunities for informal contacts between sections of the teaching staff are considerably reduced.

Committee meetings after the close of afternoon school conflict immediately with extracurricular activities and with other commitments the staff may have in teaching or in attending in-service courses, and such times prove particularly difficult for married women with family responsibilities. Some schools have faculty timetables allowing subject teachers to meet during the course of a working day, but this cannot resolve the problems of teachers with welfare responsibilities nor can it deal with the problem of staff wishing to participate because of a commitment to or interest in a particular topic under discussion.

For staff to dedicate a continuous period to discussing fully matters of major policy, it would appear necessary to look to some time other than the normal teaching day.

* Extract from LYONS, G., *op. cit.*

H*

If staff were to return to school at the end of the summer vacation one week earlier than the children, this period, when all staff would be able to interact, would provide a continuous period of time to pursue in depth major factors concerning the school's policy. It might also ensure that the first week of the Autumn Term proceeds more smoothly than is sometimes the case. Other discretionary holidays might also be used in this way. It is assumed that, for this period of work, additional payments would be made to participant teachers.

Extract from a School Handbook:

TIMETABLE NOTES 1975/76

The timetable for 1975/76 has undergone complete re-organization with the adoption of a faculty timetable through the first 4 years of the school, to be extended in 1976/77 to the first 5 years.

The timetable will be based on a ten day rotation; Monday being day 1 in one week and day 6 in the next. (See detailed timetable for exact dates).

It will now be possible to arrange meetings within the school timetable as follows:

Day	Period	Possible Meeting
1	ii	Humanities faculty meeting
2	iii	Meeting for headmaster, deputy headmaster, heads of lower, middle and upper school and director of social education
4	iii	PE faculty meeting
5	iii	Mathematics faculty meeting
9	i	English faculty meeting
9	i	Language faculty meeting
9	iii	Meeting for heads of lower, middle and upper school
10	iv	Combined science meeting

The Head of Lower School is available for the whole of Day 2 for liaison with primary schools (except when attending meeting as stated above in period 3).

Pastoral tutors may meet as circumstances require as follows:

First year tutors:	Assembly period Monday morning
Second year tutors:	Assembly period Tuesday morning
Third year tutors:	Assembly period Wednesday morning
Fourth year tutors:	Assembly period Thursday morning
Fifth year tutors:	Assembly period Friday morning
Sixth year tutors:	Assembly period As required

SCHOOL STAFF COMMITTEE

	1969–70	1970–71	1971–72
Chairman:	Mr C. Ottaway	Mr C. Ottaway	Mr C. Ottaway
Treasurer:	Mr W. Butler	Mr P. Flood	Mr P. Flood
US representative:	Mrs B. Phelps	Mr M. Gillard	Mr M. Gillard
MS representative:	Mr H. Hinton	Mr R. Avery	Mr B. Baldock
LS representative:	Mr G. Jarman	Mr A. Neville	Mrs R. McKenny

Terms of Reference

'To inquire, on behalf of any member(s) of staff, into anything which is for the good of the school in general and for the staff in particular, and to act as a liaison between the staff and the headmaster for the redress of grievances, the answering of queries and the submission to the headmaster of constructive suggestions.'

Notes

1. In order to avoid, if possible, cutting across the duties of heads of schools and heads of departments, it is recommended that:

   In any matter affecting the welfare and discipline of pupils, the query/complaint be referred directly by staff to the appropriate head of school (and also be mentioned to the appropriate head of department).

   In any matter affecting a subject or department, the query/complaint be referred directly by staff to the appropriate head of department.

2. In particular, it is the custom of the committee to be responsible for making arrangements relating to:

   (i) The staff canteen: i.e. to ensure a supply, in the staff common room, of coffee and biscuits during the mid-morning break; also tea and biscuits during the lunch break.

   (ii) A staff presentation scheme for leavers.

   (iii) A staff welfare scheme: i.e. some provision to be made in the case of:

   births to lady members of staff and to wives of male members;
   marriages involving members of staff;
   deaths involving members of staff or pupils;
   protracted illness and hospitalization of staff;
   retirement of staff.

   (iv) End-of-term full staff meetings.

   (v) An annual staff dinner dance.

(vi) The staff canteen account: The treasurer is responsible for preparing—and publishing on the CRNB at the beginning of the following term—an income and expenditure account for the preceding term.

(vii) The annual election of a staff committee.

(viii) The transfer, to the elected chairman, of past staff committee records together with a statement of account in respect of the staff canteen and the staff presentation fund as at the end of the preceding summer term.

You might like to consider the following points:

1. On the face of it, one of the greatest resources available to a school is the skills and experience of its staff collaboratively employed in the pursuit of a given task. Do any of the examples presented above seem likely to harness this strength?

2. What distinction in your experience would you draw between 'participation' and 'consultation' as applied to the decision-making process in a school? Is your view the same as that of your head teacher?

3. In your view, do teachers in general want participation in the decision-making processes of their schools?

   Can you find the time for the type of participation referred to above?

   How would a teacher view such proposals? If he views his job merely in terms of the teaching task are additional difficulties created?

4. For there to be full participation in the decision-making process in a school clearly implies a shift in the locus of power. What do you think are the likely consequences to a school's communication processes?

One characteristic of organizations staffed by professionals is that the hierarchy of command is in the shape of a flattened pyramid. The most junior member of staff thus has access to the most senior member of the staff. Also, in such organizations the chief way of doing work is by *ad hoc* committee.

(a) The committee must remain the principal way of undertaking work in schools.

(b) All teaching staff have an equal right to be consulted and to know what is going on in their schools; inspection of committee minutes is one effective way of ensuring this.

(c) The headteacher's chief function is to lay down clear ways of doing work so that everyone knows exactly where they are.

(d) The overall policy of the school should be shaped by a school committee upon which are represented all those who have interest in the school. This committee should amongst other things determine the curricular and staffing policy of the school. It should also have the power to set up working parties that would appraise the various aspects of the schools. work and it is to this school committee that such working parties should report. The academic board, which now exists at the FE level, provides a useful model."

CONTACTS

The figures in brackets refer to the numbers of staff with whom work contacts were made.

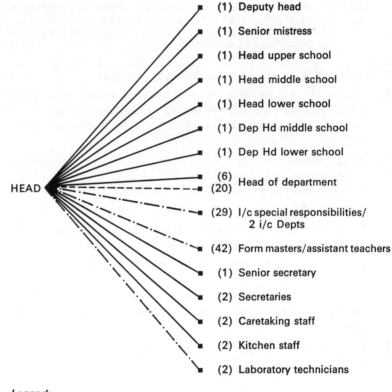

Contacts made by a head teacher and assistant teacher with other staff*

During the course of interviews on the subject of communications, teachers were asked to indicate by means of dotted, continuous and crossed lines drawn on a list of staff positions in their schools, the frequency of contact (daily, weekly or termly) between themselves and other members of staff. Only those contacts made for the purpose of undertaking work were included, all purely social contacts were excluded from the diagram. The contacts made were considered to be those with individuals or specific groups where such persons or groups were deliberately sought out. A blanket newsletter from the deputy head to all staff of the school would therefore have been excluded. The following two figures show the contact diagrams drawn by the head and an Assistant teacher in a particular school. Apart from the obviously far greater number of contacts shown on the head's diagram, it is interesting to note the way in which his contacts are structured, so as to allow daily contact with his most senior staff, weekly contact with heads of departments, and termly contact with more junior staff. The insularity demonstrated in the assistant teacher's diagram speaks for itself.

Work styles

When comparison is made between the work undertaken by the various senior staff in a large comprehensive school considerable differences emerge. It seems as though all of them specialize in different aspects of the school's work, thus the work of the head teacher, of the senior mistress, the deputy head(s), head of lower

Legend:

daily contact ———————
weekly contact ------------
termly contact —·—·—·—

* LYONS, G. *Op. Cit.*

224

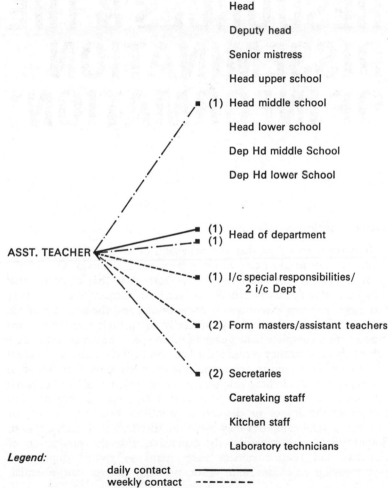

Figure 3: Work contacts made by an assistant teacher with other members of staff.

The figures in brackets refer to the numbers of staff with whom work contacts were made.

Head

Deputy head

Senior mistress

Head upper school

(1) Head middle school

Head lower school

Dep Hd middle School

Dep Hd lower School

(1)
(1) Head of department

ASST. TEACHER

(1) I/c special responsibilities/
2 i/c Dept

(2) Form masters/assistant teachers

(2) Secretaries

Caretaking staff

Kitchen staff

Laboratory technicians

Legend:

daily contact ——————
weekly contact ----------
termly contact —·—·—·—

school etc. show distinct profiles. The nature of the work, those with whom the job brings them into contact, are features that contribute to the mode by which work is undertaken, and together with personality features which any individual brings to his job help in dictating the characteristic pattern, the style of the job.

Although an individual may choose a 'style' in which to perform his job—a head may keep an 'open door', be 'available to whosoever wants him'—it is more likely that a considerable portion of the way the work is performed is pre-determined. Thus there are set procedures to invoke before a class teacher has access to the head's study, and the head's presence in the staff room would constrain the way a more junior teacher chatted to him in a way which is clearly distinguishable from that teacher's behaviour amongst his colleagues.

The two principal modes by which teachers undertake their administrative duties are, in face-to-face contact, talking to each other, and by writing. These modes usually relate to very different patterns of work, e.g. those found at different parts of a day, or perhaps constrained by the nature of the activity itself. The distribution of time spent on the various modes is by no means the same for all staff, quite different profiles being found.

The fact that 'discussing' is the way in which most work is undertaken (particularly if other verbal modes of doing work are associated with it, 'phone' and 'committee') is an important pointer to the type of institutions that schools inevitably are, and the nature of the relationships that exist within these institutions. This has a profound bearing upon the patterns of communication to emerge in a school and upon the disquiet that teaching staff appear to express towards the volume of 'paper' that now reaches them.

It seems as though small school tradition extrudes into large school practice.

You might like to consider the following points:

1. Are the conclusions to be drawn from the diagrams in this section as follows:

(a) Head teachers are busy people

(b) the position a person occupies in the hierarchy of an organization reflects his importance to that organization, and

(c) the more senior members of staff have more time to contact other people

and nothing more?

In the light of these conclusions would you justify the patterns of work that these diagrams reveal.

2. Or do you feel it is more likely that the overriding conclusion to be drawn from these examples is that the pattern of organization in a school (which includes the distribution of posts and the manner in which the incumbents perform their roles) almost wholly dictates the volume of communication and manner in which the individuals in that organization communicate with each other?

EQUIPMENT RESOURCES & THE DISSEMINATION OF INFORMATION *

Dissemination of information

It is often remarked that the provision of adequate equipment to facilitate information flows within schools is uncommon. One of the most commonly felt omissions in this respect is that of an internal telephone system. Many schools in fact have such systems, but very few have sufficient extensions to cover needs, and the problem of the location of these telephones, particularly when their scarcity is combined with a complete inadequacy of office space, becomes acute. Few schools have what they would regard as a sufficient number of external GPO telephones, and in one school the complete intercommunication system consisted of three extensions to one external GPO line. Some schools make use of a public address system, although such physical factors as the layout or dispersion of school buildings on one or between several campuses may make the installation of such a system inappropriate and/or excessively expensive. For the production of circulars and routine notices such items as stencil duplicators, photocopying machines and offset printing presses are essential,

* LYONS, G. *Op. Cit.*

although many schools again are underprovided in respect of such equipment.

The use of this equipment may require special skills and is inevitably time-consuming: it may therefore be considered more appropriate for this work to be undertaken by secretarial or technical staff than by teachers. The provision of secretarial help in most schools is quite insufficient, and the demands on secretaries' time is so great that commonly only the most senior members of staff have access to them.

There are also, in common use in schools, a variety of methods whereby information and instructions may be given out to all members of staff and pupils. Noticeboards have an extremely important function in this aspect of communication although the extent of their use varies from school to school. The location of noticeboards, in staffrooms, in departments, in tutor rooms or centrally, can be problematic when staff and pupils move frequently between different areas of the school. It is difficult, claim staff, to select from a mass of paper pinned to a board those notices which have application to a particular member of staff, and methods designed to obviate this difficulty include the provision of topic noticeboards, with an 'Urgent Notice' board, and the colour coding of notices by topic or urgency.

Such methods raise in acute form the problem of confidentiality and may involve special precautions being taken. An example of this with regard to noticeboards may involve a particular person being delegated to remove all confidential notices from the boards at the end of the day.

From a school handbook:

STAFF RESPONSIBILITIES

1. *Headmaster*

    He is responsible to the Governors and the LEA for the organization and administration of the school in all its aspects.

2. *Responsibilities of heads of department*
    (a) Responsible to the headmaster for the organization and teaching of the subject throughout the school.

(b) Responsible to the headmaster for the teaching standards of the members of the department—for ensuring that teaching is effective, preparation sound and marking thorough.

(c) Responsible for ensuring that new members of staff are settled in the school and are informed about school matters, general as well as departmental.

(d) Responsible for ordering equipment, requesting estimates and keeping a list of stock. Orders should be sent to the bursar as set out on the back of the order form.

(e) Responsible for advising the headmaster of the timetable needs of the subject—numbers of periods, use of rooms, disposition of staff.

(f) Responsible for the preparation of a scheme of work for the subject throughout the school and keeping it up-to-date. Ensuring that this scheme is followed, and that members of the department work towards common standards of presentation, and marking.

(g) Responsible for planning any courses, visits, special activities in connection with the teaching of the subject.

(h) Advising on and organizing 'out of school' activities connected with a subject e.g. English—libraries, magazine, literary competition; Geography—Geography Society, field study courses; Music—music at assemblies, choir, orchestra, etc.

(i) Responsible for encouraging a team spirit within the department, passing on to the headmaster the views and suggestions of colleagues, passing on to them decisions taken and matters discussed at heads of departments meetings.

(j) Advising the headmaster on examination policy (external and internal) in connection with the subject.

(k) Responsible for allocating pupils to groups and sets, and providing the headmaster with lists of these.

(l) He will be responsible for advising and assisting students attached to his department.

(m) He will work closely with careers staff where he may have specialized advice to offer, and with year tutors where the academic progress of a pupil needs to be considered.

(n) He will chair the departmental meetings held once every three weeks: see Appendix on Assemblies.

—Extract from *The Staff Handbook* issued by a large fully developed comprehensive school to all its staff.

A School Calendar

AUTUMN

Term begins
Year 7—Committee of
    vice chancellors
Predictive Exam
House of drama
Half-term holiday
Half-term holiday
Year 6 parents' evening

Coffee evening—Distribution
    of external exam certs
Mock external examinations
Winter O-levels begin

Year 1 parents' evening—
    Coniston and Tintern
Year 1 parents' evening—
    Raglan and Hornby
Christmas concert
Christmas concert
Term ends

SPRING

Term begins
Pantomime
Pantomime
Year V reports and
    parents' evening

Year 7 and 8 parents'
    evening
Half-term holiday
Half-term holiday
Play
Play

Year 4 examinations
Year 3 reports and
    parents' evening

Year 3 reports and
    parents' evening
Play
Play
Term ends

SUMMER

Term begins
Year 4 reports and
    parents' evening
Year 4 reports and
    parents' evening
Swimming gala

CSE examinations begin
GCE A-level examinations
    begin
Year 6—higher education—
    parents' evening
Play
Play
Spring holiday

School re-opens
Year 2 and Year 3 examinations
Year 1 reports and parents'
    evening. Coniston and Tintern
Year 1 reports and parents'
    evening. Raglan and Hornby
GCE O-level examinations begin
Year 2 reports and parents' evening.
    Coniston and Tintern
Year 2 reports and parents' evening.
    Raglan and Hornby
New Entrants' Evening
School Sports day
Junior school play
Year 3 reports issued
Year 4 reports issued
Term ends

HEADMASTER'S WEEKLY ORDERS TO STAFF
Issued Friday, 21st January

1. *School uniform*

   There has been a serious decline in school uniform standards of late. Members of staff are asked to check their forms and sets they teach, reporting any lack of conformity to DHM (Boys) or SM (Girls).

2. *Coal supplies*

   Please watch the 'Headmaster's Notices' in the staffroom to check for further news and/or directives re the next crisis.

3. *Meetings, visits, etc.*

Monday, January 24th	4.10	Sports and social committee
Tuesday, January 25th	12.40	2nd year maths, dept meeting
Tuesday, January 25th	4.10	Finance committee meeting
Wednesday, January 26th	3 & 4	4th year CHO talks
Wednesday, January 26th	12.00	6th form council
Wednesday, January 26th	4.10	Science dept meeting
Wednesday, January 26th	7.00	Nature conservancy final of quiz *vs.* Longbury Down. GS in Longbury.

4. *Deadlines*

   Tuesday, January 25th: 'A' and 'O' Level marking to be completed.
   Friday, January 28th: 4 p.m. 5th and 6th year reports to form teachers.

HEADMASTER'S WEEKLY ORDERS TO PUPILS
Issued Friday, 21st January

1. *School uniform*

   There has been a decline in the standard of school uniform recently. As from Monday, 24th January, Senior prefects and staff will make spot checks and any scarves, hats or other articles of outer clothing which in their opinion are not school uniform will be confiscated.

2. *Sports notice*

   (a) *Cross country results*   Two of our runners ran extremely well in the County Championships on Saturday, 15th January. R. Davies running in a large field in the under/14 race ran extremely well to finish 16th. F. Wilson completed the senior course in a good time to finish 9th.

Visitors to secondary schools in one LEA, Autumn Term, a Summary.

	NUMBER OF VISITS				NUMBER OF VISITORS				
	Arranged by LEA	*Arranged by PRO*	*Direct contact with school*	*Total*	*Students*	*From other LEAs*	*From overseas*	*Others*	*Total*
Comprehensive single-sex	1		12	13	30				30
Roman catholic	1		6	7	8			4	12
Comprehensive mixed	28	8	231	267	658	95	72	389	1214
Voluntary comprehensive	No Visitors								
Grammar	No Visitors								
Secondary modern	3		6	9	31			8	39
Total	33	8	255	296	727	95	72	401	1295

TOTAL—ALL SCHOOLS

Primary	148	13	450	611	1771	55	125	365	2316
Secondary	33	8	255	296	727	95	72	401	1295
Special			87	87	317	3		58	378
Total	181	21	792	994	2815	153	197	824	3989

(b) *Mixed hockey result* Our school team, weakened by injury, played extremely well against Danwell College 2nd XI on Sunday, 16th January, only to lose 4–0. For most of the 50 minutes play the match was closely fought, with three of the goals only being scored in the latter stages.

(c) *Fixtures* Boys' Swimming *vs.* Faversham High School at home, Friday, 21st January.

Boys' Cross country *vs.* Ganston GS at Ganston, Saturday, 22nd January.

3. *Examination Entries* All pupils taking CSE examinations will come to the DHM's room to check final entries as follows:

6th Form	Wednesday, Periods 5 and 6	January 26th
5:11	Thursday, Period 2	January 27th
5:18	Thursday, Period 3	January 27th
5:71	Thursday, Period 4	January 27th
5:63	Thursday, Period 5	January 27th
5:73 & 5:31	Thursday, Period 6	January 27th

Do not be late for your form's appointment

4. *Meetings, visits, etc.*

Tuesday–Thursday, January 25th to 27th: Arts trip to Whittleton (3rd years).
Wednesday, January 26th. Period 3 & 4: 4th year CHO Talks.
Wednesday, January 26th. 12.00: 6th Form council.
Wednesday, January 26th. 7.00: Final of quiz at Nature Conservancy Offices, Ganston.

You might like to consider the following points:

1. 'As schools become larger and more complex there is a need for them to formalize processes which in a small school could be constantly re-inforced or reappraised informally. This aspect of the large school, together with the impossibility of contacting everyone informally and the volume of activities undertaken, means that it is not only inevitable but *right* that the school's principal mode of communication should be 'on paper'. The real problem is that staff, pupils, parents, and all those who use the school, are not sufficiently aware of the changed nature of the new school. They must learn to commit themselves to paper. Once this is done, many of the problems will disappear. Time will thus solve many of the "communication" problems of the large school.'

   Do you agree with this opinion?

2. In order to ensure that the state of affairs referred to above can be brought about rapidly:

   (a) all new members of staff must be inducted into the school's administrative processes, and

   (b) the staff handbook of the school's rules and regulations must become a bible to staff.

   Do you agree?

   What in fact is the purpose that a school handbook serves? Would you, for example, recommend a probationary teacher in his first week at your school to read it?

3. If you did a survey of the questions that visitors, parents and pupils most commonly ask about the school, would this serve as an effective basis for a publication to distribute to them?

   Is what they want to know what you think they ought to know?

IS THIS THE WAY FORWARD?_____

It was stated at the beginning of this document that communication is no more than a manifestation of other organizational factors, and the foregoing sections have looked at different constituent aspects of school communications with a view to revealing some of their fundamental bases.

In this section it is suggested that the key to the communication problems a school may be suffering from should be sought in a study of the organization itself. Communications in a school are fundamentally a second order problem—they are a manifestation of other organizational decisions. If you get your organization right, then you have your communications right.

It is suggested that physical communication resources will always prove inadequate without sufficient staff to exploit them; that participation in the decision-making process is the only way to have effective communication in a school; and that the committees, the working parties, and so on, which are set up should be recruited from all sections of the school to aid effective interchange of information.

In producing an organizational framework to cope with the multifarious demands of school life, the school should aim for simplicity of organization. A clear description of the decision-making process and thereby of the authority structure; guidance, welfare and curricular processes that mutually re-inforce one another and are not in conflict; and sufficient staff to undertake and service these processes, are all prerequisites to a healthy organization.

POSTSCRIPT ____

this way the teacher is freed to concentrate on the learning situation itself and the problems of communication generated by the size and bureaucratic complexity of the present educational factories are done away with.

If the problems examined above all prove totally intractable, then is the following the direction in which schools must inevitably move. There is a growing literature to suggest this might be the case.

As schools increase in size the problems of policy direction and information dispersal and retrieval take up substantial and growing proportions of the school's time. The permissible time that trained teaching staff and children can spend with each other is thus severely restricted.

The school must be de-centralized. The teaching unit must be based upon the neighbourhood. Individual teachers constantly reacting with the same children in their own environment will thus be able to lead children, and others, in their learning experiences.

The school, as we know it, should disappear and be replaced by a resource centre providing the specialized help, skills and resources to the individual neighbourhood units as and when they are required. If the topic areas on which teachers spend the majority of their non-teaching time are examined, it becomes apparent that many of them may be disregarded. Problems of pupil health and welfare would be dealt with by the individual teachers in close contact with parents in easy physical reach. Buildings, grounds and their upkeep become problems of such smaller magnitude that they are solved in minutes rather than weeks. Transport problems do not exist. Extracurricular activities as such disappear since no topic is formally required and the category thus loses definition. Examinations work becomes irrelevant, as assessment becomes an ongoing process. Timetabling now becomes an unnecessary item as pupils and teacher organize their work in accordance with individual and group requirements. Equipment becomes the responsibility of the resource centre itself, and so on. In

The School Office

CONTENTS

INTRODUCTION: THE OFFICE IN THE SCHOOL

type of work is uppermost in the school at a particular time; it seems as if each week is typified by some major activity, a school play, the annual audit, half-term assessments and so on.

The office acts as a general information centre, receiving and storing information from staff, pupils and outside bodies. It issues information; it acts as a co-ordinator of the school information system; it plugs the gap of inadequate resources and, if necessary, of a poor internal communications system; and it acts as a filter and shield to the senior staff in the school.

You might care to add to this list additional functions that the office provides for a school.

"An examination of the state of the school office is like taking the organization's pulse."

The existence of the school office presupposes that what the office *is* doing is what the office *should be* doing. It is the intention of this discussion document to explore some of the ramifications of the office's existence in the school; to examine the sense of vocation that characterizes the secretary's work; to look at the office as a communications centre; and to consider the role and duties of the bursar.

The office is a permanent link between school and LEA and undertakes activities that rarely form a part of the work of most members of the teaching staff—secretaries in fact undertake work more closely identified with senior members of staff, particularly the Head Teacher; bursars are usually wholly engaged in administrative work.

The physical position of the office is interesting—all members of the school know where it is located; it is very rare for it not to be manned; and at a time of pressure or in an emergency it is an obvious place to turn to. In addition, the secretary's ability to cope with a pressure and variety of work loads serves to heighten the expectation among staff and pupils that she will be able to deal with almost all types of emergency. Further, the secretarial office is a sensitive index of whatever

A: THE SCHOOL SECRETARY___

1. The provision of secretarial help

How many secretaries does a school really need?

The demand for secretaries in a school is plainly much greater than the supply, and the distribution of secretarial help, set out below, appears to be typical in the experience of the large school.

It seems as though the availability of secretarial help will allow one secretary to service the Upper School, possibly attempting to be senior secretary to the school, being responsible for organizing the work of the office generally, and also attempting to be the Head Teacher's secretary. Another secretary (perhaps not full-time) will service the Lower School. Perhaps one further part-time secretary would be employed, attending mornings only for example, mainly to look after the clerical side of school meals.

Few schools are fortunate enough to have sufficient secretarial provision to allow a secretary to each of the major school sections, a personal secretary for the Head Teacher, and a secretary to look after the switchboard and deal with queries; in fact diary records collected by the 'Heads' Tasks' project showed on one occasion a senior mistress manning the switchboard.

Table 1 sets out the rate of secretarial provision in a sample of large secondary comprehensive schools. The number of hours worked by full-time secretaries was found to vary between 35 and 45 hours per week, although the unit used to compute the rate of secretarial provision was a more common $37\frac{1}{2}$ hours per week.

Table 1: School size, pupil/teacher ratios and secretarial provision in a sample of 16 large secondary comprehensive schools (this table is calculated on an average week of $37\frac{1}{2}$ hours)

No. of pupils on roll	Staff pupil ratio	No. of secretaries	Bursar/registrar
750	1:16.4	2.2	1
810	1:15.6	2.5	1
830	1:16.2	2.5	1
989	1:18.6	2.5	–
1020	1:19.2	3.4	–
1050	1:21.6	1.6	–
1100	1:19.0	2.6	–
1170	1:18.0	2.9	1
1189	1:17.7	2.9	–
1502	1:18.1	2.1	–
1500	1:19.4	2.5	–
1600	1:19.0	2.0	1
1600	1:19.3	4.1	1
1600	1:16.3	4.9	–
1720	1:19.6	2.8	–
2100	1:19.2	3.7	–

It is readily apparent that the rate of secretarial and bursarial provision follows no obvious pattern. Grouping schools by LEA imposes some order on the figures, but not absolutely. Even schools of comparable size, composition and history within one LEA show variation in their provision.

With the advent of relatively sophisticated duplicating/printing systems, e.g. offset litho machines, and with the increasing burden of the preparation of duplicated material that falls on the office, including the preparation of curriculum units, the dilemma is raised of whether secretarial staff should be asked to carry this extra workload or whether a separate section should be set up. Too rigid a division might bring its own problems in train. *In fact, do you think it is feasible to discuss the functions of the school office, and the duties of secretaries and bursars, outside the context of all the ancillary and support services enjoyed by the school?*

Which aspect of a school's work is most seriously hindered by lack of secretarial assistance do you think?

What is the best balance between office staff doing office work and teaching staff doing 'administration' and their own duplicating, stencil cutting and so on?

How much clerical support do the following need?

(a) Rank and file teacher, form tutor, house tutor;

(b) Year tutor, head of middle school, head of house;

(c) Head of subject department, head of faculty;

(d) Senior executives, head, deputies, senior tutors.

If your school were offered an additional full-time secretary, where would you most profitably deploy such help? On what basis would you make your decision?

2. What does the secretary do? What should she do?

It is interesting to compare the school secretary with notional ideas of secretaries in commerce or industry, a notion helped perhaps by exposure to television programmes or to films, where there certainly seems to be no lack either of secretarial numbers or of resources. The school office normally serves the complete school and in addition to this very general role the same secretaries function as private secretaries to its executives. The lack of important resources, e.g. office space, internal and external telephone lines, copying machines, recording aids, etc., may prove a serious hindrance to efficient work, since in these circumstances proper delegation of activities may be impaired, bureaucratic channels for doing work cannot be properly developed and the school secretray may become a general factotum.

Whilst it is possible to some extent to analyse the administrative work of teaching members of staff in terms of the topic being undertaken, e.g. pupil welfare, curricular activities, timetabling, etc., it must be obvious that when undertaking work on requisitions, a secretary does so from a very different standpoint, bringing a clerical or processing component to a task that has some measure of routine executive performance. It must however be added that the levels and types of work undertaken by school secretaries do vary enormously.

The secretary is usually concerned with maintaining routine processes or acting directly under instructions, and she does so by calling upon a surprisingly restricted range of activities. Set out below in Table 2, as a rate per secretary per week, are the major methods by which a secretarial service is provided to a school.

Table 2: Time spent per secretary per week on various activities

	No. of hours
Clerical work	21.4
In discussion	5.0
School meals	4.8
Information transfer	4.1
Other	2.2
Total per week	37.5

In categorizing the work undertaken by the school secretary, routine office duties account for by far the largest portion. However, it is likely that the secretary will be called upon to participate in all of the following:

Meals	Pupil careers and tertiary education
Internal and external examinations	
Finance	Pupil admittance and leaving
Pupil health and welfare	Holidays, sports and extra-curricular activities
Equipment	Personal organization
Formal and informal communications	Buildings, grounds and upkeep
Professional development and staff welfare	The timetable
	Staffing
	Supervisory duties
Curricular activities	Transport

and so on

The contacts made in undertaking this work, shown in Table 3, represent all those people with whom and for whom the school undertakes its work, and particularly exemplifies the vital link that the school office provides to the school's functioning.

Table 3: Time spent per secretary per week with named contact

	No. of hours
Self	21.6
Assistant teachers	2.8
Pupils	2.6
Secretaries and bursars	1.5
Head Teacher	1.4
Parent	0.7
Deputy Head	0.7
Heads of schools, senior mistress, etc.	0.5
LEA personnel	0.4
Sales and suppliers	0.3
Auxiliary/ancillary staff	0.3
Heads of dept., i/c examinations, etc.	0.3
Teachers other schools	0.2
House year staff	0.2
Pupil meals service	0.2
Pupil health service	0.2
EWO, probation service, police, etc.	0.2
General public	0.1
Careers	0.1
Student teachers, applicants	0.1
Others	3.1
Total per week	37.5

For many secretaries, the days of the week have a regularity and pattern to them that provides a discernible basis to the day's activities. Other events, e.g. beginning of term admissions, medicals, examinations, end of year accounts, necessarily impinge upon this pattern. It seems that a typical day would show the following sequential arrangements:

Arrive in office, open safe, files, etc., and prepare for day's work;
Open, read and distribute the post;
Issue attendance registers;
Collect dinner money, sell tickets, begin to balance and check money, registers;
Typing of correspondence;
Duplicating work;
Filing work;
Work on accounts;
Discussions with staff, Head Teacher, etc.;

Collate post for end of day, stamp, enter in post book;
Lock up office.
Throughout the day, they would also be dealing with:
External telephone;
Internal telephone;
Queries from pupils, staff, parents, visitors, tradesmen and so on;
Receiving money;
Paying out money, e.g. petty cash.
The secretary's pattern of work is further exemplified by the two diaries that follow.

Secretary's Diary (1)

9.00– 9.10	Moved out of my office to accommodate Public Health Medical Examinations
9.10– 9.55	Typing examination stencils
9.55–10.15	Entered late people in late book and registers checked for absence notes
10.15–12.00	Typing examination stencils
12.00– 1.00	Lunch
1.00– 1.30	Checking medical cards and tracing pupils for BCG skin tests
1.30– 2.10	Typing notes for registers
2.10– 2.50	Taking dictation from head of middle school and typing same
2.50– 3.20	Checking late dinner money, balancing, and entering a balance summary sheet
3.20– 4.30	Taking dictation and typing same
Plus	Phone, interruptions, first aid, etc., throughout day.

Secretary's Diary (2)

8.30–11.30	*Collection of school meals money; Seeing caretaker, lab. technician, pupils, new pupil, staff—collecting their meals money, with other secretary; Filling out late slips*
11.30–12.00	*Writing Education Welfare Officer re absentees; Dealing with queries; Dealing with phone*
12.00–12.15	*Typing*
12.15–12.25	*Listing absentees*
12.25–12.30	*Dinner check with prefects in foyer*
12.30– 1.00	*Duplicating material; More work on absences*
1.00– 2.00	*Lunch*
2.00– 3.00	*Duplicating Reception work Phone calls*
3.00– 4.45	*Correspondence, typing*
4.45– 5.15	*Packing up for end of day*

To summarize, therefore, school secretaries typically provide the following services:

(a) they undertake routine office duties of a clerical nature—copy typing, filing, duplicating and such like;

(b) they act as receptionists, telephone operators and deal with queries;

(c) one of them may act as the Head Teacher's personal secretary, arranging his diary, doing his correspondence, etc.; others, if available, may service other sections of the school;

(d) in the absence of a bursar, one of the secretaries would be senior secretary, responsible for the organization and the running of the office, and possibly taking on some bursarial duties, such as concern for some aspects of furnishing, equipment, the handling of money, etc.

Owing to the nature of the service that secretaries supply to the school:

(i) the work undertaken is particularly characterized by its volume, its pace and pressure;

(ii) the school office becomes a communications centre for the school;

(iii) secretaries, along with teaching staff, share a sense of vocation; and

(iv) the school office evolves into a focal point of the school characterized by many unintended functions.

3. Pace, pressure and volume of activities undertaken

This is one of the most outstanding features of the secretaries' work in the large school.

'There is little time during the day for thinking or planning of any kind.'

The volume of activities, at certain key periods of a day, is very high, is extremely varied in content, and is very probably an accurate mirror of work going on in the school at that moment. In one 25 minute period, one secretary dealt with queries relating to:

'Dentist, police re damage, staff unpaid leave, confidential matter, evening lettings, furniture, junior prize giving, records from other authorities, commercial suppliers and equipment maintenance, staff notice board, making up attendance register.'

It seems that it is by no means unusual to embark on typing which should take an hour or so, to find (because of interruptions) that it is still uncompleted at the end of the day.

> '*Took from 11.15–4.05 to type CSE exam paper—actual total time spent typing, only 2½ hours.*'

> '*Headmaster's correspondence attempted but nothing achieved—too many interruptions.*'

Specific delegation of duties is no certain insurance against interruption, because the amount of work to be done fluctuates, staff may be absent and scarce equipment breaks down. Part-time help proves to be only a partial ameliorator, because there is likely to be a disruption to the necessary continuity of information flow which is an essential ingredient for an efficient office.

Comments provided by secretaries suggested that if a secretary is absent then the work will almost inevitably await her return. The other secretaries would undertake it, but they do not have the time to do so. It is obvious that to cope with the pressure and to get essential work completed on time, some rationalization of activities and of work flow must take place.

> '*Had to refuse typing for head of music, too much work in hand.*'

> '*Work often done on Friday to prepare for Monday's rush.*'

Some schools have attempted the strategy of insisting that staff and pupils might be directed, insofar as it is practicable, to ask queries of the office only at certain times; inevitably, these periods are at breaks, and because of the amount of work waiting to be done, then secretaries begin working through their own coffee breaks, sometimes lunch, or reduce lunch to a half-hour period only.

> '*To lunch at 12.35—intercepted in corridor twice by boys with requests—came back twice!*'

For the very position and function of the school office makes secretarial staff readily available at all times.

It also seems fairly common to begin work some 10 to 15 minutes early, although it seems uncommon to work over at evenings or weekends. Some secretaries however occasionally do work over at these periods and one secretary was found who did three weeks unpaid overtime in August to prepare for the opening day of the Autumn Term.

In your view, is it primarily:

- **(a) the interruptions;**
- **(b) the 'peaking';**
- **(c) the overall numerical inadequacy of provision;**
- **(d) a lack of good organization**

which causes the pressure?

4. Range of activities undertaken

Few secretaries in industry would expect to undertake quite the range of activities considered 'normal' by a school secretary, and, in addition, there is at least a notional responsibility for children since, in a school, children are automatically placed in a position of dependence upon adults.

Secretaries exercise a sense of practicality and, to a male-dominated administrative hierarchy, they may bring a housewife's or a mother's touch, caring for the younger children, applying first aid, etc. If this latter conjecture is true then, where teachers are seen as figures of discipline, the secretary occupies a non-threatening role, which makes her an easy person to approach, to ask questions of and to seek guidance from.

Although most secretaries in general share communication tasks, the senior secretaries often appear to be acting at a higher level of responsibility, discussing with teaching staff current problems, rather than merely receiving and acting upon instructions. The secretaries are also, by virtue of the location of the office and the nature of their work, seen to be in possession of almost all information, not just the most important: it was, for example, to the secretary that a student teacher went for information about the detention system.

In some senses, then, the school secretaries become the embodiment of the institution, they help to humanize it; they cope with problems that have no routine channels for solution; and they bring to the organization a maternal quality, a feminine touch, as mothers and homemakers. Certainly they soften the professional nature of the organization.

'Welcome new groundsman with small chat.'

'Issue information to new staff—tactfully help them to settle in.'

The secretaries' position in the centre of the communications network, their willingness to help and their approachability entail a whole host of inquiries and calls for aid.

'Helped member of staff sort out muddle about his salary—phoned education office for him.'

'Inquiries from parents over lost property followed up.'

Their ability to cope with the unexpected is indicated by their willingness to tackle problems where no outline procedures have been adopted.

Secretaries are the people to whom children turn when accidents happen, when things go wrong. Secretaries were found for example:

Sewing boy's trousers, and carrying out all types of running repairs.
Cleaning clay off skirt and cardigan of girl and drying off her skirt.
Mending spectacles.
Mending broken sandal.
Drying clothes of child who fell fully dressed into swimming pool.

By doing something efficiently and satisfying a need, an expectation seems to be built up in the clients. The behaviour of secretaries demonstrates an ability and willingness to occupy roles necessary to the organization, but not officially filled; they may, for example, be acting as the school nurse.

'If the First Aid master is teaching and the boy's injury is small, it causes less disruption if I put on a plaster. If the accident is severe, the boy is sent to the First Aid master, and on his instructions I contact the parents and arrange transport to hospital.'

The extent of their first aid activities proves quite remarkable. One secretary in one day listed the following:

10 mins.	Pupil with discharging ear—referred to nurse.
5 mins.	Informing parent pupil sent home ill.
1 min.	Gave pupil tablet for headache.
5 mins.	Pupil feeling dizzy—taken to nurse.
5 mins.	Pupil injured in playground—referred to nurse.
5 mins.	Pupil fell downstairs—referred to nurse.
10 mins.	Called ambulance for two previous pupils.
5 mins.	Informed parents of above.
10 mins.	Traced sister of pupil to accompany him in ambulance.
5 mins.	Administer aspirin and a cup of tea to the head of lower school.

One secretary blandly wrote *'Extract pen from boy's stomach'*, presumably while she was also answering the switchboard, dealing with the Head's correspondence, and running off the 3rd-year exam papers for the Head of Geography Department.

The secretaries' maternal interest in pupil welfare, certainly their expressed interest and concern, and their access to information, appear to lead to a wider interest in pupil welfare as such.

In addition to the activities discussed so far, a secretary could also find herself acting in any of the three following capacities:

(a) as the Head Teacher's secretary

(b) as a receptionist

(c) as accountant

(a) The secretary as the Head Teacher's secretary

Few Head Teachers are able to afford to appoint one secretary exclusively for their own work, and when this does occur then the secretary can act in some capacity as a personal assistant. She will function as a co-ordinator between the Head Teacher and the school, and between the Head and the world outside school, invariably occupying a position of seniority amongst the other secretaries and crucially so when the school does not have a bursar. If secretarial provision is not so generous, she will not be so exclusively concerned with the Head Teacher's work and she will function as the Senior Secretary in the school with principal responsibility for the school office. In some schools the work is still more evenly spread with all secretaries sharing the Head Teacher's letters, dictation, typing etc.

Assuming that the Head Teacher is able to have his own secretary, then she will most probably undertake the following:

1. Open and read the Head Teacher's post each morning, filing relevant copies, and sorting the mail for his attention.

2. Take dictation from the Head Teacher, type his letters, memos, etc. and also type matters of a confidential status, e.g. reports and testimonials.

3. A daily (planned) consultation about the work to be achieved that day.

4. Arrange the Head Teacher's diary, making appointments with staff, pupils, parents, etc.

5. Make telephone calls, and receive calls on the Head Teacher's behalf. See staff and pupils on his behalf also, thus shielding him from routine work and interruptions.

6. Act in an executive capacity for matters specifically delegated by the Head, e.g. staffing. One Head Teacher's secretary saw 'staff to get details checked, saw clerk to the governors and chairman of the governors over the wording of the advertisement and the application forms, typed the advertisement, after checking with the County Offices, and finally phoned the local paper.'

7. 'Hold the fort' in the Head Teacher's absence. When one Head Teacher went home ill then his secretary received and acted on instructions about a governors' meeting and in his absence she took it upon herself to deal with some of the correspondence. This most probably related to work in hand, for it must not be supposed that her work would conflict with that of the Head Teacher's deputy.

8. In the absence of a bursar, allocate clerical work in the office and supervise its progress. She will in fact be senior secretary to the school.

9. She may also provide some secretarial service to senior staff, e.g. type letters for the deputy head.

(b) The secretary as receptionist

All secretaries appear to share in reception and telephone duties although the level of involvement varies. Reception may be as simple as:

'receiving from a parent ingredients necessary for Home Economics lesson this morning, and forgotten by her daughter.'

Although few schools are able to afford the luxury of a switchboard operator, it must not be assumed that the operator does nothing other than handle telephone calls. She is most likely to be handling routine clerical duties simultaneously, although junior assistants and part-time secretaries are likely to be doing more of this sort of work.

The switchboard of a large school is a very busy place. Secretaries at one school made a record of the number of telephone calls they handled in a week, shown below in Table 4, and this very probably, because of the difficulties of recording information, under-represents the true figure.

Table 4: Number of telephone calls handled in a week in one large school

	Mon.	Tues.	Wed.	Thurs.	Fri.	Total
Internal calls	60	40	50	46	30	226
GPO external calls	98	65	75	75	70	383
Total	158	105	125	121	100	609

If each call lasted for only one minute then that would represent some ten hours work per week, but not every member of staff in a school is on an internal telephone, in fact, not all schools sampled had an internal telephone system.

> 'Each external phone call entailed (a secretary) writing out a message sheet, and delivering to staff or to their pigeon hole.'

If this latter situation is operative, then the amount of work caused by a telephone call is considerably increased. Where a school does not have a switchboard operator or an automatic exchange, then the telephone can cause interruptions to any work at hand and heightens the pressure. One of the greatest problems seems to be in tracing staff for phone calls, urgent messages, etc. It seems as if a great deal of time must be spent walking around the school searching for people, although the difficulties of internal communications are reflected equally in the problems of information retrieval:

> 'Asked head of PE to inform me when groundsman returns after being on sick leave—learnt he has been back several days.'

This appears to reflect a situation in which the secretarial staff and aids to communication are matched to the number of teaching staff as though they were the only occupiers of school premises. In fact, although the pupils impose no direct burden on these services, the obstacles to communication are more fairly represented in terms of an office building occupied by the number of pupils on the school roll and all other additional staff.

Because of the size of the schools, the lack of resources and the difficulty of internal communications, at least at the time of the sampling, then what could have been a simple information transfer may become an irksome, time-consuming piece of work. This would appear to be particularly true where activities are not absolutely routine and where the geography of the school becomes an important variable.

Secretaries are also on occasions used as messengers outside school.

The functions of a receptionist in a large business organization or in other administrations, e.g. hospitals and hotels, are clearly delineated and the receptionist has an identifiable place of work. This ensures a reduction in both the number of interruptions and the disruption of the work not only of the main office, but, if the administrative offices are laid out as in our diagram, then also to the work of the Head and Deputy Head.

(c) The secretary as accountant

It has been mentioned above that the Senior Secretary in a school where there is not a bursar is likely to assume responsibility for the running of the school office, and to take on functions which would otherwise be assumed by a bursar if available. The handling and responsibility for money in school is an example of such a duty.

The table below shows the amount of money handled in one half of a week, Monday-Wednesday, at one large comprehensive school.

Table 5: Money handled in school office in one half-week

Dinner money, each Monday	£500·00	
Amount involved in school play	287·73	
		£787·73
Sales in Tuck Shop, milk and orange	34·62½	
Visits	23·82½	
Book subscriptions	6·00	
School photographs	2·10	
Ski trip	25·50	
French exchange visit	74·00	
Sale of books	1·12½	
Transport by minibus reclaimed from LEA	2·62½	
	169·80	
Deduct Petty Cash	6·55	
		163·25
Total Handled		£950·98

A more detailed breakdown of the likely transactions of the school office involving money over the course of a year is given below in Table 6.

Table 6: Likely money transactions into and out of the school office over a year

MONEY IN	MONEY OUT
Daily	*Daily*
Tuck shop items issued and sold, money and stock totalled and balanced for banking	Petty cash payments
	Stamps issued
Money for stamps and postage account balanced	
Weekly	*Weekly*
Dinner ticket order forms (Nos. of tickets, free dinners, staff dinners, cash paid)	Dinner tickets issued
Termly	*Annually*
Payments into school fund	School magazine distributed to each pupil and staff member on approved payment
Subscriptions for commercial magazines supplied at reduced rates	
Intermittently throughout year	*Intermittently throughout year*
Money for charities	Payments to charities
Advertisement fees from advertisers in school magazine	Payments to pupils and staff
	Money to LEA
Money for projects, needlework sales, woodwork, etc.	Payments for running costs
Money from LEA for running school minibus	Deposits, bills and insurance premiums
Money for school visits	Money for school visits and functions
Money for miscellaneous items (staff telephone a/c, lost property poundage, staff presents, income from dances etc.)	Money to be banked
Money drawn from bank	

5. Summary

The secretaries' nearness to those who hold authority in the school probably ensures that some reflected authority is invested in them. However the hierarchical distinctions within the school office are never very marked and at time of maximum pressure the school secretary or any of the office staff will perform any of the varied functions which fall to them. Although secretaries are associated particularly with the routine processes of running a school it can by no means be assumed that they are exclusively so concerned. For the sense of vocation and dedication which enables the teaching staff to undertake their work is equally shared by secretaries.

The position of secretary may lead to a situation of potential conflict (as might, for different reasons, that of the Bursar—see below), for, whilst professionally they must be junior to any member of the teaching staff, their usefulness to the organization is likely to contradict this relationship at times; in the controlling of resources, for example, sometimes the entreaties of even the most senior members of staff must be denied.

It seems as though the school must look to the secretaries' sense of identity with the organization and to their sense of vocation, in order for work to be completed on time during the very busiest periods. There is plenty of evidence of this vocation and in fact this characteristic of the school secretaries' work seems to be one of the attractions motivating some of them to undertake the work in the first place.

'I would like to place on record that I personally do not feel "hard done by" by the pressure and pace of the work, and in common with most school secretaries I feel it is part of the job and would not wish to change it.'

They are often amongst the longest serving members of staff of the school.

Secretaries plainly share the commitment and professional values of the teaching staff in a school.

Does this in your view represent any danger to your school?

Do you think secretarial duties should be much more tightly defined?

How might the problems you see best be resolved?

B. THE BURSAR___

As a school becomes larger, so the volume of administrative work of a kind bearing no relation to teaching increases, to the point where it seems beneficial to make a full-time appointment to the administrative staff—this seems to be the assumption underlying the appointment of a Bursar.

Traditionally, bursars are not necessarily associated with large schools, but are a product of the early days of Grammar Schools when the payment of tuition fees and staff salaries was not a matter of a transaction between state and the various banking institutions that it is today. Finance is no longer the bursars' sole concern—they are expected to undertake administrative tasks requiring the exercise of initiative which is not normally demanded of secretaries. The bursar, in common with such people as the counsellor or social worker, is in a somewhat anomalous position in a school, in that he is regarded as having similar status to the teaching staff, but without necessarily having any teaching commitments; his duties are not clearly defined in the way that those of, say, the matron are; and his position might be regarded with some caution and even suspicion by the teaching staff who might feel their position eroded by the appointment of a person taking on some aspects of their duties without having their professional competence as teachers. In some ways the bursar may represent to teachers a potential threat—the threat, that is, of 'the full-time administrator who would gradually take over a school and run the organization to the benefit of other administrators without proper regard to educational ends.'

Does the potential conflict between administrators and academics have any basis in reality in the secondary school?

How much power does/should the bursar really have?

Does he aid the school as a cutter of red tape? Or, is he an agent of the LEA in the school—for whom does he work?

How do you control him?

1. What should the bursar do? What does he do?

It seems that Head Teachers would like the bursar to be regarded as a member of the senior staff of the school. However, when comparison is made with the teaching staff, it is seen that the bursar's pattern of work is very different.

They do not have the same working hours or holidays as teachers, their office tends to be near the school secretary's office, and in many ways the kind of work they do shows more similarity to a school secretary's work than to that of the teaching staff.

In surveying what bursars did in a sample of schools no clear job description emerged.

What the bursar does

A research project (Lyons, G. *op. cit.*) which surveyed bursars' work found the following:

(1) In comparison with teachers' activities, bursars are heavily represented in tasks that do not necessarily feature teaching staff (Table 7).

(2) The methods by which the bursar undertakes his work show a marked difference when comparison is made with the principal methods of senior teachers' work (Table 8). The bursar is a writer.

It follows that the characteristic way for a bursar to work, is 'working alone', and that the most frequent contacts made are with secretaries. Trade contacts, although representing only six per cent of his time, are far greater than those made by members of the teaching staff (Table 9).

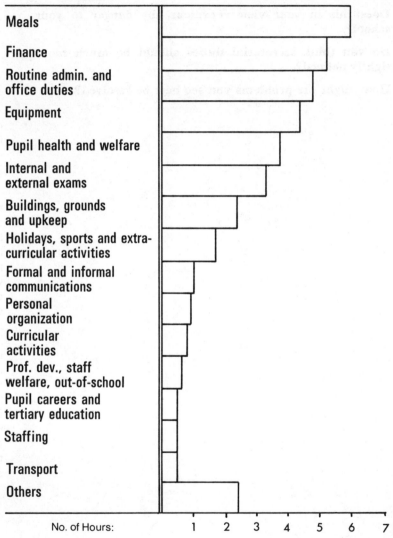

Table 7: Number of hours spent by a bursar each week on various activities

Meals

Finance

Routine admin. and office duties

Equipment

Pupil health and welfare

Internal and external exams

Buildings, grounds and upkeep

Holidays, sports and extra-curricular activities

Formal and informal communications

Personal organization

Curricular activities

Prof. dev., staff welfare, out-of-school

Pupil careers and tertiary education

Staffing

Transport

Others

No. of Hours: 1   2   3   4   5   6   7

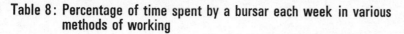

Table 8: Percentage of time spent by a bursar each week in various methods of working

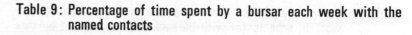

Table 9: Percentage of time spent by a bursar each week with the named contacts

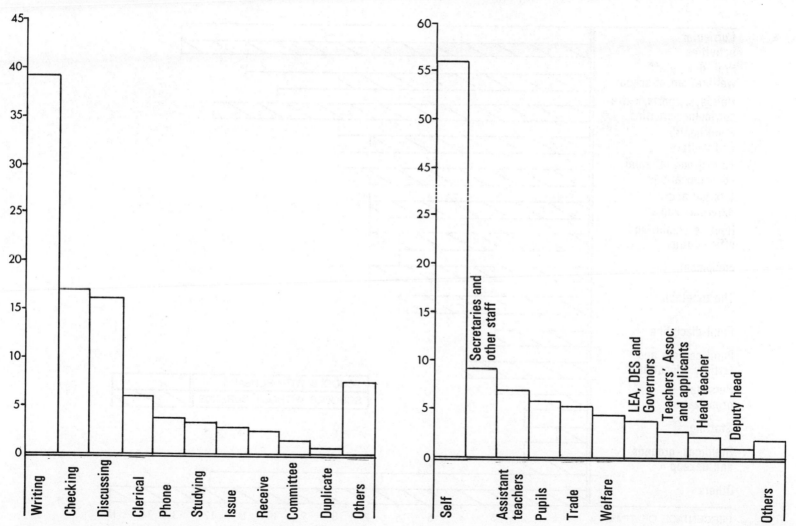

245

Table 10: Percentage of time spent by senior staff on administrative work in schools (a) with bursars and (b) without bursars

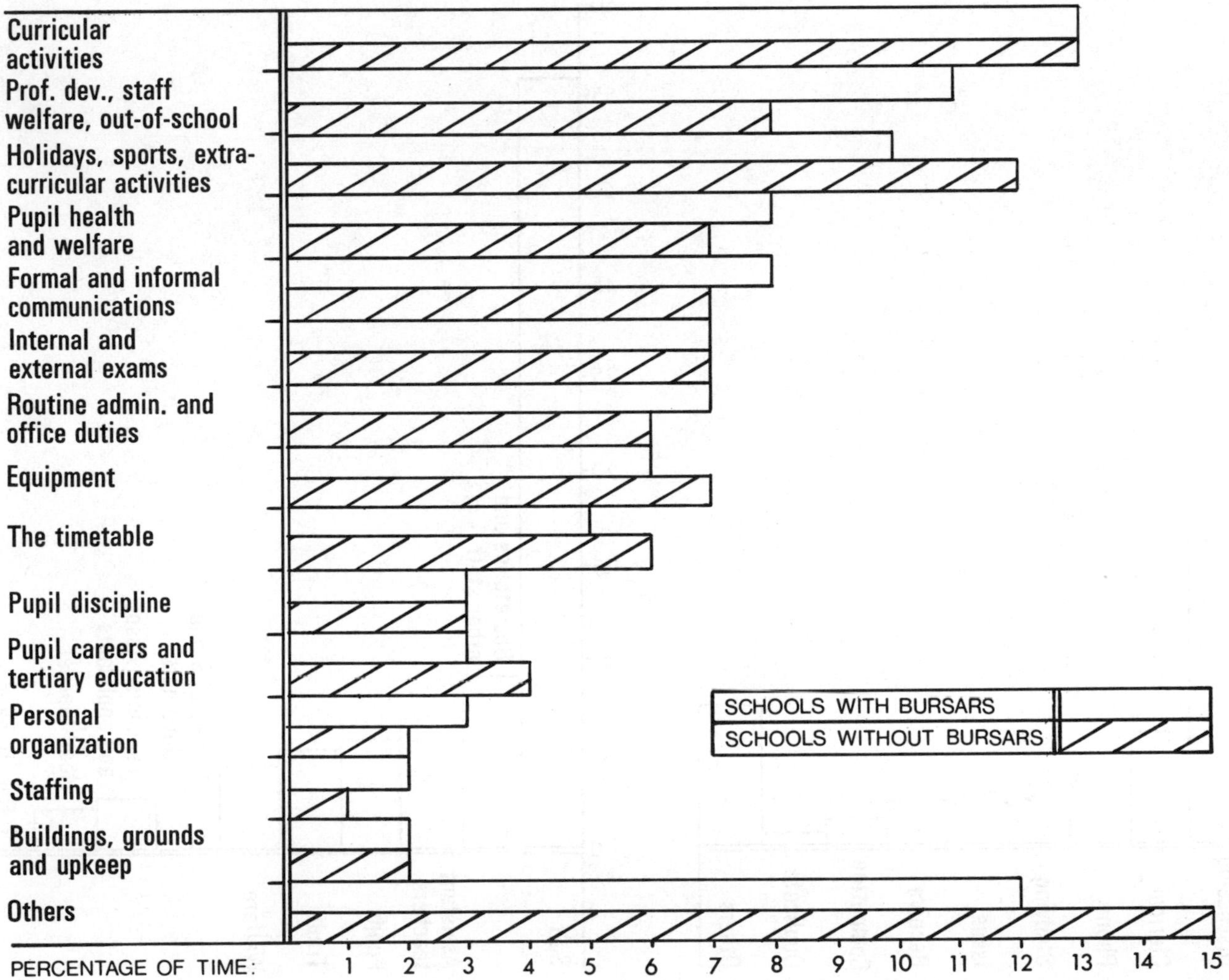
Curricular activities
Prof. dev., staff welfare, out-of-school
Holidays, sports, extra-curricular activities
Pupil health and welfare
Formal and informal communications
Internal and external exams
Routine admin. and office duties
Equipment
The timetable
Pupil discipline
Pupil careers and tertiary education
Personal organization
Staffing
Buildings, grounds and upkeep
Others
SCHOOLS WITH BURSARS
SCHOOLS WITHOUT BURSARS
PERCENTAGE OF TIME:
1 2 3 4 5 6 7 8 9 10 11 12 13 14 15

2. Schools with bursars—schools without bursars

If a comparison is made between the amount of time senior teaching staff (including the Head) spend on the various categories of school administration in schools where there is a bursar and schools where there is none, generally little difference is found between the two samples (Table 10).

Since senior staff in schools where no bursar is present do not conspicuously undertake the bursarial type of activities, certainly when measured in terms of the hours of effort, it becomes interesting to ask who actually is undertaking this type of work.

It is immediately apparent that the work is of two categories:

(1) *accepting responsibility for tasks, i.e. administrative or executive responsibility, and*

(2) *physically undertaking the routine aspect of whichever task is to hand.*

Almost certainly senior teachers in schools without bursars would have a burden of signing invoices, ordering equipment, taking responsibility for stock books, initiating building maintenance, recruiting ancillary staff, etc., while the routine burden of the task operation would fall upon the secretarial office. To introduce a bursar into a school may therefore free senior staff from routine responsibilities which, although not taking up a disproportionate share of their time, are nevertheless distractions from the work in hand; the bursar will also be able to offer help with the clerical side of some tasks. Thus the main beneficiaries from a bursar's introduction in terms of potential work capacity will apparently be the secretarial office.

Where the school does not have a bursar secretaries seem to undertake the same tasks but at a higher level of responsibility, reporting directly to the senior member of staff most involved.

In schools which did not have bursars, secretaries were involved in the following activities that had quite clearly been identified as undertaken in other schools by bursars:

Detailed financial and account work;

Preparing accounts for presentation to auditors;

Issuing salary cheques to staff;

Dealing with problems about staffing and ancillary staff;

Placing orders and stock taking, etc.;

Statistical returns to LEA;

Attendances;

Admissions, including interviewing and documentation;

and activities of service responsibility normally assumed by bursars, such as:

School transport arrangements;

Fire drills;

Laundry.

Work upon buildings, grounds and their upkeep is one area of activity which, in the absence of a bursar, is not undertaken by secretaries beyond the routine typing of, for example, repairs proformas.

It was interesting also to note at one school which did have a bursar, but who was absent at the time, which other members of staff had to be contacted in order to initiate action. It was necessary for the caretaker to supply keys, for the deputy head to sanction the use of a tape-recorder, secretaries checked accounts with the relevant members of staff, and 'because of bursar's absence (the secretary) welcomed new groundsman'. The secretary and caretaker dealt with a problem of repairs, and also went to the bank with money.

Now follow two diaries which cover a day's work in two fully developed comprehensive schools. Also attached are two job specifications for bursars from two other fully developed comprehensive schools.

Does this information allow you to judge whether any of these bursars are undertaking the type of activity, in content or load, that you would have anticipated?

Bursar's Diary (i)

Time	Mode	With	Event
8.15– 8.40	Check	Self	Preparation of registers
8.40– 8.50	Discuss	Pupils	General queries
8.50–10.15	Check / collect	Self	Collect registers and record absentees
10.15–10.30	Discuss	Cook Supervisor	Dinner numbers
10.30–10.45	Receive	Pupils	School funds
10.45–11.30	Write / check	Self	Update dinner registers, late payments
11.30–12.10	Check	Self	Pupils absent for more than 3 days
12.10–12.40	Write	Self	Lists of pupils absent for more than 3 days for form tutor's comments
12.40– 1.30			Lunch
1.30– 1.40	Check	Self	Preparation of registers
1.40– 2.30	Check / collect	Self	Collect registers and record absentees
2.30– 3.00	Discuss	Form tutors	Pupil absences
3.00– 3.45	Discuss	LEA	New application for free meals
3.45– 4.15	Write	Self	Prepare weekly record of school meals
4.15– 4.40	Write	Self	Prepare daily record of meals actually taken

Bursar's Diary (ii)

Time	Mode	With	Event
9.00– 9.50	Write	Self	Correspondence
9.50–10.45	Check and distribute	Pupils	Classroom stationery
11.00–11.30	Write	Self	Financial arrangements for forthcoming Spring Fair
11.30–12.30			Preparing and banking monies
12.30–12.45	Discuss	Teacher in charge of audio-visual aids & technician	Future policy about audio-visual aid equipment
12.45– 1.20	Discuss	Senior pupils	Accounts of upper school tuckshop
1.20– 2.00			Lunch
2.00– 2.40	Discuss	Tradesman	Printing of receipt books, stationery, etc.
2.40– 3.30	Write	Self	Outgoing mail, preparing registers, receipt forms, money bags, etc., for savings collection on Monday morning
3.30– 4.30	Discuss	Teachers and caretakers	PTA Spring Fair on following day

What types of work do you think bursars ought to be undertaking?

It has been suggested that the three main areas of work for a school bursar should be: finance; institutional management; and the servicing of committees.

Do you agree?

Or: Is his principal function to man the office in the long summer vacation?

Bursar's duties (School 1)
From the school's handbook

1. *Overall responsibility for administration and organization*

2. *The reception and distribution of incoming correspondence. He will draft many routine letters*

3. *Finance—overall responsibility*

   (i) Control of expenditure of annual school allowance through the allocation of amounts to depts. (determined by H/M); the keeping of up-to-date estimates of monies spent; the placing of orders; checking of receipts and keeping of accounts to be presented to the auditors.

   (ii) The control, accounting and payment of monies from private school funds; private music lessons; school sales and staff beverages.

   (iii) Responsibility for the collection, book-keeping and banking of school meals money.

   (iv) The distribution of salary cheques for teaching and non-teaching staff.

   (v) Assisting the headmaster in the preparation of estimates.

4. *Supervision of furniture, buildings and grounds*

   To deal with repairs to the fabric through contact with the Clerk of Works; maintenance of grounds through contact with the groundsman; repairs of furniture through contact with LEA designated contractors; etc.

5. *Non-teaching staff*

   Control of laboratory assistants; cleaners; caretakers; school meals supervisors, and assistance of cooks with school meals staff.

6. *General administration*

   (i) The preparation of statistics for the Headmaster and statistical returns to the Department of Education, and the LEA.

   (ii) Supervision of attendance registers; admission registers; returns on attendance, and admin. work involved with leavers. Interviewing and documentation concerning admissions.

   (iii) Responsibility for annual stocktaking of equipment and furniture.

   (iv) All clerical work concerned with lettings.

7. *Transport*

   (i) Liaison with school social worker and any admin. for master i/c school buses.

   (ii) Organizing transport for school games, and control of school minibuses.

8. *General Correspondence*

   All that correspondence not directly the concern of the Headmaster, the deputy or the heads of schools.

9. *To receive all those people visiting the school on admin. or business matters—travellers, etc.*

10. *Ordering of office equipment and general school stationery for both upper and lower schools, and arranging for servicing and repair of office machinery*

Bursar's duties (School 2)
From the school's handbook

1. *Status of bursar*

   As a middle range head of department, with comparable department.

2. *Main areas of responsibility.*

   (a) In immediate charge of the office—an office manager.
   (b) The administrative officer for other non-teachers.

3. *Organization of office work* (specialization rudimentary)

   (a) Official accounts
   (b) Dinner accounts
   (c) Materials and service to staff
   (d) Specific Headmaster
   (e) Unofficial accounts
   (f) Common share:
       (i) Telephone/reception
       (ii) Filing
       (iii) Miscellaneous

4. *Specific tasks of bursar*

   (a) General role of organizing the office
       (i) Able to take overall view of work load and to distinguish the wood from the trees
       (ii) To arrange smooth flow of work
       (iii) To let staff know what is expected of them and so avoid irritations or unpleasantness which might arise.
   (b) Dinner money—collecting and accounting
   (c) Ordering and distribution of basic consortium stock
   (d) All non-official accounts. Examples include monies for educational visits, residential visits at home and abroad, visits to school involving payment, drink vending machines, school shop, concerts and plays held at school for which monies are collected and payments made, fund raising events, staff committee fund, bursaries for the deprived fund, photograph sales, and all usual ad hoc school fund accounting. *NB* Drink vending and staff committee involve employment of ancillaries paid for from unofficial funds.
   (e) Operation of the school bank (involves training scholars)
   (f) As a frame of reference for staff and heads of department on administrative matters where it is thought unnecessary to involve the Head
   (g) Opening of post and syphoning off routine advertisements, invoices, etc.

5. *Bursar as clerk to governors*

   (a) This has always been an appointment outside the control of the Head and not on the staff of the school.
   (b) In this appointment he is a servant of the governors and LEA whilst at the same time being on the staff of the school under the direct control of the Head.
   (c) Confidential nature of the task may involve seeing the Head in conflict with the governors, or with the LEA, or the governors in conflict with the LEA.
   (d) Knows when to seek the advice of the Head on correspondence stemming from a governors' meeting.
   (e) The question of loyalty to the Head could be absolutely crucial.

6. *Communication between bursar and other staff*

   (a) Pigeon holes
   (b) Morning staff meetings
   (c) Head of department meetings

Advantages of employing as bursar someone who has had teaching experience

   (a) Teaching staff prefer an ex-schoolmaster, as this lessens the potential professional versus administrator conflict.
   (b) Teaching staff can be confident that he will be sensitive to the problems of the teacher.
   (c) Teaching staff will not ignore him, but will take him seriously as one with ability and authority, which will minimize the likelihood of the Head still carrying his old burdens.

Do you agree with the specification of duties presented above? What changes would you make?

3. Training and recruitment

The sources of recruitment are likely to be quite varied. They can include such diverse fields as ex-service officers, school secretaries, practising LEA staff who are placed in the school for a term of service before subsequently moving back into the LEA. There seems to be a current tendency to appoint serving teachers to the post of Bursar.

There is also a confusion of terminology. Similar posts are described as bursar, registrar, senior secretary, etc. . . . deputy head, even.

What, in your view, would constitute relevant experience for a candidate appointed to the post of bursar?

Do you anticipate a career structure for bursars?

How would you anticipate bursars being trained?

4. The introduction of a bursar

The immediate problem for the bursar is to distinguish his work from that of secretaries in a situation where the work naturally overflows from the office.

The most senior of the secretaries is probably effectively in charge of the office and, through senior staff, has been responsible for its organization, particularly at a day-to-day level. Almost certainly she will continue this.

One solution is for the bursar to take over all aspects of a particular task. The bursar may, however, work closely with the secretaries and in this case the work pattern may show a greater similarity to that of secretaries, characterized by intensity of effort and a greater variety of tasks. Perhaps he might also help the secretaries with their duties.

It seems apparent, however, that the bursar stands in a position of authority over secretaries, being responsible for co-ordinating work in the school office and leaving secretaries largely responsible for the clerical side of any task at hand.

If it is possible that the bursar may take over tasks which were formerly the responsibility of the LEA or of Senior Teachers;

if it is possible that the bursar may be seen as taking over responsibilities which were the responsibilities of the senior secretary;

if it is possible that the bursar will undertake work which was undertaken either by teaching staff or the secretaries;

if it is possible that the bursar may be seen as a threat, that is, the threat of a full-time administrator, by some members of the teaching staff.

then his introduction into a school may be fraught with conflict.

In your opinion:

What should the bursar do?

What can he most profitably undertake?

How would you go about introducing a bursar into your school?

What power would you give him?

Would you include him in the 'cabinet'?

Overview

You might like to consider the following:

'Lots of people are willing to take on secretarial work, the problem is to organize them, to get the work out of them.'
(A Head Teacher)

Who should monitor and control the work of secretaries and bursars?
Who should they report to?

Upon what should a judgement as to the efficiency with which they undertake their work depend?
Should it depend upon a job specification?

How do you determine at what point the work of the bursar differentiates from that of the secretary?

If your school were offered the choice between one bursar or two full-time secretaries, what criteria would you use to make a decision?

How do you select a person who needs:

a considerable knowledge of office routine, motor skills, or inter-personal skills, or organizational skills, and a sensitivity to the relationship that the office has to the ethos of the school? Would you call upon the expertise of the registrar of the local College of Further Education to do the interviewing for you?

Bishopton
High School

Bishopton High School an outline of a simulated school to aid discussion of previous chapters.

BISHOPSTON EDUCATION COMMITTEE
Bishopston County High School

The school was originally formed in 1961 from the merging of two secondary modern departments (Boys and Girls), accommodated in adjoining premises. In these early years the presence of a selective central school as well as a Grammar school gave rise to a double creaming but the central school combined with the merged boys' and girls' schools and a bilateral school began to emerge. New purpose-built premises with extensive playing fields and room for further expansion were taken over in 1968. A fully comprehensive intake was then officially declared by the LEA. This goal was achieved at the beginning of the present academic session when catchment areas for the comprehensive secondary schools were redrawn and adhered to with some rigidity.

The new school serves a mixed residential area, has some pupils from a rural area brought in by bus each day and also takes pupils from the centre of the town where poor housing conditions exist. Many of the parents are either skilled craftsmen or members of the armed forces although the beginning of the comprehensive intake is expected to see a considerable increase in the numbers of children of professional and other white collar workers entering the school. Mobility of population is a marked feature often to the detriment of an individual pupil's educational career.

Last September saw the first of an 8 form entry intake with over 1200 pupils on roll, taught by a full-time staff of 67 and five part-time teachers. (23 have graduate status, pupil/staff ratio of 18.1.1).

The Headteacher, Mr V. Gregory, BA, leads an enthusiastic staff and is ably assisted by Mr J. Lincoln, BSc, Deputy Head, and Miss E. H. Morris, BSc, the Senior Mistress.

The teaching work of the school is organized through the subject departments, the majority of which are based on the normal range of school subjects; each has a head of department and in almost every case a number of specialist teachers, some of whom teach in more than one department. The head of department has responsibilities for the effective teaching of his subject, the content and method of the syllabus, the amount of homework set, and he is also expected to supervise the work of his colleagues within the department. Assessments, internal and external examinations, the maintenance of records, requisitioning of books, stationery and other materials are also his concern. In all these matters he works closely with the deputy headmaster.

Curriculum and internal organization are designed to meet individual children's needs and varying abilities. In the first three years the children are split into parallel bands each covering approximately.the same range of abilities with a single, separate remedial form in each year. Within each band there are four forms.

These teaching forms do not predominate in the timetable organization. The use of 'sets' in English, maths and French for example allows the heads of the subject department to arrange different groupings within each 'band' so that the group taught by one member of the staff in his subject may not exist for other subject teachers.

During the first three years nearly all pupils follow the same curriculum, but in the fourth and fifth years the basic course occupies only about 60 per cent of the time, the remainder of the pupil's timetable (2/5ths) being devoted to a wide range of examination and non-examination options. Extensive consultations take place in the second half of the third year involving pupils, parents and staff before an individual's programme for the fourth and fifth years is achieved. Inevitably choices are influenced by future career decisions so that careers staff are intensively involved in all these discussions. The sixth form is open to anyone remaining after the completion of a fifth year and for whom a worthwhile course can be arranged. This may vary from a full three A-level course to one in which external examinations do not figure at all.

The school has a large number of thriving clubs and a full programme of extracurricular activities.

All pupils in the school belong to one of six houses but those in the first year, although assigned to a house, are treated as a separate unit— the lower school. Each house therefore contains all IInd-VIth form pupils within a specified range of surnames, with a house head, assistant house head and a number of tutors. With the exception of part-time teachers, who are assigned to a House largely for administrative purposes, all the staff belong to a house and serve as its tutors. Within the house, pupils remain in one particular tutor group in their second and third years, moving to another for their fourth and fifth years, and finally, if they remain, into a sixth-form tutor group. The heads of houses and the head of lower school are responsible for a wide range of pastoral and administrative duties.

Summary of Staff

Headmaster, deputy headmaster, senior mistress
Head of department posts

Scale 5	... ...	2
Scale 4	... ...	3
Scale 3	... ...	7
Scale 2	... ...	3

i/c subjects

Scale 2	... ...	2

Head of lower school

Scale 4	... ...	1

House heads

Scale 3	... ...	6

Deputies to house heads

Scale 2	... ...	1

Subject teachers

Scale 2	... ...	4
Scale 1	... ...	35

Mr A. S. E. Priestly, House Head (Scale 3) is on secondment as Teacher in Charge of the Local Development Centre, and his post as Head of House has been protected. The temporary appointment of Mrs V. Day was made as from Easter 1973. As Mr Priestly has now been appointed Head of St John's School, the appointment of a permanent successor to him as House Head will now be necessary.

There is a vacancy for an Assistant in Mathematics.

There is also a vacancy for a counsellor (Scale 2)
Secretaries: Mrs T. Wilson, Mrs A. Greenfield.
School Caretaker: Mr Edwards.
Canteen Supervisor: Miss Willett.
Lab Technicians: Mrs T. J. Brever, Mr F. McMichael.